Sacred Gaia

Here is a book that is really needed. Hurrah for it!

(Mary Midgley)

Anne Primavesi's affirmation that life is a continuous gift, in the myriad dimensions she describes, is grounded in a provocatively new and thoughtful understanding of theology as an earth science. If theology took evolutionary theory seriously, as *Sacred Gaia* suggests, the implications for religious proclamations and understanding would be profound.

(Heather Eaton, St Paul University, Canada)

a tour de force. ... This is a book to widen anyone's horizons.

(Ruth Page, University of Edinburgh)

James Lovelock's Gaia theory considers the earth as a whole, with its evolution and the evolution of life upon it merging into a single process. From this dynamic system emerged conditions favourable for sustaining life in every organism and species, including our own. In this important book Anne Primavesi develops the religious implications of this theory and presents for the first time a coherent theology rooted in 'awe at the sacredness of the whole earth system'.

This is a remarkable and thought-provoking book: while offering challenging ideas, it remains effortlessly coherent.

Dr Anne Primavesi is former Research Fellow in Environmental Theology at the University of Bristol.

Sacred Gaia

Holistic theology and earth
system science

Anne Primavesi

Pertenece a:
Maria A. Belisario
OTTAWA, 2001

London and New York

First published 2000
by Routledge
11 New Fetter Lane, London EC4P 4EE

Simultaneously published in the USA and Canada
by Routledge
29 West 35th Street, New York, NY 10001

Routledge is an imprint of the Taylor & Francis Group

© 2000 Anne Primavesi

Typeset in Galliard by Taylor & Francis Books Ltd
Printed and bound in Great Britain by Biddles Ltd, Guildford and King's
Lynn

British Library Cataloguing in Publication Data
A catalogue record for this book is available from the British Library

Library of Congress Cataloging in Publication Data
A catalog record has been requested for this title

ISBN 0–415–18833–4 (hbk)
ISBN 0–415–18834–2 (pbk)

To dearest her who lives alas! away

Una
beloved sister and friend
1932–1995

Contents

Foreword   xi
Preface   xiii
Acknowledgements   xx

1 **A single evolutionary process**   1
   Autopoiesis, metabolism, boundaries 2
   Organism, environment, and structural coupling 3
   Gaia as autopoietic entity 5
   Humans as autopoietic entities 6
   Poiesis and partiality in perspectives 9
   Theology from a coevolutionary perspective 12

2 **Coevolutionary organisms**   15
   The family of organisms 15
   Ourselves and other organisms 17
   Theology becoming an earth science 19
   Human history/Earth history 21

3 **Description and distinction**   24
   Evolutionary nature of description 27
   Margulis' descriptions and their character 28
   Metaphor and the function of paradox 29
   Division or distinction? 32
   Theology divided from, or distinct from science? 34

4 **Contemporary theological circuits**   37
   Coevolutionary impact 37
   Unique creation 39
   Independent incarnation 40

Made in God's image 42
The 'end' of evolution 44
Natural selection, or natural drift? 46

5 **Evolutionary description**   50
Scientific distinctions 51
Evolutionary narratives 53
Evolutionary competition and capitalism 54
Sociobiological reflections 55
Theological reflections 58

6 **Poietic process**   60
Metaphoric process and emergent perceptions 62
Metaphorical imagination 63
Imagination and emotion 64
Distinction and differentiation in religious description 65
Contingency and hope 68

7 **Justice and judgment**   72
Distinguishing justice 73
Judgment now 76
Justice now 77
Coevolutionary judgment 79

8 **Justice North and South**   81
Energy and access to its sources 83
Quality and inequality 84
The ecological footprint 85
Environmental space 87
North/South and theology 89
Liberation and ecology 91

9 **Freedom for theology**   93
Situated knowledge North and South 94
The option for the poor 97
The function of 'God' in liberation theologies 99
The function of 'God' in capitalist societies 101
Liberating theology 106

10 **Freedom from competition**   108
Competition rules 109

Poiesis and mimesis 113
Liberation from competition 116

11 Women and the ordering of Nature   121
Hierarchy as a principle of order 122
Modes of hierarchical ordering 126
The place of Nature and women in hierarchical ordering 128
Effects of hierarchical ordering 129
Women and Nature 131
Defining Nature 133
Belonging to the Gaian order 134

12 The ordering of God   137
Hierarchical relations between God and world 140
Omnipotence and identity 144
Christianity and identity 145
Identity and land ownership 147
Validation of suffering 150
An alternative feminist vision 150

13 Life as gift event   154
The nature of 'gift' 155
The nature of gift event 158
Scapegoats today 161

14 Sacred gift   168
The concept of the sacred 168
Discerning the gift 172
Gift as grace 175
The 'first' donor? 178

Bibliography   180
Index   188

Foreword

Neither Newton nor Darwin would have thought it odd to be asked to write a foreword to a book on theology but present-day scientists might find it so. This is because for many years science and religion have been antithetic. The outstanding success of reductionist science in explaining the details of life and the universe has given science authority as a source of knowledge which in past times was left to the churches. It has sometimes led practitioners of science to hubris – to a belief that science can explain all there is to know. Modern science has developed a dangerous tendency to be certain.

The change in science since Newton and Darwin's time has been the concentration on reduction and this has put science out of balance. It is almost as if, in medicine, physiology and the study of the whole live person were given second place to the introspective sciences of biochemistry, cytology and molecular genetics. In favouring specialization science has, like the churches, fragmented into sects, each of which is certain that it alone has the truth. The landscape of modern science is too often like a scene from *Star Trek*, a triumph of expertise over wisdom.

Science may have displaced religion as the source of information about life and the cosmos but it offers no moral guidance, indeed it often claims to be ethically neutral. President Havel of the Czech Republic first noticed that Gaia is a part of science with a moral dimension. The Earth is something tangible that we can revere and want to care for and Gaia can punish us if we transgress, for the theory stresses that any species that adversely affects the environment of its progeny will perish.

Anne Primavesi has subtitled her book *Holistic theology and earth system science*. It is refreshing to read scientific arguments posited by a theologian and it is a splendid book, well written and accessible to both scientist and theo–logian. When my first Gaia book was published in 1979 I was astonished to receive twice as many letters from those interested in its religious aspects as from those interested in science. When I wrote the book I did not intend to address religious topics. It was a book to express in lay language a new theory about the evolution of the Earth – a subject that I saw as wholly scientific. What I failed to see was that a theory of the Earth that sees it behaving like a living organism was inevitably theological as well as scientific. Looking back, I now see why my friend the novelist William Golding suggested that I call the theory Gaia.

Gaia theory looks at the whole Earth from outside and sees it as a live entity; modern science looks at the surface details and gives us an inventory of the parts. Think of a faceted diamond suspended by a thread. Seen from a few feet, all of its sparkling elegance is visible but close up only the territory of a single facet can be seen. In a sensible world we need both of these views if we are to understand our planet and respect it. There is more to Gaia theory than a change of viewpoint; the theory enters the realm of emergent phenomena, a place where the whole is always more than the sum of the parts. Modern scientists brought up in the reductionist tradition find emergence, where an ensemble behaves coherently and becomes a new and characteristic entity, difficult to understand. Life emerged from an ensemble of chemical cycles and consciousness emerged from the operating system of the mind. The understanding of emergent phenomena like these will not come from a wholly reductionist approach.

Let me illustrate by an anecdote just how difficult mainstream scientists find the phenomenon of emergence. In the middle of the last century the engineer James Watt demonstrated a model of his steam engine governor at an exhibition in London. It was one of the first successful self-regulating devices and it regulated the speed of a steam engine. It consisted of a pair of spinning balls mounted on a vertical shaft whose rotation by the engine caused them to spin out and so move a lever that partially closed the valve supplying steam to the engine. If the engine went too fast the balls swung further out and shut off the steam; if too slow, they fell inwards and increased the supply of steam. It worked wonderfully well and among the audience watching the demonstration was James Clerk Maxwell, perhaps the greatest physicist of his time. He said three days later that he had been kept awake trying to analyze mathematically Watt's invention, he had no doubt that it worked but its analysis eluded him. If it was too difficult for Maxwell to analyze then it is hardly surprising that the more complex system Gaia is difficult to explain using reductionist science.

I now see why thoughts of Gaia are as much in the realms of theology as of science. Anne Primavesi is among the few of my friends to understand Gaia but understanding is intuitive and often can not be easily explained. Theologians have that wonderful word ineffable; perhaps scientists will adopt it to acknowledge that they can never explain everything. I have enjoyed reading this thoughtful book and I hope that scientists and theologians will read it and find how much they have in common.

James Lovelock

Preface

The horizons of this book are uncommonly wide and some explanation seems called for as to why I expanded them as far as I have. In *From Apocalypse to Genesis: Ecology, Feminism and Christianity*, published in 1991, I deliberately gave priority to ecology. I was convinced then, and am even more convinced now, that if theology is to have a positive input into the important environmental debates of the day then theologians have to use or at least to familiarize themselves with scientific environmental language and with its implicit understanding that the ecosystems to which we all belong interconnect within a greater whole. This linguistic landscape was opened up and made common ground by the political and scientific processes leading up to the 1992 United Nations Conference on Environment and Development in Rio and by the gradual, if patchy, implementation of some of its policies ever since. Over the years this has provided the general public, including non-scientists like myself, with a crash course in such concepts as environmental degradation, sustainable development and the loss of biodiversity. It has also altered irrevocably our perspective on the actual landscapes we inhabit.

The move to an ecological perspective within theology might seem, then, no more than a cultural shift. But for me it signals a moment when theological terms must and can be translated into a commonly used, science-based language, making theology and its concerns accessible to the largest possible number of people. For I believe that the truths glimpsed in theology (what we say we know about the relationship between the world and God) as well as the truths glimpsed in science (what we say we know about the nature of the world) are pertinent to all our lives, and are meant to be available to everyone, specialist and non-specialist alike. I also believe that constructive dialogue between scientists and theologians is not only possible but necessary. For we all, one presumes, want to live in an environmentally friendly fashion. Science, ideally, helps us to understand how the complex relationships within our environments are sustained and how we contribute to them, positively and negatively. Theology, ideally, can help us to understand how and why our lifestyles reflect and are validated by some of our most deeply held, if often unarticulated, beliefs about our relationship with God.

Seeking such understanding over the years, James Lovelock's Gaia theory jolted me awake to the phenomenological aspect of theology: to the collective experience of an entire field of relations between organisms and environments recorded in human evolutionary history and now manifest in my personal experience. Within that relational field, and nowhere else, I learn what it means to be alive and to die, and also what it means to be good, just and loving. I learn uncomfortable things about my own species, not least my dependence on other life forms to provide me with the energy needed to sustain my life. The discomfort arises because I behave most of the time as if my lifestyle and concerns are independent of the relations and processes which sustain not only myself, but the whole encompassed by Gaia. And if my independence from the rest of the earth community is not a biological reality in any thoroughgoing sense, can it be a theological one? The theological discomfort increases when I see the visible effects of an assumption of independence and realize that it is underwritten by doctrines which claim that my species alone is created in God's image. What kind of image is that supposed to be?

Gaia theory has helped me question prevailing images of God (and their function) by offering a scientific understanding of the world accessible to scientist and non-scientist alike, one I can engage with and discuss with others at whatever level suits us. It reveals facts about our environments and their continuing evolution which give me a different perspective on them and a different contour to human history. For this theory takes its bearings from the benchmark of the evolution of life on this planet, and from that vantage point, the contour made by the human species is seen as an integral part of the planetary landscape rather than its distinguishing feature. Against that horizon, the human person is seen as one which emerged through and from continuing evolutionary processes. This reconfigures any descriptions of our place and role in the planetary landscape, and involves translating theological descriptions into 'ordinary' language which stays close to real life.

Such a translation is, however, fraught with difficulties, some of them inherent in the nature and evolution of language itself. Brian Friel's play, *Translations*, set in a Gaelic-speaking part of Ireland where in 1833 the British carried out an Ordnance Survey mapping of the district, reveals the enormous impact on those who live there (as well as on those doing the translating) when familiar names for physical landmarks are changed. The native Irish are, by the very process – and even the translator himself dimly perceives this – evicted from their customary dwelling within the landscape. Translating the Gaelic place-names into English names means, for them, forfeiting their place in the landscape's history as well as their ability to record their life events on its contours. The British soldier charged with the task of translation (this was a military exercise) tries to learn Gaelic, for he knows that 'something is being eroded'. At the same time he is excited by the fact that as he names a place, it leaps into existence and becomes congruent with his reality. He echoes the primal excitement and sense of power contained in the Genesis narrative of

Adam 'naming' the animals when he exclaims: 'Welcome to Eden!' The reality for the soldier, of course, is that of the printed page (Friel 1981: 30–45).

That reality is particularly relevant for Christian theology. One could say that its canonical texts are assumed to have mapped theological reality with the thoroughness of an army, in this case that of the Holy Roman Empire. The prototypical translator here is Jerome, charged by Pope Damasus in 384 CE to produce a uniform and dependable text of the Latin Bible which would revise those Latin texts in circulation, using the Greek original for this purpose. Jerome was not only clever enough for this formidable task. He was clever enough to see what it entailed. He responded to the Pope's mandate by saying that while he accepted the task as a labour of love, it was at the same time both perilous and presumptuous. 'How can I dare', he asked, 'to change the language of the world in its hoary old age, and carry it back to the early days of its infancy?' He anticipated that both the learned and the unlearned man, perceiving 'that what he reads does not suit his settled tastes', will break out immediately into violent language and call him, Jerome, 'a forger and a profane person for having had the audacity to add anything to the ancient books, or to make any changes or corrections therein'.

His fears were not unfounded. Augustine records that during a service at Oea, a town in North Africa, when the congregation heard that Jonah rested under *hedera* (ivy) instead of the familiar *cucurbita* (gourd), there was such a tumult that the bishop nearly lost his flock. Jerome responded vigorously by referring to his detractors as 'two-legged asses' who think that 'ignorance is equivalent to holiness' (Metzger 1977: 333–4).

The reaction foreseen by Jerome, both of his readers and of the congregation, will have come as no surprise to those who later, like Wycliffe and Luther, translated the biblical texts into the vernacular of their day. It comes as no surprise now to those present in congregations when new hymnbooks are introduced into traditional services, or God is first publicly addressed as 'Mother'. But as Jerome said, that cannot stop us adding, changing and correcting theological texts in the light of present knowledge. This process is as much part of the evolution of Christianity now as it was in the fourth century, even if carrying it back 'to the days of its infancy' means looking at scientific narratives rather than the Greek of the Septuagint.

So I would hope that now, as then, there are some who, having left the congregation because it seemed incapable of change, might return to it and contribute positively to that change. Those too who see, or rather hear theology as irredeemably prescriptive may be pleasantly surprised by the importance attached to its descriptive aspects and by the experience of hearing them translated into a contemporary idiom. I would even hope that people who don't think theology concerns them at all might also be pleasantly surprised to find that it does, not least because the more we understand of how theological assumptions underlie many secularized institutions and theories, including those of science, the better able we are to discern them and deal with them positively.

A case in point occurs in a recent book by the scientist Steve Jones, in which he says that 'the birth of Adam, whether real or metaphorical, marked the insertion into an animal body of a post-biological soul that leaves no fossils and needs no genes'. This, as one reviewer remarks, 'is almost identical to a line in the recent encyclical about evolution written by the Pope!' (Dylan Evans reviewing *Almost Like a Whale: The Origin of Species Updated* in *The Guardian*, 18 September 1999). Resistance to the loss of privileged status for our species takes various forms, and often many of them, as we shall see, depend on usually well hidden theological presuppositions.

Unlike the case of Jerome, today's impulse to change does not come from papal edict – quite the contrary – but from the material/physical/chemical environment of theology: from the landscape itself. Its degradation speaks to all of us at varying levels and in different degrees as we become aware of the accelerating rate of environmental change through human agency, and of the visible and all too often deleterious impact of this change on biological communities. Post-Rio research on human communities reveals that this impact is heaviest on those within them least able to do anything about it – women, children, indigenous peoples and the poor. This revelation has deepened and strengthened commitment to and calls for social and environmental justice and has made them part of the contemporary political landscape.

Feminist analyses and critiques have contributed significantly to this, highlighting the fact that women, a majority of the world's population, receive only a small proportion of its opportunities and benefits. A recently published *Human Development Index* establishes that in no country in the world is women's quality of life equal to that of men, once life expectancy, educational attainment and income are taken into account (Nussbaum 1999: 31). On the theological map women's lives feature much less prominently, but nevertheless have become a force for change there too as feminist theologians struggle to establish, to name and to describe women's place within that landscape and to claim validity for this particular knowledge base. The ecofeminist theological perspective which informed *From Apocalypse to Genesis* changed my perception of the Christian landscape by throwing into sharp relief emergent contours scarcely visible before. For where Christianity is alive, its landscape changes. Where the landscape changes, so does Christianity. Else it finds itself, to use one of Friel's images, imprisoned in a linguistic contour which no longer matches the landscape of fact.

A further step for me into this changing landscape, and a decisive one towards writing this book, came when I was asked to teach on James Lovelock's opening course at Schumacher College in 1991 and on subsequent courses given there by the ecophilosopher Arne Naess. The participants, from many countries and a wide range of backgrounds but nearly all working in or familiar with the physical sciences, shared in varying degrees an understanding of the material world based on our interdependence with all life forms. On this basis, they also shared a commitment to living nonviolently, seeing this as a rational response to the perceived fragility of living beings and their environments.

Nonviolence, as the term is consistently written here, is unhyphenated because it is more than the negation of violence. It is a powerful commitment to living in a way conducive to the long-term, universal reduction of violence (Naess 1974: 60).

Such a positive commitment connects (at the same time as distinguishing between) what we say we know about the nature of the world, what we say we know about God and how we live. This nonviolent connectedness has always been a prominent feature of Buddhism and of a lifestyle modelled on Gandhian principles. My hope in this book is that Gaia theory and its connective discourse can build such a bridge within a western theological landscape. It would be a standpoint from which to review such questions as: What kind of God is discernible in a planetary environment which evolved chemically and physically over billions of years, and what kind of continuous relationship between it and God can we posit? Can this God be concerned with anything less than the entire field of relations which sustain my life and every variety of life on earth? How does that affect my perception of the place I occupy within that relational field and what is the lifestyle appropriate to it? Does it fit in with theological claims to be given dominance over other species and to be dependent only on God? Does this God sanction the suffering I impose disproportionately on other living beings – or share that suffering?

Theology becomes, from this perspective, another earth science, one which raises important questions about human status before God as we see ourselves within the context of consistent and continuous relationships between organisms and their environments which constitute our world. They contribute, we must assume, each according to its kind, to continuous and consistent relationships between God and the world which can never be reduced to what we ourselves see and experience of that world, but cannot, for us, be divorced from it either.

Therefore we learn to consider the Earth as a system, emphasizing the whole system over its parts while paying particular attention to those interactions between organisms and their environments which have been constitutive of life on earth over a vast time scale. God, on any reckoning, could be commensurate with no smaller a scale. And since the whole system and its processes have affected and continue to affect us, even as we now affect them, we too can be concerned with no less. Whatever we may say about our environment, or about God, will relate God, ultimately, to every process or organism seen within the evolution of life on earth. Seeing myself embedded there will affect how I speak about God. But how should I perceive and describe myself within this single evolutionary process?

This last question decides the structure of this book. In the opening chapters I use Humberto Maturana and Francisco Varela's concept of *autopoiesis*, or self-making, to explore and describe the evolution of human identity. They highlight both dependence and limited autonomy as characteristic of continuous interactions between organisms (including ourselves) and their environments. Grounding us in biological processes, they place us within a continuum of patterns of evolution ranging from microbial, subvisible organisms through to the evolution of recognizable species and individuals. These patterns will, as far as we know, continue into the future as long as life persists on earth. They have enabled us to develop, in common with all other living beings, not a pre-specified form but our present constituent structure – including our capacity to relate to others in a just and peaceful way.

However in contrast to this wide-ranging view, western Christian theology, even to the present day, has remained focussed on the role of the death and resurrection of Christ in proclaiming and establishing a certain once-for-all divine/human order on earth, and on comparing and contrasting this with a previous world order epitomized in an individual called 'Adam'. The range of theological enquiry has been confined to whatever has been deduced and recorded about the span of human history between these two individuals, and to what can be and has been said about it subsequently. Theology within those parameters remains practically a human and a social science, but one conducted as though its environment, if considered at all, were marked solely by the time/space continuum and interpretative symbolic structure which has distinguished western history. That is, up to now.

Gaia theory represents the second of two major changes in western cultural perception which have, potentially at least, altered the landscape of western Christian theology. Both have centred on the evolution of our species. The first, associated with Darwin, moved its timescale back beyond any individual 'Adam' to a shadowy and uncertain past where we, as one species among others, cannot point, in any strict sense, to a precise starting point for our own. As we saw with Steve Jones, scientists as well as theologians are reluctant to forfeit this 'alpha' moment. Its continuing role is to claim a special place for ourselves outside the evolutionary process, one where our most distinguishing feature, 'a post-biological soul' [*sic*], leaves no fossils and needs no genes, thereby making us intrinsically different from other living species.

Like it or not, however, we cannot assume (as creationists do) that God put us on earth in a pre-specified form at a particular moment and point in time and by some special act of creation. We too, like every other living entity, emerged out of ongoing evolutionary processes on earth. And if we want to deny this, we have to ask why. What is the function of this denial? Does it make us care more, or less, about what happens to other species? And if, as some would hold, it should make us care more, then where is the evidence that it has had this effect? In fact the evidence (the loss of other species through human violence) is to the contrary.

The second shift, associated with James Lovelock's work, has moved the timescale of our evolution back still further: back to the evolution of the first living organisms on the planet. There, ultimately, lie the 'days of our infancy', but days so far removed from us in time and in emergent processes as to distance us almost completely from those life forms from which we originated. Gaia theory takes us back beyond recognizable species to the evolution of those planetary conditions which made life, in its most rudimentary form, possible. It takes us to 'the back of beyond', to an evocative point on the horizon which recedes as we approach it.

Both these evolutionary shifts in perspective have profound theological implications, and throughout this book I look at their effects on three interrelated issues. The first, as I said, is our self-perception. Gaia theory requires me to take theological account of the evolution of life through the tight coupling of organisms and their environments. Where were we indeed, as God asks Job, throughout the enormous timescale this implies? And where was God in this gap between the origins of life and our lives? What can we say about God's relationship with the material environment we share with other organisms, whether this be the air we breathe or the oceans and rocks which surround us, when they are all either the direct product of living organisms or else have been greatly modified by their presence? And in particular, what must we say when we see the changes to the material environment caused by our presence, even within the relatively short lifespan of our species?

From this question emerges the second theological issue: that of justice to the whole earth community. This is considered from the perspective of those who visibly suffer injustice. They are the subject of liberation theologies today. Seeing them suffer the effects of our lifestyles, the concept of structural sin acquires detailed and explicit meaning. We come to realize that they, and all living organisms including those yet to emerge, are affected by our ability to modify, use and abuse the material environment, including the genetic makeup of the organisms themselves. In many instances those modifications have led to extreme suffering for large sections of the human population and for non-human species. They embody some of the contemporary 'landscape facts' whose causes theologians must seek to understand and to remedy, not least by stressing the need for nonviolent, that is, nonconsumerist lifestyles.

Throughout the book I continuously review both these issues in the light of a third inseparable from them: the function served by our God-concepts. Are they used to validate human violence – or to alert us to the suffering and death it causes? Do we impose an apartheid system on the living beings before us, segregating some we call sacred from others we call profane and then using this binary code to devalue and destroy what we label 'non-sacred'?

In the light of such questions, I find my theological orientation has shifted toward a God concerned with and for all living organisms throughout earth's history. The central theological task has become that of describing the paradoxical nature of this 'God' as perceived from within this larger frame: one who is infinitely close to, and infinitely far from each living being; one who is not to be confused with, or separated from our home environment, earth; one both visible and invisible in the sacredness of the whole of existent reality.

Acknowledgements

This book has evolved over such a long time that it is not possible to mention all who contributed to it in one way or another. They include, for instance, people I met during my time as a member of the European CEC/CCEE Project Group on Environment and Development (1992–1995) and while I was teaching in the Department of Theology and Religious Studies, University of Bristol (1994–1997). There are however others directly involved in the final version who can and must be thanked. Among them are my first editor at Routledge, Adrian Driscoll, who saw my original proposal through to its final form. Since taking over the editorship Roger Thorp has provided prompt and expert guidance towards the book's completion. Wallace Heim not only recommended essential reading matter but often provided it as well. Tim Ingold sent me pertinent articles of his I would otherwise have missed. The readability of the present text owes much to Jennifer Henderson's careful scrutiny and to Mary Midgley's reading through the manuscript and suggesting ways of improving it. Finally, my thanks to Glynn Gorick for his scientifically precise and beautiful cover illustration.

It is clear that James Lovelock's work and his courteous readiness to discuss it with a nonscientist like myself have been crucial to the arguments developed here. Ultimately, of course, in this instance as in all others, I alone bear responsibility for the particular form they take. His friendship and that of Sandy his wife not only inspired me but took practical form in a grant from the Gaia Charity and an invitation to join the Gaia Society and attend its biennial conferences. There, thanks in no small measure to the kindness of those present in their professional capacity, my grasp of the scientific implications of Gaia theory has been stretched to its limits and beyond. Discussions over the years with Mark, my husband, have helped define and refine my understanding of the relationship between science and theology. His many contributions to the book itself include time spent in reading different versions, countless hours of word-processing, formatting and indexing, and large doses of encouragement when most needed. The whole of his input remains, however, far greater than any sum of these parts. So the book can stand for the interdependence, and, in this instance at least, the compatibility of science and theology.

I am grateful to Asphodel Long for permission to use her translation of an Orphic hymn quoted in Chapter 13 and to the following publishers for permission to reprint the following material: Milkweed Editions for 'All the Elements of the Scene' and 'Eating Death' by Pattiann Rogers from *Firekeeper: New and Selected Poems* (Milkweed, 1994), and 'Animals and People: "The Human Heart in Conflict with Itself" ' by Pattiann Rogers in *Eating Bread and Honey* (Milkweed, 1997); World Council of Churches Publications for the poem 'From Air and Soil' by B. K. Mason, contributed by Richard Lawrence to *Five Loaves and Two Fishes* (WCC, 1998); Orbis Books for the extracts from 'The Faith of the Poor' by Hugo Assmann in *The Idols of Death and the God of Life: A Theology* (Orbis, 1983); Kreuz Verlag for the verses by Dorothee Sölle from *The Window of Vulnerability* (Fortress, 1990).

1 A single evolutionary process

Hearing the rising tide, I think how it is pressing also against other shores I know. ... On all these shores there are echoes of past and future: of the flow of time, obliterating yet containing all that has gone before; of the stream of life, flowing as inexorably as any ocean current from past to unknown future

(Rachel Carson 1955: 215)

'Are we made of organs, or metabolic systems, or cells, or atoms, or memories, or passions, or all of the above?' This question allows for many different answers as to what, on earth, it means for us to be living beings. The biologist Tyler Volk raises it because of the dilemma we face when, as Gregory Bateson observed, the division of the perceived universe into parts and wholes becomes convenient and/or necessary, even though no necessity determines how it shall be done. Indeed, with living systems, the number of simultaneous levels at which they are discerned compounds the problem. We deal with it, as Bateson implies, by dividing the universe we perceive, or indeed ourselves, into certain parts and wholes and not others. The choice of which wholes, or which parts, depends on our overriding perspective; on the way in which we grasp the disjointed parts as a comprehensive whole. This grasp of the whole enables us to partition multilevelled biological and physical processes according to some interactions and not others (Volk 1995: 132; Primavesi 1998a: 74).

Volk's answer is implicit in his question, offering as he does various ways of describing ourselves that are comprehensible to him and to others, both scientists and non-scientists. Two other scientists, Humberto Maturana and Francisco Varela, spent many years attempting to answer two questions which at first sight appear to be different to his, but in fact address the same problem. They asked: 'What is the organization of the living?' and 'What takes place in the phenomenon of perception?' Bringing the questions together enabled them to concentrate on the root problem: 'How do we, as living beings, perceive anything?' Including ourselves.

Autopoiesis, metabolism, boundaries

Their answer was an abstract description of the systemic organization of single cells common to all living systems. It is this which makes perception, in the broad sense of a living individual's response to an environment, possible. It is this which creates, literally and figuratively, the single evolutionary process in which organisms and the material earth evolve together.

Maturana and his colleague coined the term *autopoiesis* (self-making) for their abstract description of systemic organization in living beings. The term refers to the dynamic, self-producing and self-maintaining network of production processes within live organisms. Whatever their components, an indispensable aspect of living beings is that the function of each component is to participate in the production or transformation of other components in the network. In this way the entire network can be said to continually 'make itself', even though its surroundings may change unpredictably. The living being maintains its structural integrity and organization by using solar energy, either directly or at one or several removes, to remake and interchange its parts. Metabolism is the name given to the chemical activities of living systems, to the incessant buildup and breakdown of subvisible components which include solid, gas and liquid exchanges in activities such as breathing, eating and excreting.

This metabolic activity refers us back to one of Tyler Volk's possible choices for self-description. We may view ourselves as metabolic systems, and are, from this perspective, networks of chemical and energetic transformations. Our cell metabolism produces components which make up the network of transformations that produced them. Some of these components form a boundary, sometimes a visible one, which sets a limit to this network of transformations. But the boundary remains a part of the network. A membranous boundary (for example skin, bark, etc.) participates in the transformation network that produced its own components. The interaction between boundary and metabolism constitutes the discrete entity we call a cell. (See Maturana and Varela 1998: 43–52; Capra 1997: 98; Margulis 1997: 267f.; Maturana 1971, quoted in Luhmann 1990: 3. I shall be using the work of Margulis 1997; Margulis and Sagan 1995; Capra 1997, and Luhmann to comment on Maturana's own formulations.)

The minimal autopoietic entity is a bacterial cell. (The largest, according to Margulis and Capra, is probably the system Lovelock calls Gaia. See Margulis 1997: 267. See also Volk 1998: 114f., for what he calls the geometries of global metabolism in Gaia. More of this later.) All autopoietic entities metabolize continuously, that is, they perpetuate themselves through chemical activity, through energy expenditure and, in Margulis' colourful phrase, the 'making of messes'. Autopoiesis is, she says, detectable by that incessant life chemistry and energy flow which is metabolism. In order to qualify as an autopoietic entity, that is, as an individual organism, any such material-metabolizing entities must be bounded by membranes made by their own metabolism – plasma membranes, skin, exoskeletons or bark. The breaching of the boundary signals disintegration or loss of autopoietic status. Maintaining the boundary maintains the entity, maintains 'the self' or 'sense of self' or 'live individual' (Margulis and Sagan 1995: 23f.; 1997: 65f.). This way of describing what it is to be alive also gives us, of course, another way of describing death: dissolution of the boundary.

Organism, environment, and structural coupling

Autopoietic entities have a tendency to interact with other recognizable autopoietic entities, and with their environment. Maturana and Varela define the latter as the medium that constitutes the ambience in which the entity emerges. The entity interacts with this medium from within it, as well as with other autopoietic entities, and by extension, with their media/environments also. The interactions occur at and through the membranous boundary, which is always, to a certain extent, permeable. One sort of interaction is what we call perception, that is, sensory response to the local environment or to another autopoietic entity.

The environment, in its relationship with an autopoietic entity, has structural dynamics of its own, operationally distinct from those of the living being. This distinction between organism and environment, and the paradoxical nature of that distinction, is of crucial importance for Maturana and Varela's theory. *As observers*, we distinguish two structures that can be considered operationally independent of each other: living being and environment. But between them there is, at the same time, a necessary structural congruence in which the evolution of organism and environment merges. This independence/coincidence of living entity and environment is integral to coevolutionary description. The distinction between organism and environment made by an observer serves to underline the fact that in their interactions, perturbations from the environment trigger an effect in the living entity. But those effects, or changes, will be determined by the structure of the entity. The same holds true for the environment: the living being is a source of perturbations to it and not of instructions. As long as this congruence between them continues, as long as there is mutual triggering bringing about changes of state, we have an ongoing process called 'structural coupling' (Maturana and Varela 1998: 94–105).

This, in Gaia theory, is called 'tight coupling': the close relationship between the evolution of living organisms and the evolution of their physical and chemical environment which constitutes a single evolutionary process. Through this process, there are changes in both organism and environment which take place in each one as an expression of its own structural dynamics and because of its selective interactions with the other. Whenever the term 'coevolutionary' is used in the following chapters, it always refers to this single process. The prefix serves as a reminder of the two interactive components which coevolve within the process, although it is often necessary to describe them separately (Lovelock 1991: 25).

Similarly in autopoietic theory there is deliberate stress laid on the structural integrity of both living being and environment within their mutual transformation, thus safeguarding their relative autonomy while positing transformative interactions between them. (This methodological move is especially important, as I shall show, when discussing notions of freedom.) A cell membrane continually incorporates substances from its environment into the cell's metabolic processes. An organism's nervous system changes its connectivity with every sense perception. These living systems are, however, autonomous. (This simply underlines the 'auto' element in 'autopoiesis'.) The environment only triggers the structural changes; it does not specify or direct them. The central characteristic of an autopoietic system is that it undergoes continual changes while preserving its web-like pattern of organization. Margulis sums up: 'It changes in order to stay the same.'

The components of an autopoietic system continually produce and transform one another in two distinct ways. One type of structural change is that of self-renewal. Every living organism continually renews itself, with cells breaking down and building up structures, tissues and organs to replace themselves in continual cycles. Many of these cyclical changes occur much faster than one would imagine. Our pancreas replaces most of its cells every twenty-four hours, our stomach lining self-renews every three days. Our skin replaces its cells at the amazing rate of 100,000 cells per minute. In spite of this ongoing change, we as organisms maintain our overall identity, our identifiable pattern of organization (Capra 1997: 213f.).

The second type of structural change in a living system is that in which new structures are created – new connections emerge in the autopoietic network. These changes – developmental rather than cyclical – also take place continually, either as a consequence of environmental influences, or as a result of the system's internal dynamics or its interactions with another autopoietic system. An example of the latter would be sexual interaction and the consequent emergence of a new autopoietic entity. Such necessary transformations and/or changes of state from conception to death characterize each of our life histories. But in each case, the environment of that life history has also played a decisive role (Maturana 1987: 74–82).

The double-sided character of coevolutionary interaction is evident in the inherent association between differences and similarities in conservation of organization and structural change. It is evident also in tendencies toward cohesion and radiation, autonomy and bonding. This inherent association makes coevolutionary interaction highly complex and resistant to simple description. Therefore, in this and the following chapters, the constant elements of organism, environment and their recurrent interactions will be described in as many ways as possible. Some conclusions can then be drawn as to what it means to be aware of the planet and ourselves as autopoietic entities, and what it means to accept that our perspective on the world is formed by evolutionary processes.

Gaia as autopoietic entity

At the large end of the scale, James Lovelock's Gaia theory presupposes that the planet itself is an autopoietic entity, that is, one which possesses features of organization analogous to (not identical with) the physiological processes of individual organisms. Margulis, one of his closest collaborators, describes the Earth as symbiosis viewable from space: a very complex living system of interacting living and non-living components that has cycled the elements through 3.5 billion years of evolution, during which symbiogenesis generated different arrangements within that symbiosis (Margulis and Sagan 1995: 156). Lovelock takes a similarly long view of the Earth as a tightly coupled, bounded system where its constituent organisms and their environment evolve together (Lovelock 1995: 37–39). Tyler Volk discusses the interconnected dynamics of Gaia under the rubric of four primary pools, or substances – life, soil, air and water – overlaid with biogeochemical cycles such as that of sulphur. Having analyzed their interactions, he distinguishes life as something special, with air, ocean and soil as matrices which surround life, harbour life, nourish life and, not least, serve as dump sites for the wastes of life. (This correlates with Margulis' definition of autopoietic entities, including Gaia.) Furthermore, he says, because the matrices are themselves products of life, he calls them biogenic matrices. Again we have the 'self-making' organizational pattern (Volk 1998: 114–24).

All the scientists quoted see each life form today, including ourselves, as a product of those billions of years of interaction between chemical-based systems and their environments. Our ancestors were not brought into this terrestrial environment from outside it. Rather, they, and we, have coevolved with it into the living beings they were then and we are today. The different components of our planetary physical environment and their systems of interaction, broadly categorized as cosmosphere, atmosphere, lithosphere, hydrosphere and biosphere, have, over billions of years, continuously recycled and reorganized the elements which eventually generated the homosphere, that particular arrangement within which human life became possible and sustainable (Galtung 1982: 13–19).

From this perspective, the surface of the planet itself is seen as alive with a connective metabolism of temperature and chemical modulation systems (Margulis 1997: 93–99). Within this biosphere almost every living organism, including the human, exists today. I say 'almost', since the organisms which live around the geothermal vents deep in the ocean subsist in a different atmosphere, and because artificial homospheres which operate beyond the Gaian system have been created for and used by astronauts for some years now. One result of calculating the cost of creating artificial homospheres has been that economists are able to compute the benefits to us, without apparent cost to us, of the naturally occurring biosphere we inhabit. It also gives them a way of computing the cost of its destruction through, for example, our overuse of fossil fuels and the release of ozone-depleting gases.

Humans as autopoietic entities

At the smaller end of the scale of autopoietic entities, we humans evolved and continue to reproduce from nucleated cells which themselves (according to the scientists quoted) evolved from bacterial interactions. As with different classes of organism (bacteria, protoctists, animals, fungi and plants) we come into being from a special single cell and grow through a process of structural coupling marked by class identity. Our lives depend on the evolution of other communities of cells, of food webs and other aggregations held in balance by the stability of their environments; by the constancy of atmospheric conditions favourable for life. Though constant in that they remain stable within a certain temperature range, they are dynamic too, hovering between equilibrium and disequilibrium, and as a consequence we too hover between vulnerability and impermeability, between death and life (Lenton 1998: 439).

This dynamism holds within species as well as between species, where the death of some organisms sustains the life of others. Our own physical sustenance is largely maintained by the ceaseless labour of living and dying organisms, notably through the activity of plants which photosynthesize the sun's energy for us, something we cannot do for ourselves. Our survival in extreme climatic conditions depends to a great extent on organisms long dead retrieved as fossil fuels, and in the future perhaps, if the technology can develop fast enough, it may depend on those living in the geothermal vents. Such facts about ourselves prove the truth of Vernadsky's dictum, quoted by Margulis, that 'human independence is a political, not a biological concept'.

Nested as we are within material environments which range from the planet to the home, from the Gaian to the personal metabolic system, their differentiation is difficult to describe when the English language uses one term, *environment*, for all of them. In fact, there are as many dimensions of environments spoken of and described as there are those who may or may not be aware of them. Usually we differentiate between our spatially near (personal) environment, in which our basic needs are met, and the larger one (regional, continental or global) within which it is set, and go on then, through a variety of media, to examine our relationships with these. But completely isolating one environment from another in any fundamental sense is untenable from a Gaian scientific perspective. Similarly, isolating one type of relationship with our environment from another in any complete sense is not sustainable in autopoietic terms because our interactions with our personal environments are simultaneous and continuous rather than occurring at isolated intervals.

However, it is often convenient, and in this book necessary, to divide that all-encompassing experience of environment into parts and wholes, or more accurately, into more or less comprehensive wholes. This is especially the case when we want to discern and understand the nature of our environmental interactions and communicate those perceptions to others. The choice of which wholes I choose to describe in this book follows from an autopoietic understanding of relationships between organisms and their environments. From this perspective our personal bodily boundary can be seen as itself delineating our environment while our perception of it is shaped and constituted by manifold interactions across that boundary which couple us to our environment's social, physical, chemical, cultural, religious and poetic dimensions.

The manifold nature of these interactions can easily be lost sight of since, as I said above, the English language uses the one term 'environment' inclusively for all of them: while at the same time scientific and popular usage limits its meaning to our external physical and chemical environs. This has in turn limited our perception of the complexity of interactions between organism and environment posited by autopoietic theory. To counteract this I shall differentiate quite sharply between certain dimensions of those interactions, while at the same time insisting on their interrelatedness through various metabolic exchanges. The scientifically recorded rise in atmospheric pollutants has led to a general if inchoate perception of the complex biogeochemical cycles described by Volk which couple us with the material, earthly dimension of our environs. But there are other dimensions – social, linguistic, religious, political, imaginative and emotional – which also help make us what we are and allow us to develop through time. It will become clear that they too influence our 'making' our physical landscapes what they are.

In this chapter I shall delineate four of these dimensions which roughly correspond to our individual, social, biophysical and expressive experience of structural coupling, while aware that the interactions between the individual and the social, for example, are such as to make distinctions between them hard to sustain. But here the value of the distinctions outweighs the difficulty of maintaining them, since they allow me to highlight one of the crucial characteristics of an autopoietic entity: its individual autonomy. This is crucial for its structural integrity and for its freedom to act in accordance with that structure. It is particularly crucial for us as a condition of possibility for our acting responsibly in relation to our environments: for our building a bridge between what we say we know about the world, what we say we know about God and how we live. In all this I am not arguing for a stratified form of differentiation between the dimensions. I am merely trying to describe a functional, or rather interfunctional form of relationship.

Inevitably this becomes an exercise in 'thick description', a term Clifford Geertz borrowed from Gilbert Ryle to characterize the use of multiple complex conceptual structures with many of them superimposed upon or knotted into each other. Their copresence, Geertz says, always needs clarifying (and here will be continually recalled), but that does not mean that they cannot be separately formulated and appraised (Geertz 1993a: 3–30). To do this I shall attach variable prefixes to the basic term 'Scape' (shorthand here for the metaphoric/literal use of 'landscape' in the Preface) to describe various dimensions of a human organism's experience of its environment.

The first dimension, *SelfScape*, centres on the boundaries around the autopoietic self at any particular time: body and place together. Capitalizing the basic term signals a notional boundary between the two parts, while at the same time the absence of punctuation between them signals their being integrally connected to or knotted into each other. Personally this dimension can extend as near or as far within the compass of my horizon as I settle for at any one time (my desk, the garden, the canal bank beyond), because however large or small, I am always at its centre and I carry that centre with me wherever I go. I am never 'detached' from my *SelfScape*, since I cannot exist outside it. And in a very special sense, it does not exist without me. It corresponds to the scope and compass of my personal perspective, of my subjectivity. It is the triangulation point from which I survey the world and through which information about it is fed back to me. It gives my perspective its distinctive contours, shaping my view of all other dimensions of my environment. It is the place where my immediate metabolic needs are met, or not.

The second dimension, *SocialScape*, provides me with generalized media of exchange ranging from food to Internet access (cybercafés are a neat expression of these interactions), and includes language, ritual, sex, education, play, culture and religion, all of which enable me to affirm my subjectivity but at the same time curtail the scope of my *SelfScape*. This contradiction occurs because there is a necessary difference of perspective between my *SelfScape* and that of others who share my environment: but at the same time I need a universally accepted social environment in which my basic needs are met, my experiences are validated and my inclinations to act in a particular way are approved (or not). Within the bounds of this *SocialScape* I receive positive or negative feedback not only on what I am, but also on what I perceive and express (Luhmann 1986: 12f.).

The distinction between my *SelfScape* and my *SocialScape* is part of my personal boundary. Preserving it is vital for any discussion of autonomy within structural coupling and, as we shall see, recognizing that boundary is crucial for living as nonviolently as possible. Oscar Wilde (although this was not his immediate purpose in telling it) reveals the identity and difference between the two dimensions in a parable:

> When Narcissus died, the flowers of the field were desolate and asked the river for some drops of water to weep for him. 'Oh!' answered the river, 'if all my drops of water were tears, I should not have enough to weep for Narcissus myself. I loved him'. 'Oh!' replied the flowers of the field, 'how could you not have loved Narcissus. He was beautiful.' 'Was he beautiful?' said the river. 'And who should know better than you? Each day, leaning over your bank, he beheld his beauty in your waters.' 'If I loved him,' replied the river, 'it was because, when he leaned over my waters, I saw the reflection of my waters in his eyes.'
>
> (Quoted in Ellmann 1987: 336–7)

The *SelfScape* perspective of the river is thrown into relief against the *SocialScape* view expressed by the flowers. The clash of perspectives is skilfully disclosed by Wilde by his closely connecting and at the same time precisely distinguishing between them. The copresence of more than one perspective (the river's,

Narcissus' and the flowers') is revealed in such a way that we can see how violence would be done to the others if only one was allowed to be expressed.

The third and most generally perceived dimension of environment is what I call here its *EarthScape*, its physical/chemical/earthy dimension. It too presupposes boundaries (permeable in some respects) between itself and the two previously named dimensions, as well as constant interactions between all three. Every breath we draw and use for every word we speak, as well as every meal we share or every step we take depends on this tight coupling. Tim Ingold's comments on Jakob von Uexküll's use of the German term for environment, *Umwelt*, are particularly useful for illustrating both the boundaries and the interconnections of the *EarthScape* dimension. Ingold remarks that a stone, for instance, is no more than an object with certain essential properties of shape, size, hardness and crystalline composition. Thus described, it would be an example of what von Uexküll called 'neutral objects'. But at some time or other, the stone may be coopted into various animals' projects. 'A crab may have concealed itself beneath it; a thrush may have used it to break open snail shells; an angry human may have picked it up to hurl at an adversary.' Within the *EarthScape* of the crab, 'the stone is a shelter, within that of the thrush it is an anvil and within that of the human it is a missile'. Von Uexküll insisted, Ingold says, that these qualities are not attributes of the object itself, but are acquired (from our perspective) by the object's having entered into diverse relationships with subject organisms. Each organism ascribes functions to the objects it encounters and thereby integrates them into a coherent system of its own (Ingold 1992: 41f.). In my terms, into its *SelfScape*.

Hence our *EarthScape* can be seen as our 'mapping out' of our *SelfScape* (and in many cases our *SocialScape*) onto the world outside and around our bodily boundaries, and at the same time, as the coopting of that world into our projects. The continuous interactions between all three dimensions constitute what is usually called 'the environment', each contributing to and distinguishable within the complexity of our autopoietic relationships. Through them our perspectives are shaped. Through them we learn to see the world, and to see it differently from one another, but always as significant to us in some respect.

Poiesis and partiality in perspectives

The fourth dimension I want to highlight is the *PoieticScape*, the linguistic, poetic, intellectual, creative, imaginative and expressive dimension of our coevolutionary environment: the place where we 'make' and remake our images of ourselves and of our relationships and express them through various media. Human *SelfScape* perspectives are expressed and communicated to others in words, spoken and written; in art; in music; in computer graphics; in ritual and gesture; in scientific experiments and mathematical equations. The *PoieticScape* dimension in subject organisms (whether myself, the crab or the thrush) always implies and is closely bound up with the *SocialScape* dimension, but I want to mark it off from that as the space where the 'poiesis' in autopoiesis becomes actively present. There we become poets, writers, makers, narrators, inventors, musicians, lovers, dancers, actors and imitators. For us, the faculties of language, logic, movement, art and imagination, driven by emotion and by passion, generate descriptions and reflections on them, reflections which may then affect how we act (Maturana and Varela 1998: 28f. The different ways in which this process expresses the selves of other organisms is necessarily backgrounded here). The *PoieticScape* is the place where translations between media and transactions between matter and form are worked through. It is also the place where we integrate the other dimensions of our structural coupling – *SelfScape*, *SocialScape* and *EarthScape* – and make them manifest in various ways.

Theologically, the *PoieticScape* corresponds to the relationship between faith and praxis, or belief and practice. It is particularly important for the kind of theology I envisage here. Generally speaking, we become aware of God (*theos*) in our *SelfScape/SocialScape* most effectively through the use of words about God (*logos*). By effectiveness I mean that through our God-concepts we ascribe functions to God in relation to whatever we encounter within our *EarthScape* and thereby integrate it into a coherent system. Functions ascribed to God and accepted in our *SocialScape* (creator, father, potter, judge, hierarch, mother, king) play a crucial role in our social and religious evolution. They determine to some extent the kind of distinctions we make between the components in our environment (what is sacred, profane, good, evil) and how we use them and/or relate to them. And it is through such interfunctional distinctions that we coopt God into our relationship with the *EarthScape* dimension of our lives, not as 'a neutral object', but as the validator of our attitudes and policies. A good example, which will be explored in some detail later, is the claim that God created our species alone in 'His' image, and has given us the land for our sole use and benefit. All too often this has served to validate violence within the *SocialScape* and the *EarthScape*.

Together, the other three dimensions shape my *SelfScape* perspective, the primary personal focus through which I see the complex interactions of my life as a meaningful whole. It remains individual and partial, that is, more or less comprehensive, because my view is mine alone. This determines my choice of one among a number of valid, but only partially comprehensive descriptions of the components of those interactions, or of the interactions themselves. Acknowledging the partiality of my perspective (in the double sense of preferred as well as incomplete) reduces its autofocussing power over me, encouraging me instead to place my own views in question by considering the partial basis on which I hold them. It also enables me to acknowledge, and to allow for, the same process at work in others. For in the proverbial couple who looked out through prison bars, one saw mud and the other, stars. Presumably they saw the same view and had the same keenness of vision. But their individual perspectives determined what they saw as significant in the world before them. They also made it difficult, at best, for each to discern or accommodate the other's view.

Descriptions of the *SelfScape*, *SocialScape* and *EarthScape* will vary as greatly as the *PoieticScapes* of those who do the describing. In the third of his *Four*

Quartets, named *The Dry Salvages* after a small group of rocks off the Massachusetts coast, T. S. Eliot observed and reflected on the same Atlantic seaboard as Rachel Carson. She trained and worked as a marine biologist, and was fascinated all her life by the mysterious nature of the sea and its inhabitants. Her meticulous scientific observations and descriptions of marine organisms and their interactions with each other, and with their environments, convinced her that nothing, neither the sea nor herself, lives to itself or for itself alone. She saw her *EarthScape*, the sea's shores, its tides and its chemistry as parts of a comprehensive whole: of a world which brought her forth and kept her alive (Carson 1955: 14–39). Her *SelfScape/SocialScape/PoieticScape* gave her the ability and the desire to describe living entities in ways which respected their radical difference while acknowledging her interdependence with them.

Eliot's third Quartet was read at Carson's memorial service. What a different *SelfScape* it expresses! He too sees the sea's drift from past to future, but in terms of an individual's wailing, withering and enduring pain and loss. The sea evokes from him too reflections on past and future. He sees them, however, in terms of their conjunction in the here and now rather than their flowing continuously into an unknown future. Our own past, he says, is covered by the currents of action, but, looking at the furrow left in the wake of a liner, we cannot think that the past is finished, or the future before us. Rather, the 'impossible union of spheres of existence' is made actual in us. It is, he says, only a superficial notion of evolution which would allow us to disown the past (Eliot 1968: 31–43).

Wordsworth's perspective on a 'host of golden daffodils' differed in significant respects from that of a flower girl selling them in Covent Garden. And, perhaps, from that of the person who looked at her, saw her poverty and bought them. For we see that part of the world open to us as significant *to us* in some way, a significance made actual in words and deeds. Our behaviour differs significantly according to our perspective at any one time. We can, if we wish, see things as metabolic systems; as a means of feeding our children; as objects of pity or wonder; as a metaphor for human existence; as a chemical industry's resource bank; as sacred text written in fire, stone and water. And maybe as all of these, and more, depending on time, place and circumstance.

This partial dimension of possible human perspectives on the world – the physically bounded, social, cultural and intimate perturbations which shape, motivate and are expressed in our *PoieticScape* – is one I want to highlight in this and the following chapters. Our perspectives evolve in and through us as we interact with different environments at different stages of our lives. Therefore we necessarily live and work, individually and together, in and with partial perspectives. Therefore no one person, at any one time, can claim to have *the* perspective on the world, much less the putative viewpoint of 'no one in particular' or 'of God'. Demonstrating this false notion of 'objectivity' and drawing conclusions from its falsity has formed part of the radical feminist agenda for some years now.

Volk, recounting the story of a round-table discussion by scientists from different disciplines on how to describe the human body, says that gradually they moved toward a conclusion: a truth of no one truth. 'Instead, we decided, the truth resides in the very fact of the multiple viewpoints' (Volk 1998: 99f.). This is *not* the same as saying, as is sometimes held, that if my truth is as good as your truth, there is no such thing as truth. It *is* saying that an individual encounter with or response to a shared environment cannot express the whole truth of that environment. What the truth of multiple viewpoints holds is that by our very nature, an individual's perspective on truth is partial. Therefore it needs to be complemented by *SocialScape*, by the perspectives of others. The world I bring forth in my *PoieticScape* always depends on what is being looked at, who is looking at it, and why. It also depends on the *EarthScape*, the time/space within the stream of life *where* I find myself.

The acceptance of this 'truth within situations' by scientists today means, for them, that 'the epoch of certainties and absolute oppositions' is over. Ilya Prigogine aligns himself with this truth by quoting Merleau-Ponty's description of knowledge as both objective and participatory. So long as we keep before us the ideal of knowledge in the absence of any viewpoint, then, says Merleau-Ponty, our situation is a source of error. But once we acknowledge that through my situation in life I am geared to all actions and knowledge that are meaningful to me, then my contact with others is revealed to me as the starting point of all truth, including that of science. '[A]nd, since we have some idea of the truth, since we are inside truth and cannot get outside it, all that I can do is define a truth within the situation' (Merleau-Ponty in Prigogine and Stengers 1985: 299).

Theology from a coevolutionary perspective

The overarching coevolutionary perspective I have been describing tries to take account of the multiple environments within which that perspective has evolved. It relies on us seeing ourselves *as* members of biological communities structurally coupled with diverse environments through time and space. The overriding theological understanding is that the patterns of events throughout the evolution of life on earth have been, and are, continuously revelatory of Godself (Primavesi 2000). We see them now, at whatever stage of our evolutionary lineage we have reached, *as* continuously un-veiling and re-veiling the mystery we call God. We respond to, express and communicate that mystery according to our partial capacity. And each of us does this in our own particular and special way.

Two related things follow from this. The first is that unless western Christian theologians acknowledge the situatedness, the time/space dimensions of our theological traditions, especially their prior shaping by literate and urban male elites, we are liable to confine discussion of God within the frame of a particular perspective; to confine divine presence, or activity, or inspiration to a particular time, text, environment and group.

The second point follows: if we acknowledge the partiality of theological perspectives, we cannot claim absolute truth for any particular theological formula or narrative. The truth of multiple viewpoints applies above all to a truth, which is, by definition, beyond human grasp. If we glimpse it at all, it is through a glass, darkly.

This theo-logic, which presupposes theological validity in more than one set of perspectives or expressions, thereby removes one of the greatest sources of inter-religious violence. Theological descriptions based on this presupposition can be crafted and offered for discussion in ways which are essentially and intentionally nonviolent. Especially when a warrior God, or one who condemns living creatures to death for an offence they did not commit, is seen to be as much the product of a partial human perspective as the one Feuerbach alerted us to: God as a being who can do everything which is impossible to Nature, to reason and to us (Harvey 1995: 61). It is in this light that I read Pannenberg's comment that the meaning of the word 'God' in modern times can only be determined by anthropology (Pannenberg 1993: 81).

This leaves theologians, however, with more, rather than less, ambiguities in what we can say. For if we cannot decide conclusively between thoroughly valid, but only partially inclusive models of the world which we observe, how can we succeed in describing satisfactorily a God who, by definition, cannot be observed? The word 'God' itself, as theologian Karl Rahner remarks, refers to the 'ineffable (indescribable) one', the 'nameless one' who does not enter into the world we can name as part of it (Rahner 1978: 46f.).

Yet we know that God does 'enter' the world, most effectively in western culture through the dimension of it I call the *PoieticScape*, and that this affects our 'mapping' of or perspective on the *EarthScape* and our coopting it into our projects. Therefore an important part of the theological task is to make transparent the function ascribed to 'God'. Explicitly or implicitly, how is the concept, or the name 'God' systematically integrated into the diverse relationships maintained with and by the *EarthScape*? And how does this affect even those descriptions not explicitly claimed as, indeed sometimes denied as theological?

In one of Darwin's most forceful, and for me most uncomfortable of images, he compares the face of Nature to a yielding surface, with ten thousand sharp wedges packed close together and driven inwards on it by incessant blows, sometimes one wedge being struck, and then another with greater force (Darwin 1996: 168). Who drives the wedges? Carefully, he does not say. For many, if not most of his contemporaries, it could only be 'God': and themselves as God's 'instrument'. Some in America, engaged in the settlement of New England as 'New Canaan', proclaimed that the God of Exodus, of 'the mighty hand and outstretched arm', sanctioned their alteration of the landscape. This, the face of 'fallen' Nature, was to be subdued, redeemed through plough and shears (Merchant 1996: 36–44). Rachel Carson's carefully chosen epigraph for *Silent Spring*, taken from E. B. White's writing one hundred years after Darwin, states pessimistically: 'Our approach to nature is to beat it into submission.'

What concerns me here is that Christian belief in God did, and still so often continues to add righteous sinew to the human arm driving the blows into Nature's countenance (see White 1967).

Does the word 'God' have to leave furrows of violence, traces of pain on the face of Nature, and on the faces of all living beings, including ourselves? And if so, why? The word itself, as the Jewish philosopher Emmanuel Levinas reminds us, is at once the most familiar and the most obscure name known to us, subject to every use and abuse. Even its deliberate obscuring, as in the extract from Darwin, does not save it from abuse, in the sense of sanctioning abuse. What, or who this word names has been fiercely contested throughout history. Whatever its meaning, wherever it appears it is clothed in values which cannot be weighed precisely against any generally accepted counter-measure. This imprecision, to use Seamus Heaney's luminous phrase, tilts the scales of reality towards some transcending equilibrium (Heaney 1995: 1–16).

The balance is held if we see ourselves within a single evolutionary process; as members of biological communities contributing to the sustaining of life in whatever environment we inhabit. This gives us a maximum perspective on the function of God concepts within those communities. Do those concepts, through a positive conjunction of sacred, technological and political power, sustain reverence for, and so safeguard the living systems which form our communities? Or negatively, do they continue to sanction violence against any of them?

This may appear a minimum criterion, but, as the history of religions shows us, it is none the less radical for that. If, for example, we distinguish, from among all living creatures, ourselves alone as being made in the image of God, do we not then see ourselves as of greater value to God than others and, as a corollary, see them as of lesser value? And if so, what kind of behaviour does this sanction? Does our theological lectionary rule out non-conceptual, non-verbal ways of knowing God? Do we tend to universalize our perspective as true for everyone, regardless of their environments? Or rather, do our words resonate against the shadowy contours of what cannot be said, reminding us that the task of language at certain levels of discourse, whether scientific or religious, is to express (as clearly and comprehensively as possible) what is, ultimately, inexpressible?

In response to such questions, whatever is said about God from a Gaian perspective will be said, as far as possible, descriptively not prescriptively. It will suggest rather than define. This approach respects the diversity of interfunctional relations with God and the differentiation of religious perspectives within a diversity of environments. Such respect restrains us from reducing the complexity of those environments to what can be said about them within human society, or within any one group there. Each of us, as Rachel Carson reminds us, emerges from and passes through the stream of life from and to a certain place and at a particular pace. The stream itself moves us, together with biological communities past and present, with and through the ministering flow of evolution.

2 Coevolutionary organisms

The miracle of life is that, despite the best grip we can get on reality, it continuously manages to surprise us. The beauty of science is that, notwithstanding all our tacit assumptions, these surprises can get through. ... Our surprise is a measure of our tendency to underestimate the flexibility of living organisms. ' "Organism" is a code word – not simply a plant or animal but the name of a living form, of object-as-subject.'

(Evelyn Fox-Keller 1983: 183; 200)

True to its nature, the miracle of life eludes complete description and definition. Yet as we saw in the previous chapter, 'thick' descriptions which highlight rather than underestimate the complexity of living organisms and their environmental interactions give us surprising glimpses of that miraculous reality. The focus in this chapter is on the evolutionary history of living organisms, and the surprise is due in large measure to the fact that when this history is opened up for us, we find it part of our own. Science technology, in the form of time phase photography and the electron microscope, now enables us to read some evolutionary texts formerly subvisible to us, and as we look at them they arouse in us the kind of wonder Descartes called 'the surprise of the soul' (Fisher 1998: p. 45f.). We find ourselves paying close attention to rare and extraordinary objects, and as they demand our attention and reflection we come to see them, and ourselves, in a totally new way.

The family of organisms

One scientist whose moments of seeing involved very close attention to the history of living organisms was Barbara McClintock (quoted above by Fox-Keller), whose life's work on genetic organization in corn plants earned her the Nobel Prize in 1983. Her work first surprises us when we find that she classifies both animals and plants as organisms which move in different ways. The ability to move had been taken, and often still is, as a defining characteristic of animals, indeed of 'animacy' itself (Ingold 1994: 2). But plants, McClintock points out, have a sophisticated form of movement in response to light, and today time lapse photography reveals to all of us their usually imperceptible progress. Her scientific experiments, conducted over long periods of time, disclosed that movement is not the only characteristic plants share with animals. During her research, she isolated transposable elements found in genetic organization within bacteria, yeast, flies, mice and men. 'Organism' for her was a code word, in which 'every component of the organism is as much of an organism as every other part', a more or less comprehensive whole. Her work on this multilayered, multifaceted reality within organisms convinced her of the inadequacies of our models when faced with the complexity of natural, actual order. It gave her a deep reverence for nature and a capacity for union with the living forms she studied, a capacity she summed up herself as 'a feeling for the organism'.

The first surprise then, of a Gaian perspective, is that on the basis of our physical components, we cannot, as she said, draw a convincing line between plants and animals, or between our lineages and those of other living organisms. (Is coral a plant or an animal?) We do, of course, make such distinctions for convenience sake, and in order to appreciate the subtlety of unique configurations of components in different living forms. Above all, we differentiate our kind from other kinds by our ability to think, to speak and to act freely. This becomes problematic, however, when on this basis, theologians claim that this God-given ability enables us alone to seek, to respond to and to speak about God. The planet's history and the evolution of life on it before we became its dominant inhabitants (at least in our own eyes) are treated as prologue to God's revelation to the world. The dialogue between God and world begins, we assume, with our entry on the scene. This presupposes a radical discontinuity, which works in our favour, between our potential for meaningful relations with God and that of the billions of other species which preceded us, accompany us and, perhaps, will supersede us. This is epitomized in the ascription to us alone of an immortal soul which relates us directly and eternally to God.

This theological platform has occupied the high ground right up to the present day. Coevolutionary theologians, however, burrow beneath it to test its foundations. They delve into the fact that our species, like all organisms now alive on earth, has evolved through biological processes which place us within a continuum of patterns of evolution (which simply means change through time) ranging from microbial, subvisible organisms with cellular boundaries through to the evolution of individual organisms and species, including our own. The physical environment which has coevolved with these organisms is the biosphere, that part of the earth where living things, including us, normally exist. The biosphere is itself maintained within Gaia, the planet-sized system where the living and non-living components interact as two tightly coupled forces, each one shaping and affecting the other through systemic feedback loops. This system includes the rocks, air and oceans; has continuity with the past back to the origins of life and extends into the future as long as life persists (Lovelock 1995: 20).

A Gaian perspective, therefore, does not support a view of ourselves in radical discontinuity with other species. On the contrary, our common origins with other multicellular organisms bind us ineluctably to past and present communities of life forms on earth. We share the capacity for movement, sensory behaviour and potentially unpredictable response both with our microbial predecessors and with larger animals. With the latter, we share a unique developmental pattern from fertilized egg into embryo (Margulis 1997: 93–95). Every animal and human person encapsulates not only the motor and sensory capacities and responses of our microbial predecessors, but the originary microorganisms themselves. This perception of our multilayered, multifaceted *SelfScape* can, and does change our perspective on ourselves. What am I, indeed, that God is mindful of me? What kind of God is mindful of me, such as I am? And over what time span, and through what changes, has God known me?

From this maximum perspective, another foundation of the traditional theological platform, the drawn lines between life forms which rank them or stack them in a particular order, appears increasingly unstable. At a basic biological level we see that all life on earth, including human and plant life, derives from common ancestors – tiny bacteria. We are, from this perspective, interlocked with all living organisms in a matrix of bacterial ancestry. We can see this under an electron microscope, where the fundamental division (and connection) in life forms is not between plants and animals, but between bacteria (organisms composed of small cells with no nuclear membrane surrounding their genes) and all other life forms (including humans) composed of cells with nuclear membranes.

Looking through this window on the miracle of life, the biologist Lewis Thomas remarks that a good case can be made for our non-existence as entities. We are not made up, as we had always supposed, of successively enriched packets of our own parts. At the interior of our cells, driving them, providing the oxidative energy that enables us to do anything, are the mitrochondria. Strictly, they are not ours, or us. They are separate creatures, the colonial posterity of primitive bacteria that swam into ancestral precursors of our eukaryotic cells and stayed there. Ever since, they have maintained themselves, and their ways, by replicating in their own fashion, privately, with their own DNA and RNA quite different from ours. Our genomes are catalogues of instructions from all kinds of sources in nature, filed for all kinds of contingencies (Thomas 1974: 2). Primary coevolution, from this perspective, relies on the remarkable capacity of bacteria to combine their bodies with other organisms, and so form alliances which may become permanent – and human. Fully 10 per cent of our own dry weight consists of bacteria, some of which – such as those in our intestines – we cannot live without. 'Our' bodies are actually the joint property of the descendants of diverse ancestors (Margulis and Sagan 1995: 192; Thomas 1974: 82–7).

Ourselves and other organisms

This means that far from being radically distanced from microorganisms on the evolutionary ladder, we are surrounded by them, partly composed of them and dependent on them. This perspective on life forms subvisible to us, but essential for our survival, shows the inadequacy of the commonly held view of evolution as a chronic, bloody competition among individuals and species. Life did not emerge initially solely by what appears to us as combat or predation, but also by what is recognizable as co-operation and networking. From the beginning, emerging life forms responded to each other and to their physical environments by interacting in many different ways, multiplying and diversifying through different structural couplings which required, in some instances at least, co-opting others rather than killing them. Thomas observes that in contrast to our routinely violent and aggressive behaviour, which has been accepted as conforming to 'a law of nature', most of the associations between living things subvisible to us are essentially cooperative, symbiotic in one degree or another. When they do have an adversarial look, it is usually a stand-off relation, with one party issuing warning signals. Bacteria, he points out, live by collaboration, accommodation, exchange and barter. They and fungi, probably with some help from a communication system laid on by viruses, comprise the parenchyma of the soil. They live on each other, beside each other, inside each other, with some microbial communities extending so deeply into the affairs of larger forms of life as to seem like new kinds of tissue in plants and animals (Thomas 1974: 6–10).

This understanding of subvisible microorganisms strongly and consistently interacting with each other and with us has not yet surfaced in a major way in theology. This is hardly surprising, since, as biologist Lynn Margulis points out, it has yet to migrate significantly beyond the world of microbiologists. Even there, and from the start, bacteria have had a bad press, routinely associated with infection, studied and marked as agents of death and decay in us. The culmination of this process can be seen in our development of 'biological' weapons, reinforcing the image of micro-organisms as 'virulent others' to be destroyed lest they destroy us first. In recurring crises in the Gulf, wide media exposure is given to the lethal and long-term effects of Saddam Hussein's biological weapons. All of which obscures and leads us to discount the enormous importance of bacteria to the well-being of all forms of life (Margulis and Sagan 1995: 68f.). Even the experience of iatrogenic disease, usually resulting from indiscriminate destruction of bacterial colonies in our bodies through overuse of antibiotics, has done little to balance the account.

The discounting of what Thomas calls 'the biologic revolution' is due to other factors besides the 'bad press' already mentioned. More subtle is the intuition that, if taken seriously and pursued to its logical and practical conclusions, like all revolutions it will subvert the accepted order of things. As McClintock pointed out, it will reverse the subject–object relationship, and, more subversive still, will put our own supreme subjectivity in question. Thomas hinted at this when he spoke of the sense of being non-existent, of being a 'non-entity'. This would depose us from the top of the evolutionary ladder we have constructed to support our self-esteem, toppling us into a disorienting world where 'top' and 'bottom' are inverted. Rather than seeing ourselves as stand-alone, self-energized individuals, we would discover ourselves always to have been dependent on what he calls the 'obscure little engines inside my cells'.

These mitochondria and chloroplasts, from this subversive viewpoint, appear as the most important things on earth. In effect, he says, 'they run the place'. They move about in my cytoplasm, breathe for my own flesh, but remain strangers. They are much less closely related to me than to each other and to the free-living bacteria in the soil. The same creatures, precisely the same, are out there in the cells of sea gulls and whales, in dune grass, in seaweed and hermit crabs; in the leaves of the trees and in the fly on the window. 'Through them', he says, 'I am connected; I have close relatives, once removed, all over the place. There is something intrinsically good-natured about these relations; nothing resembling predation; no pretence of an adversarial stance on either side' (Thomas 1974: 81–7).

Yet still we feel threatened by the fact of our common origins with all life forms; by our continuing dependence on those inhabiting ourselves and our environments. Thomas says succinctly: 'I had never bargained on descent [*sic*] from single cells without nuclei. I could even make my peace with that, if it were all, but there is the additional humiliation that I have not, in a real sense, descended at all. I have brought them all along with me, or perhaps, they have brought me.' His sense of being humbled is highly significant. The awakening to such dependence is disorienting for a species which has believed and preached that God has given it dominion over all living creatures. Or, in a secular version, that our brains/technology/higher consciousness have given us the ability to dominate every other life form and the right to exercise that dominion.

Feeling humbled is, therefore, a logical response to the perception that organisms too small for us to see do exist, have existed and will exist happily without us. And that the reverse is not true. We would not exist at all, happily or otherwise, without them and their self-maintenance. It was bacteria that made the planetary environment supportive of life. On a global scale, the living tissues made by microbial mats – whether as living carpet or growing stone – may be as important to biospheric functioning as lungs and liver are to us. Bacteria took over the world and still run it, using their decentralized planetary metabolism and capacity for worldwide intraspecies gene transfer. This has enormous implications, not only, as Margulis asserts, for our self-perception, but also, I would hold, for our perception of God (Margulis and Sagan 1995: 68; 1997: 74–82).

Theology becoming an earth science

This self-perception destabilizes hierarchical images of God and creation which traditionally support claims to our God-given sovereignty over the rest of nature; to our inhabiting a 'higher' level of being, implicitly closer to God. The orienting metaphors of top and bottom, of 'above' and 'below' begin to shift in ways which make hierarchical categories of higher and lower, near and far, redundant. Within this maximum perspective, is not God, by definition, infinitely near to and infinitely far from every living being? The ability of each to respond to God 'according to its kind' shifts us from a belief in ourselves empowered by our souls as the prototype of proper response to a more egalitarian view, one of a world which allows for and empowers a multiplicity of responses to God. In theological terms, we play one part in a polyphony of response orchestrated by all that exists. We do not, and cannot sing solo.

Theology at this level is an earth science. This simply affirms that the systematic organization of human knowledge, in this case knowledge of God, now includes in its remit and discussions the environment in which that knowledge is systematized. It includes the perception that space and time, as we experience them on earth, preserve distance from and nearness to God for all living beings within a single evolutionary process. It accepts that our knowledge of God, and whatever God-descriptions emerge from our *PoieticScape*, emerge ultimately from our *EarthScape*. Gaia theory shows us that while space and time may in one respect appear to keep us at a distance from other species, in another respect all living things on earth are in physical contact at one remove through its water, atmosphere and soils, exchanging gases and other chemical compounds with the water, atmosphere and soils of the planet (Margulis 1997: xxii). This is the *EarthScape* in which we express the hope of knowing God according to our kind, knowing too that knowledge of God is shaped by our *SelfScape/SocialScape* and is, therefore, partial.

This wide-angled view reveals the structural fragility of another foundation of traditional theology: the assumption that God's relationship with the world is focussed on and solely determined by us and by our conduct. This assumption props up certain doctrines of sin in which it is stated that because one man, Adam, sinned, all living creatures were doomed to suffer and to die. A Christian revisionist version, fine-tuned to today's environmental sensibilities, is that Christ's redemption of us from the effects of sin also redeemed fish, fowl and four-leggeds. But this continues to define, as contingent on human relationships, the response to God of life forms which evolved long before we emerged – and which will continue to evolve after our species has had its allotted span and humans disappear from the earth. It still presumes that their goodness, their intrinsic value is dependent on ours. Adam's new clothes are supposed to cover not only himself, but every living thing trailing along behind him.

This view also assumes that the whole human race was, and is, arrested at some point of evolutionary change, a point beyond which it did not and cannot go without direct divine intervention. With that intervention, some would even claim that the concept, if not the reality of evolution became redundant. 'Is not the Christian faith destined, is it not preparing to save and even to take the place of evolution?' (Chardin 1965: 326). Christians not only applaud the new clothes, but make them uniform for those humans who wish to live forever with God. For this outfit has the very special property of making its wearers immortal. They draw a very heavy line, marked 'death', between themselves and all other living organisms. Even though, on this view, death is not natural for the latter either, but is the punitive effect on them of Adam's sin – an effect which, unhappily in their case, endures forever. This enduring effect is usually attributed, by us, to their lack of a human soul.

Coevolutionary theory leads to a very different view, one in which human-kind, in common with other organisms, is by nature alterable and able to alter. This seems a rather obvious thing to say, until one realizes that traditional doctrines of original sin, in their emphasis on an intrinsic flaw in human nature which can only be redressed by direct divine intervention, deny us the possibility of change. Or at least, of change for the better. The concept of evolution itself however, by definition, assumes change through time. We have some bench-marks, such as the abolition of slavery in the nineteenth century, to encourage us about the direction of change. In the twentieth century, we have had some individuals, such as Helen Keller, Gandhi and Aung San Suu Kyi, who give us hope in human progress through nonviolent means. In regard to death, that too is change, a natural change from one state to another. It is not negotiable with God. Within the court of evolutionary law we cannot, as we well know, argue an exemption for ourselves on the grounds of pre-Adamic or post-Christic precedent. Rather, as Lewis Thomas says, we have to give up the notion, prevalent in our society, that death is catastrophic, or avoidable. Tragic, heart-wrenching and painful as it may be for those of us left bereft by death, we cannot avoid it. Everything in the world dies, and almost everything we see is in the process of dying. If it were not for the constant renewal and replacement going on before our eyes, the planet would turn into stone and sand under our feet (Thomas 1974: 113f.).

Human history/Earth history

In rewriting the evolutionary record to give us a unique let-out clause, Christian theology has effectively cut it down to one short story: human history. A traditional western biblical interpretation abridges that history still further to that of a particular group of people at a particular moment in time. Particular events, such as Exodus from Egypt, are taken as a definitive revelation of God's will and purposes for that people and their descendants, both physical and/or spiritual. This methodological move relies on a normative concept of revelation-as-human-history, or human-history-as-revelation. It is unfortunate, to say the least, that the history chosen to describe the revelation of God's purposes is all too often that of conquest, land acquisition, oppression of and violence towards the conquered, sanctioned on the assumption of God's love for some peoples and not others. Most of us today would want to think that Egyptians and Canaanites, Hittites and Perizzites were also God's people.

In theology narrated from a coevolutionary perspective, the relationship between God and the world cannot be reduced to some groups within human history, or to human history alone. Our *SocialScape* never has coincided with the whole *EarthScape*. Instead, evolutionary science obliges us to 'study a world from whose history we are largely absent. We must survey an antiquity in which we have no place' (Beer 1983: 21). God's revelation, the unveiling and reveiling of Godself to the world, can then be taken as part of the evolution of life from its inception, however established. This does not exclude human understanding and expression of that revelation, but it cannot be reduced to it either. Nor can it be reduced to human speech, or, even more reductionist, to one set of texts or words in one particular language (Primavesi 2000) The texts themselves surprise us with this truth. Before any human voice was heard, sun, moon and shining stars praised God; the sea roared, the floods clapped their hands, the hills sang for joy; fire and hail, snow, frost and stormy wind fulfilled God's commands (Psalms 98; 104; 148). These responses continue, and will continue until, perhaps, in Yeats' phrase, God burns up the world – with a kiss.

Different kinds of question, then, emerge from an *EarthScaped* theology, behind which stands an overarching question, 'Why have we made and why do we insist on certain 'orders of merit' in God's relations with us and with all other living creatures in our environments?' Various answers will be suggested which beg a prior question: In whose favour does each distinction operate? Can these distinctions, as presently invoked, not be seen as having a validatory function, sanctioning present unsustainable and explicitly violent lifestyles? (Primavesi 1991: 85–11; 195–222). This question directs attention to the function of these self-elevating distinctions. It also highlights the positive task of a Gaian theology: to make distinctions not in order to degrade other life forms, but in order to respect them, a respect which calls for a maximum perspective on them whenever possible, one disclosed to us today in large part by the earth sciences.

One of the tools the earth sciences give us is a different set of distinctions between life forms. These taxonomies (of which this whole chapter is an exemplar) are based on the premise that the correct context for discriminating between one life form and another is the whole ecosystem and not merely the notionally demarcated species. Furthermore, the focus is secondarily on its use to us, and primarily on its relationships with other organisms within the ecosystem and therefore with the ecosystem itself. In Gaia science the correct context ultimately includes the planetary system and its life cycles, and within that, the relationship between an organism or species and its material environment, including other organisms. Marine algae are a typical case where this relationship extends to cloud formation and can include, eventually, planetary water and sulphur cycles (Lovelock 1991: 122–6).

In science there is (usually) no overt assumption that algal bloom relationships can be confined to, or defined by those relationships of utility they have with us, or we with them. However as they are often implicitly viewed in this way, we find, as Margulis observes, that scientists are just as reluctant as theologians to give up the kinds of discrimination which assume an absolute barrier between ourselves and other living organisms: just as reluctant to acknowledge our real geophysiological relationships of interdependence. And this reluctance is reinforced, often unconsciously, by religious taxonomies which posit relationships between God and certain people in our *EarthScape*, or between us and certain parts of it, which isolate them from the whole and allow us to assume God-given power over them or to deny, more or less explicitly, that their life cycles are there for any other purpose than our use and benefit. Such religious taxa are pagan or heathen persons, unclean animals or pro-fane/unconsecrated land, buildings, food, materials or artifacts – allowing us to assume that they have no intrinsic value to God and therefore can/must be destroyed, exploited or used as we wish. The theological *PoieticScape* then functions as a validation of violence.

Theology within a Gaian *EarthScape*, however, subverts the foundations of a narrowly human-centred one, arouses powerful (and often confusing) emotions and expands the imaginative and compassionate capacities of our *PoieticScapes*. A world infused with a sense of wonder and awe, strange and yet familiar, is disclosed against the horizon of one in which new theological questions arise. This 'fusion of horizons' between the world of theology and the *EarthScape* in which theologians find themselves is akin to that which occurs when, according to Seamus Heaney, the poet must submit to the strain of holding in balance present circumstance and glimpsed alternative. From the fusion of the coevolutionary and theological horizons emerges one bright particular star: the hope that, as a species within diverse environments, we may evolve towards a consistently nonviolent way of life. The background against which that hope shines is, by and large, a dark and violent one. But it shines all the brighter for that. It is, I believe, the theologian's task no less than the poet's to place a counter-reality in the scales of environmental discussion today. It gains weight because for us, as for the poet, that counter-reality is imagined within the gravitational pull of the actual violence evident in intersubjective and interspe-cies relationships. Theological hope in nonviolence has the added exigence of being testified to against the backdrop of religious institutions and concepts which have justified and continue to justify, in the name of God, violence inflicted on others, both human and non-human.

3 Description and distinction

Suppose I had never distinguished myself
to myself from the landscape
so that reaching out to touch a leaf
of chickasaw plum or a spiny pondweed
underwater were no different to me
from putting my hand on my knee or pulling
my fingers through my hair.

(Pattiann Rogers 1994: 220)

The poet Pattiann Rogers is credited with creating a complex natural theology in language which is scientifically precise. Her poem quoted above, entitled *Eating Death*, meditates on how we would meet death if, as she says, we had never distinguished ourselves from the *EarthScape*, from the landscape to which we return in that 'last event' of our lives. Rogers recognizes this event, coming to us from our own depths, simply as a further aspect of ourselves. She alerts us to the fact that life, or death, cannot be observed, or, as she says elsewhere, caught hold of, if we lose what was defined in the preceding chapter as our autopoietic identity. How then do we, as observers, distinguish ourselves fruitfully and appropriately from the landscape we inhabit and observe?

In this chapter, I want to consider that distinction against the background of the structural coupling of organism and environment. Maturana and Varela are precise in delineating their interaction, its variables and its constants. They point out however that organisms and environment vary independently: the organism at each reproductive stage and its environment according to quite different dynamics. This variable dynamic affects both their interaction and the evolution peculiar to each. When the environment changes slowly, over long timescales, phenotypic stabilization in the organisms will emerge. When the environment changes abruptly, diversification and extension emerge within the organism. But whatever the variables, organism and environment remain in a continuous structural coupling (Maturana and Varela 1998: 3f.). This year, for example, only some of the tadpoles from March spawnings in our pond metamorphosed into frogs so that now, in early October, I still see tadpoles swimming about. Abrupt temperature changes seem one likely explanation.

A brief description of my personal experience of change through time triggered by environmental variables coinciding with different stages of my development may serve as exemplar of autopoietic identity. I can and do distinguish myself, through and across the boundaries of my *SelfScape*, from the *SocialScape*, *EarthScape* and *PoieticScape* with which I am coupled. I retain my class identity as a human person by being an autonomous, living, bounded, self-producing, self-maintaining network of production processes. As an emergent human being I continuously interact with but am structurally distinguishable from the dimensions of environment out of which I emerge and which I inhabit, and from other autopoietic entities and their environments. Variables within my environment have triggered changes within me, some of them abrupt enough to be noticeable (such as moving from Ireland to Britain), others slow enough to be almost unnoticed (for example, the growth in multimedia inputs). My close coupling with different dimensions of my environment and different rates of change within them trigger different changes within me at different times, but throughout these complex environmental interactions I can, if I wish, distinguish both stability and variation, independence and dependence, wholeness and partiality which is peculiarly my own. This individual *SelfScape* marks me off as different from others within the *SocialScape*, *EarthScape* and *PoieticScape* we share: it forms part of my class identity and shapes my perspective.

Given this multidimensional character of my coevolutionary experience, there are many ways open to me to describe it. One kind of description, however, is not an option, that is, one which would eliminate the effects of all the diverse experiences triggered by variables within my own life, whether they come from my personal development or from interactions with my environment. The descriptions emerging from my *PoieticScape* express and reflect the evolution of my *SelfScape* in its interactions with my *SocialScape* and *EarthScape*. As I said in the Preface, varying rates of change in the global *EarthScape* over varying periods of time (due, among other things, to two hundred years of industrialization, technology and capitalism coinciding with a certain stage in ten thousand or so years of climatic change) led to the emergence of the United Nations Environment and Development Programme. And its emergence within my *SocialScape* triggered important changes in the *PoieticScape* within which I theologize.

This personal account of my experience may seem no more than stating the obvious. What I am saying is that dynamic variables, within themselves and within their environments, have affected scientists and their descriptions of interactions between organisms and their environments, just as they have always affected theologians and their God-descriptions. This means for them that in spite of the amount of work done on trying to reconstruct the biblical worldview (more or less successfully depending on your purpose and point of view), it does not accord with the *SocialScape* or *PoieticScape* of today. Biblical

Hebrew, for example, had no word for what we call 'Nature', a complex unity which only later became an object of study and experiment. 'Nature, the phenomenal world in all its strangeness, beauty and power, was just *there*, to be admired and occasionally feared, to elicit the praises of God, and to provide – in the aphoristic literature – analogies and lessons for human behaviour' (Blenkinsopp 1995: 41).

Theological observations and descriptions continually evolve, subject as their authors are to the natural drift of time and history and to their tight coupling with certain environments and not others. Yet some contemporary theologies of creation use classical terms such as 'original creation' to describe God's creating the universe in a state of perfection later disturbed by us; and continue to use these terms presumably on the assumption that classic theological texts alone retain this state of perfection.

In a poem reminiscent of Wilde's parable, Rogers displays her awareness of evolutionary linguistic potential:

> Here am I in this scene too, my shadow wrinkling
> On the water of the pond, my footprints making pools
> Along the bank. And all that I say, each word
> That I give to this scene is part of the scene. The act
> Of each thing identified being linked to its name
> Becomes an object itself here …
> This poem, as real as the carp sliding in green
> At the bottom of the pond, is the only object
> Within the scene capable of discussing both itself
> And the scene.
>
> (Rogers 1994: 44)

We distinguish organisms from each other by linking them to names we or others give them. But they can be, and have been differently linked by others. We, and the organisms, belong at once to a plurality of linguistic codes. Only the Latin taxon, perhaps, of the sliding green carp would be used by a zoologist observing the same pond as Rogers. Claude Monet might have given a specific name to the green colour he'd need to paint it. Physicists, with the spectroscopic instruments available to them, could discuss the colour's wavelength. Thomas Seboek, looking at living systems from a semiotic perspective, paraphrases a striking passage from Lévi-Strauss about transitions from code to code. '[F]rom many different versions, rendered simultaneously, there might flow a sense richer and more profound than each of the partial and distorted meanings that any single version, taken in isolation, might yield to us' (Ingold 1994: 67).

Evolutionary nature of description

I assume that theological sense too flows, indeed overflows from a mingling of linguistic codes, in this case scientific and theological codes. Scientific descriptions of evolution come in many versions, and for me one of the 'thickest', the autopoietic version, will be examined in this chapter, with others summarized in succeeding chapters. This plurality of codes is necessary because of the systemic character of structural coupling and because, as Rogers clearly sees, we, the observers, are inextricably enmeshed in it. This systematically limits the precise measurement of conjugate variables (such as position and momentum, or energy and time), and means that whenever we observe or describe these variables, we are ourselves immersed in a network of interactions which themselves affect and effect our own perspectives, observations, descriptions and behaviour. These complex interactions account for the fact that our descriptions of the world will always have precisely that mixture of regularity and mutability, of solidity and shifting sand, of precision and vagueness typical of human experience (Maturana and Varela 1998: 241; Bateson 1991: 98f.). But this dynamic mixture, by its resistance to reductionism, fuels our desire and continuous search for more accurate terms and for more precise descriptions. Theological hermeneutics, the science of continuous interpretation and redescription of foundational texts, is partly fuelled by a similar desire.

Whether we write, or paint, or sing, or ritualize our descriptions for others to engage with, yet another interaction must be taken into account. Rogers indicates this by addressing her reader directly:

> And see, reader, you are here also, watching
> As the poem speaks to you, as it points out that you
> Were present at the very first word. The fact of your
> Cognizance here is established as you read this sentence.
>
> (Rogers 1994: 44)

Manifold interactions between observer, describer and reader, and between their individual perspectives, keep the circuit of language open to new linguistic couplings. This ensures that the *PoieticScape* evolves. From Sappho to Pattiann Rogers, 'description' in an autopoietic context means, precisely, that each time an observer describes the interactions that occur between two or more organisms and their environments, the meaning she attributes to them in some way affects the course of those interactions (Maturana and Varela 1998: 209). This emphasis on attribution is not, as we have seen, a mere semantic exercise. Attribution assigns and accepts responsibility for the meaning attributed, and for the violent/nonviolent potential of the description. That responsibility cannot be off-loaded onto 'no-one in particular'. Attribution accepts that the description cannot be divorced from the perspective, the context, the assumptions of the person selecting it. 'Meaning' cannot stand alone, independent of the one finding it. Attributing meaning to a description is another way of talking about the function of descriptions, whether scientific or theological. Which is another way of speaking about their significance.

Margulis' descriptions and their character

How does autopoietic description function? Margulis, as observer/describer of autopoietic interactions and their meaning, starts in true scientific fashion by isolating certain criteria in an autopoietic system. Firstly, she says, it has an identifiable boundary around discrete components. Secondly, it is an entity in which the component interactions and transformations are determined by component properties. Next, the boundary of the entity is determined by relations among its components. Thus the boundary and system components are produced by component interactions and transformations (Margulis 1997: 93). This, for her, also identifies an ecosystem.

She then tabulates six properties and aspects of autopoietic systems and gives technical examples of their biochemical/metabolic correlates. The property of *identity* has the aspects of structural boundaries, identifiable components and internal organization. The property of *integrity*, or unitary operation, has the aspect of a single, dynamic functioning system. The property of *self-boundedness* has the aspect of a boundary structure (skin, bark, exoskeleton) produced by the system. The fourth property, of *self-maintenance/circularity*, has the aspect of components and boundary structure produced by the functioning of the system. The properties of an *external supply* of component raw materials, and of energy, have the external aspect which presupposes *interactions* with the dynamic stability of the surrounding environment (Margulis 1997: 268).

Margulis attributes the meaning of the interactive, recursive relations between the internal and external aspects of autopoietic systems (which make them constitutive of the coevolutionary whole) to their mutual and binding differentiation *and* unity. Her descriptions *connect* the internal and external aspects of the organism and its environment, while at the same time the language itself, of identity, internality, externality and boundedness, *distinguishes* them. We, the readers, take note (at some level) that an autopoietic system is intrinsically connected with its component parts, thus making their integration and self-boundedness define the system as an entity. At the same time, we take note (at some level) that by identifying the parts, she differentiates them within and from the system which makes and maintains them. Yet we know that the systemic connection between them is part of the identity of each component. Finally, we take note (at some level) that these internal, separate elements of the autopoietic system are known to be dependent on and interactive with the external, separate energy-giving properties of the environment beyond the system's boundary. That environment is, therefore, a constitutive component in the life of the autopoietic system.

Her descriptive conjunction of connection and distinction, of dependence and separation means, for us as readers, that the dynamic relations between us and our environments are shown to be such that they belong to the basic description of what we are. These autopoietic relations are an essential component, for me, of what I am in myself and of the world in which I live (Primavesi 1995b: 102). They are, for anthropologist Tim Ingold, 'the creative unfolding of an entire field of relations within which beings emerge and take on the forms they do, each in relation to the other' (Ingold 1998: 170). They are, for Pattiann Rogers, the recognition of 'night and day as my own slow breathing in and slow breathing out of light' (Rogers 1994: 220).

Such a relational self-description may seem, at first glance, nothing more than a common-sense observation about me as an individual, or a poetic insight into us as a species tightly coupled with our surroundings. Yet, it is not so simple, for the paradoxical nature of Margulis' descriptions keeps their meaning opaque, resistant to immediate understanding or simple verbal expression. They are paradoxical, and therefore difficult to express or grasp, because they invite us to hold together dual and logically exclusive aspects of relationality: connection and differentiation; autonomy and bonding; distinction and its obliteration; dependence and separation. Or, in a dominant descriptive word-pair of western culture, competition and cooperation.

This holding together goes against the law of contradiction, which assumes (rightly) that we cannot, in the same breath, both affirm and deny that we are connected. Conceptually also, affirming connection normally denies differentiation, just as affirmation of differentiation normally negates connection. Paradox as a language form uses sequential proximity of mutually exclusive concepts to subvert our common-sense understanding of sequential causation. Causes usually precede their effects. Connection 'causes' bonding. Separation 'causes' break-up. To link 'connection' with 'separation', or vice versa, immediately negates the first effect and subverts rather than upholds our common-sense understanding. Locating the source of this distorting pressure and correcting it is, for some philosophers, one of the tasks confronting philosophy.

Metaphor and the function of paradox

Against this requirement stands the fact that our experience of multiple environments is not sequential, but simultaneous: 'all at once'. The language form 'metaphor' evolved to express this simultaneity, and paradox is a particular metaphorical form which works within the bounds of sequential logic by subverting it. Metaphor, as a primary expressive medium of our *PoieticScape*, bridges the boundaries between *SelfScape*, *SocialScape* and *EarthScape* by crossing between linguistic codes and, by alluding to one in the context of another, conveys information about these different dimensions of experience far in excess of the terms used. It clusters together processes, subjects, meanings and perspectives, and then uses the cluster to inform ourselves, and others, about something more than or other than the terms themselves convey. In this book, it is the primary building block of the 'bridge' between what science says we know about the world, what theologians say we know about God, and whether we live violently or nonviolently.

The metaphor 'All the world's a stage', informs us that our life in the world can be described in terms of roles, parts, scripts, directors, beginnings and ends, climaxes and anti-climaxes, etc. But at the same time, it relies on our knowing that the world around us is not, and cannot be reduced to, a stage. This 'is/*is not*' relationship is the centripetal force holding the metaphor together, the twin supports of its reference. Evolution, as we shall see, is/*is not* the natural drift of water drops down a hill (Maturana and Varela), just as it is/*is not* a gardener selecting some strains of vegetables rather than others (Darwin). The word cluster can be as small as a sentence, as extended as Gaia theory (earth and the life it bears is/*is not* a system which has the capacity to regulate the temperature and the composition of the earth's surface and to keep it comfortable for living organisms), or as enduring an image as 'the tree of knowledge' in the Genesis text.

The study and theory of metaphor itself constitutes a sprawling heap, from which I shall pick up only a few salient items. The first is that a metaphorical cluster can be added to at different times, sometimes from other clusters. Its contents can be sifted and shifted into different arrangements and patterns to satisfy the requirements of the one using it. It grows or shrinks accordingly, in ways which allow it to demonstrate different things to or for those looking at it from different perspectives. As long as this process continues, the metaphor is 'alive': it keeps what Ricoeur calls 'the power of disclosure', the ability to describe reality in a meaningful way (Ricoeur 1975: 29–147).

Literalism works as a centrifugal force in metaphor, leading us to ignore or be unaware of the '*is not*' pillar holding up the bridge of split reference. The metaphor 'God is our Father' remained untouched for so long that it no longer has the power to disclose the fact that God also, by definition, *is not* our father. 'Man is a machine', or 'the brain is a computer' are explicit and implicit metaphors in much popular science today, especially where genes are described as the motor or software. This reductionism/literalism leads to such textbook statements as one quoted disapprovingly by Margulis: 'Evolution … is change over time in gene frequencies (by gradual accumulation of mutations) caused by natural selection in natural populations' (Margulis 1997: 272).

The metaphorical heap called paradox retains its power of disclosure because the centripetal force of the is/*is not* relationship remains intact and potent. It keeps side by side mutually contradictory words and concepts, and, by doing so, usually highlights the '*is not*' aspect. It forces it on our attention, subverting our tendency to literalism. Paradox, by removing the fixed focus offered us by human logic, compels us to swivel from one lens to another and so reveals the perplexing nature of our world. At the same time, it demonstrates the relativity of our different frames of reference as we focus alternately on other possible patterns of relationship.

These referential frames are (to change the metaphor to one of Sir Arthur Eddington's about science) two-inch fishing nets used to detect the whole of reality. If reality is the ocean, the net will not catch anything smaller than two inches. It is presumed therefore, that nothing smaller exists. Further, if the ocean, and fish larger than two inches, constitute the whole of reality, then birds, stars, grass, butterflies and elephants remain undetected.

In general terms, paradox functions to place in question the ability of discursive reason (or sequential discourse, written or spoken) to express adequately our coevolutionary experience of the world. It subverts our capacity for self-deception, for believing that by our placing certain aspects in logical, that is, spoken or symbolic order, either of causation, value, precedence, number, letter or magnitude, that that is how they are in reality. It keeps descriptions mutable, open-ended, subject to constant revision and, ultimately, non-prescriptive.

In autopoietic descriptions of coevolutionary relationality, paradox conveys a particular kind of meaning, communicates a particular kind of consciousness of ourselves as distinct from (the *auto* component), yet intrinsically connected to our internal and external environments (structural coupling through *poiesis*). This recursive symmetry of our self-reference, which, paradoxically, can only be stated asymmetrically, is validated in descriptions which convey the truth that while in some contexts we experience and stress the connectedness, and in others the distinctness, we exist by virtue of a coevolutionary process which holds together both at once (Luhmann 1989: 144). We mean both at once, even if we can only express one at a time.

Theologians use paradox specifically to subvert any attempt to say the 'final' word about God, and positively, to point to One who is not conditioned by human reason, or by any human order, but is experienced in doubt and faith, hiddenness and presence, transcendence and immanence. Word-pairs like these, and others such as sameness and difference, rest and motion, straight and crooked, light and dark, right and left, necessity and spontaneity, are alluded to by Plato in the *Timaeus* as elements abstracted out of the generated world to provide an account of the existence of that world. (Shades here of Bateson, Margulis and Volk.) Everything that exists in our universe is taken to be the joint, simultaneous product of whichever pair is being discussed. The word-pairs light and dark, good and evil, male and female, life and death, rest and motion have particular relevance in the accounts of creation. In both Plato and the Genesis narrative, these 'principles' are not 'parts' of the generated world. Most importantly, the ordering of these principles, or elements, is bi-causal, not temporal. It is not the case that at some moment in time the first principle (first in order of expression) produced the second. The production is not subject to time. Rather, the first could not be conceived and/or exist as a principle without reference to the conception and/or existence of the second (Samuelson 1994: 169–77). The same simultaneous generation, as I understand it, obtains for the Chinese principles of yin and yang.

Some famous examples in science of conceptual problems resolved through paradoxical formulations are the wave/particle theory of electrons and the dead/alive nature of Schrödinger's cat. Both of these (raised by familiarity almost to the status of cliché) bring home to us the limitations of rational logic characterized by a linear, sequential structure. They force us to realize that the problem lies not in whatever reality it is under discussion, but in our need, as observers, thinkers and describers, to divide the perceived universe into principles, parts and wholes. This need arises out of the nature of our perception of the universe. It is always structurally, physically, socially and linguistically coupled to whatever *SocialScape*, *EarthScape* or *SelfScape* we inhabit; to whatever poietic medium we are using to express our experience; to whatever metabolic exchanges supply components and energy to and set boundaries for our thought and vision. They, and our descriptions of them, necessarily do not grasp the whole.

Scientists themselves acknowledge that this inadequacy extends to that 'rationality' which, as we shall see in Chapter 4, is taken to be the most highly valued element in human nature: indeed, the element most akin to the divine. Ilya Prigogine, addressing a European Commission Conference on environmental ethics, stressed the 'boundedness' of our capacity for formulating and solving complex problems. These are precisely those which arise in environmental ethics, where we are forced to relate human conduct to the laws of nature, especially as reflected in the structure of our environment. He uses Herbert Simon's concept of 'bounded rationality' as a guiding principle, one which takes into account the limitations of human knowledge and computational ability and therefore accepts that we cannot assume that we are always capable of making optimal choices. The best we can hope for is methods of choice which are as effective as our decision-making and problem-solving means permit. This 'procedural or bounded rationality', says Prigogine, stands in opposition to the ideal of classic rationality, for it takes into account not only the limits on classical science but also the nature of the observer, including the limitations of his [*sic*] computational ability and the amount of information he can handle.

This is particularly the case, he says, when we deal with the dramatic variations in climate and global environment in the past and are attempting to forecast its future trends, especially since nothing in the evidence at our disposal indicates that this variability is about to cease. We are faced here with diverse types of behaviour in different classes of dynamic systems, some of which, unlike those which meet the requirements of classical rationality, lead to instability, unpredictability, and breaking of temporal symmetry – in other words, a basic contingency (Prigogine 1989: 89f. This will be discussed further in Chapter 5.)

Division or distinction?

Given that premise, how best can we break up the whole, the paradoxically limited whole, into more or less comprehensive wholes? Since we need to make distinctions, how should we do it? Briefly, in scientific and theological description, by careful and precise use of metaphor, particularly in its paradoxical form, to convey both differentiation and connection, and, having done so, to use the differentiation in order to convey respect both for the part differentiated, and for the whole with which it is intimately coupled.

Introducing the notion of 'respect' (or the lack of it) introduces emotion, or what one might call personal and social emotional coupling between the describer, whatever is being described and the one hearing or reading the description. This, for both science and theology up to now, has been considered at best regrettable, and at worst, repugnant. It is a fact that one of the reasons why *Silent Spring* met with outright hostility from a number of scientists was their revulsion at Rachel Carson's extended metaphor of 'Spring' in pesticide-land. Using scientific codes with precision, she combined them with evocative literary descriptions of a landscape drenched with poison. Their emotional impact was such that they persuaded readers not only of the interdependence of all life, but aroused in them the will and desire to act for its protection. She helped them, in E. B. White's terms, to view the planet appreciatively. One of the main charges used by chemical corporations against her was that she wasn't 'a proper scientist', but 'an emotional spinster' – as though the two are mutually exclusive.

James Lovelock experienced a scientific backlash when he used the metaphor of Gaia for his scientific theory. One delegate at a conference, when Lovelock was asked a question, interrupted to say: 'Gentlemen, we are here to discuss serious science, not to listen to fairy stories about Greek goddesses.' Lovelock responded with the nicely judged comment that such objections are an irrational and improper attempt to censor a metaphor. Indeed, personifying the planet is seen by scientist Freeman Dyson as a hopeful sign of sanity in modern society, precisely because it does engage our emotions. 'Intelligence determines means to an end. Emotions determine what our ends shall be.' In a remark which underlines the social character of the expressive environment, Dyson points out that emotions belong to the group, to the family, to the tribe, to the species, and that our emotional bonds with Gaia must be preserved as a means of keeping the planet fit for life. 'Respect for Gaia is the beginning of wisdom' (see Primavesi 1998a: 82f.).

I shall return to this question of emotion but want to concentrate here on autopoietic metaphorical processes. Maturana and Varela conclude from their studies in biology that the uniqueness of being human lies exclusively in a social structural coupling, in the *SocialScape*. This coupling occurs publicly primarily through languaging, generating (a) the regularities proper to human social dynamics, for example, individual identity and self-consciousness, and (b) the recursive social human dynamics that on reflection enable us to see that, as human beings, we have only the world which we create with others – whether we like it or not, whether we like them or not. These dynamics are inextricably bound up with emotions. Dividing emotion from language is only possible in language. (Those who train public speakers know this well, since they only attribute about 30 per cent importance to text, and overwhelming importance to what they call 'body language' which connects the speaker's emotions with those of the audience.) The words 'coupling' and 'generating' used as scientific terms retain latent emotional content. Maturana and Varela make it patent.

If we find, happily, that we love those with whom we create the world, then this deep-rooted biological dynamic becomes a stepping stone to interactions which make our social lives coherent. To dismiss love as the biological basis of social life, together with the ethical implications of love, would be 'to turn our backs on a history as living beings that is more than 3.5 billion years old'. *Every* emotion (fear, anger, sadness, etc.) is a biological dynamic. We may resist the notion of love in a scientific reflection because we fear for the objectivity of our rational approach. But why should the emotion of fear benefit our science anymore than that of love? Especially since love expands our cognitive domain (Maturana and Varela 1998: 246f.). Love dissolves the presumed division between emotion and rationality. Theologically, this revives Spinoza's concept of *amor intellectualis Dei*, a rational, understanding love – of God or of Nature.

How do I make distinctions (scientific or otherwise) in order to respect what is distinguished? By appreciating difference and identity at the same time. This entails understanding that whatever I distinguish from myself is both distinct from me, and at the same time intrinsically connected to me. The primary function of making distinctions then becomes linguistic coherence in the service of coevolutionary cohesion: a way of communicating a particular consciousness of ourselves as distinct from, yet intrinsically connected to whatever is being described. I use this kind of distinction-making to distinguish between certain aspects of environment discernible within the total field of relations characterized by our structural coupling.

Ecofeminist philosophy and theology has been particularly concerned to uncover distinctions with a contrary function: those religious taxa associated with negative feelings which can be used in order to degrade or devalue, particularly those made on the basis of traditional hierarchical paradigms in western thought (Primavesi 1991; Plumwood 1993). They have relied on, and have routinely employed linguistic decoupling; that is, stressing the distinction, the *is not*, in such a way as to deny any connection with the 'is'. Then it becomes possible to denigrate what the distinction separates off. In western religious and cultural history, matter has been distinguished from mind; nature from culture; woman from man; body from spirit; emotion from reason; earth from heaven in order to devalue one compared with the other, the devalued being described as unclean, polluting, inferior and/or profane. This de-valuing or de-grading has meant that emotion, matter, nature, woman and earth could then be treated as of lesser value, lesser importance. This degradation, in the case of women, nature and the earth, was taken to justify their exploitation.

Theology divided from, or distinct from science?

Within Christian theology there is a subtle theological division, generated by thought and reinforced by strong emotions, which for some people places the whole methodology of this book in question. They distinguish, in order to degrade, knowledge of God mediated through the natural world from knowledge of God mediated through Christian texts and teaching. They divide themselves and their Christian biblical revelation from Christians who accept that knowledge or awareness of God existed, and exists, before and after the textual record of revelation through Jesus Christ alone. The division runs deepest today between those who accept, and those who do not, that, as a corollary to the first proposition, we can, or cannot know God through 'Nature', or by nature. Glimpsed at the bottom of this chasm, by those with a Gaian perspective, is the presupposition that Nature itself could, in its own way, know God.

The division is old as well as deep, old enough to have bred lineages which give class identity to their descendants either as so-called 'natural' theologians or as 'orthodox' ones. The latter, as well as dividing divine revelation off by time, place and group, also divide the world, and human nature, into pre-Adamic (original creation in a state of perfection) and post-Adamic (tainted by original sin). Human nature then, by definition, needs redemption from the effects of original sin. Therefore Jesus, for those to whom he is revealed in Scripture and Christian teaching, is their Redeemer. However an intrinsic flaw remains in human nature which makes it impossible for us to have 'natural' knowledge of God. Therefore the truth about human nature, and about God, can be found only in texts which describe revelation of God in Jesus Christ.

This divisive Christian absolutism, which, implicitly at any rate, does not accept the common view of human evolution (although some of its adherents happily subscribe to it in every other respect than in their understanding of Christianity), has perennial appeal. This derives in large measure from its intellectual divisions being intensified by latent emotions, not least the feeling of 'security' which comes from being on the 'right' side of the divide. The fact that these same Christians pray to 'the one God and Father of all', a most comprehensive statement of common identity, is ignored. Those on the 'wrong' side are also, at best, ignored. More often, they are reviled in ways which can, sadly, be used to justify violence against them. Conflicts between Christians, between Christians and Jews, between Christians and Muslims, divide the children of the One they call God. What does it mean to them that the Christian Scriptures say: 'Our God has no favourites?' (Deuteronomy 10: 17; Acts 10: 34; Romans 2: 11; James 2: 1).

This absolutism can also, covertly and overtly, divide Christians and scientists. In general, those who accept the concept of natural knowledge of God are open to the concept of the truth of multiple viewpoints. Those who do not accept either of these concepts divide themselves, internally and often externally, from those who do; from those who understand all boundaries, whether membranous, political, religious or disciplinary, to be in some degree permeable. Instead, they stand guard over their chosen area and regard those outside as potential raiders or invaders. The division runs, in this form, not only between theologians, but between some scientists and others, as well as between scientists and theologians. In particular, it is evident in scientists who insist that anything which escapes physical examination does not exist, or that questions asked about the nature of the universe which cannot be answered by the laws of physics and material causes do not merit serious consideration.

Today, theologians hear questions raised and statements made by scientists which would once have been their province. A notable example is Stephen Hawking's assertion that science may one day, if not already, help us 'know the mind of God'. The reliable information offered by science about the world and ourselves predisposes people to listen to such questions and answers. They deal with universal aspects of knowledge pertinent to, and made available to all members of society, regardless of their religious affiliation. Most pertinent now for coevolutionary theology is the way in which, through exploration of the interdependence of organisms and their environments, earth sciences stress our connectedness with the whole *EarthScape*, our planetary environment. Theologians can be helped by this to realize that their work too, in common with that of other disciplines, is dependent on and interactive with the external, separate, energy-giving properties of the environment beyond their system's boundary. And, perhaps, to realize that independence is not a theological concept either.

4 Contemporary theological circuits

> In the real world, there was no stopping the circulation of meaning, no cutting of what Lacan calls the circuit of language. In the 1960s, metaphor, not material exchange, provided the primary vehicle for this circulation. In other words, it was the metaphorical use of *information* – as it criss-crossed among these two sets of disciplines (molecular biology and cyberscience), among their practitioners, and among their subjects – that provided the principal vector for the dissemination of meaning.
>
> (Evelyn Fox-Keller 1995: 103f.)

This quotation sums up the final point in the preceding chapter and at the same time introduces the one to be addressed here, which is whether or not theology has shared, or can share, in the metaphorical networks Fox-Keller has in mind. And if not, does it break the circuit of language between itself and the real world, and, by doing so, stop its own 'circulation of meaning'? A powerful contemporary circuit of meaning is constructed by and around evolutionary theory, and it figures as a pre-eminent metaphorical network in the 'real' world. It covers the cluster of processes, subjects, observations and perspectives which, after Darwin, is used to describe the complex history of transformation in living beings. Is this the world in which Christian theologians operate? Does the information offered by this theory provide a vector for the dissemination of meaning within the theological circuit? And if not, why not?

Coevolutionary impact

There are four main ways in which Christian theology has short-circuited evolutionary theory. Firstly, it has not accepted that our species evolved in the same way as every other species, that is, it assumes that ours was created in a once-for-all-time state of perfection. Secondly, it assumes that our species is unique in that God became a member of it at a particular moment in time, and that this incarnation was in some way outside the flow of evolution. Thirdly (and this is often, though not always, correlated with the preceding assumptions) it assumes that our species alone is made in the image of God. And finally, in a mirror image of the first assumption, it assumes that we alone know, through divine revelation, how our species began and furthermore, what will happen to us as a species at the end of our individual lives, together with what will happen at the end of time itself. 'Man alone perceives and communicates God's analogical ordering of the world' (Beer 1983: 20).

From the perspective of traditional Christianity, events are plotted along a line with an unambiguous beginning, middle and end, with the incarnation, or 'Christ-event' as 'hinge' or temporal mid-point of the entire process. This event is endowed with extraordinary explanatory force, setting the figure of one man, Adam, typifying sin and death, against that of another, Jesus Christ, typifying grace and life (Romans 5: 12–17). 'For the believer, the revelatory figure of Jesus is the intelligible event that makes all other events intelligible' (Taylor 1984: 59–65.)

What concerns me in this chapter is not so much the fact that theologians have held and taught, implicitly and explicitly, these presuppositions about our species, since they were commonly held in western society. My concern is the way they now function in our perception of God and of the natural status and function of death within life. Present knowledge of coevolutionary process before and throughout human history makes it impossible to isolate one individual, Adam, out of that process and attribute to him the pivotal role in that history then brought to a triumphant conclusion by Jesus Christ. To continue to believe this account requires belief in 'Adam' as an individual who brought death into the world. But this is a denial of contemporary understanding of life processes emergent in every living organism since life began on earth.

It is also a denial of pre-fifth century attitudes to death and life, as the twelve-year debate between Julian of Eclanum and Augustine demonstrates. The former held that death is not a punishment for sin, but a natural process. Unfortunately, the fifth-century church canonized Augustine's interpretation of the text of Romans, even though it was based on a mistranslation of Paul's text. Augustine read it as: 'death spread to all men because of (Adam) *in whom* all sinned', rather than '*in that* [that is, because] all sinned' (Romans 5: 12). It is beyond the scope of this book to set out why Augustine's interpretation was taken up and is still authoritatively upheld as a true and orthodox assumption about human life, and not only by theologians (Primavesi 1991: 224–30; Webster 1995). My present concern is that this misconception of 'Adam's' role be seen for what it is, and countered by stressing our common evolutionary history rather than our putative exclusion from it, or one man's lethal and disproportionate effects on it. Hopefully, this sense of our embeddedness in coevolutionary process would gradually redress the balance of Christian violence not only against those of our own species who do not accept Christ as 'a second Adam, greater than the first', but also against members of other species now condemned to death and/or extinction by us, not by Adam, day after day.

Unique creation

In the era after Aristotle and before Darwin, the fixity of species was a core belief. Each was considered to be uniquely created by God to fit a particular ecological niche (or so we would now see it). As the revolutionary import of Darwin's views has been absorbed into cultural consciousness in varying ways, and those views clarified, corrected through his successors engaged in scientific research and disseminated through the information revolution, this doctrinal pillar has become increasingly shaky. Our own species, not just non-human ones, is now seen as undergoing transformations over long periods of time through structural coupling with its environments. At the same time, it is becoming clear that these interactions with our physical environment are triggering perturbations within it and recursively on ourselves in ways which have no predictable outcome. Loss of biodiversity, human overpopulation, deforestation, overfishing and our disturbance of the delicate balance of the earth's atmosphere through chemical pollution are seen as having incalculable long-term effects, not only on our environment, but on us. The 'beginning', that putative moment indelibly inscribed on Christian consciousness, is no longer a sure source of knowledge about ourselves now, or about our present relationship with the world or with God. Knowing, or believing we know from the Genesis narrative what the 'first' man and woman did, or did not do, or where and how they lived, no longer tells us enough about human beings today and their proper relationship with their environments.

Increasing information about evolutionary change and perceptible transformations in ourselves and in the physical environment have had profound effects on traditional Christian believers, effects most evident perhaps in the increasing numbers who have relinquished their beliefs. The effects are also, however, reluctantly acknowledged by some who still profess to hold them. The reluctance is understandable, as it involves accepting that religious truth itself evolves and is not immutable. This lies at the heart of what is known theologically as the acceptance/non-acceptance of the development (evolution) of doctrine. Rachel Carson, living as she did during the development of atomic science, the Russian launch of the first satellite into space and increasing evidence of the loss of wilderness through human activity, noted the effects of these cognitive developments on her views of herself and her environment, and noted also her reluctance to accept the consequent change in perspective. The changes, she said, put thoughts into her head which were so unattractive that she rejected them completely. 'The old ideas die hard, especially when they are emotionally as well as intellectually dear to one.' It was pleasant to believe, she explained, up to the launch of the Russian satellite, 'that much of Nature was forever beyond the tampering reach of man – he might level the forests and dam the streams, but the clouds and the rain and the wind were God's. ... It was comforting to suppose that the stream of life would flow on through time in whatever course God had appointed for it, without interference from one of the drops in the stream – man.' She had clung to these traditional beliefs, she said, because to have them even vaguely threatened undermined everything she held dear. She realized, however, that it was worse than useless to 'go on repeating the old "eternal verities" that are "*no more eternal than the hills of the poets*" ' (my italics). She decided that she might as well be the one to write about 'Life in the light of the truth as it now appears to us' (Carson quoted in Lear 1997: 309f.). It is significant that she intended doing so by writing a major work on evolution, an intention which she was prevented from fulfilling by first having to research and write *Silent Spring*, and then finally, sadly, by her illness and death.

She came to accept the mutability of truth through time and space long after her scientific acceptance of the mutability of our species. Whichever aspect first impinges on us, traditional believers confronted with Darwin's description of evolutionary process have to grapple with the realization that the process itself precludes the possibility of *any* species, or the first or any member of that species, including our own, being 'independently created'. (See Thomas Huxley's essay, *A Piece of Chalk*, for a lucid exposition of this impossibility.) Darwin condemned such a claim to independent creation as 'erroneous'. For he saw that if evolutionary process applies to one species, it applies to all. Furthermore, once 'species are not immutable' became the basic axiom of evolution, no line could be drawn between humans and others. The acceptance of a shared evolutionary origin for our own species meant, in Darwin's words, that 'those belonging to what are called the same genera are lineal descendants of some other and generally extinct species, in the same manner as the acknowledged varieties of any one species are the descendants of that species. Furthermore, I am convinced that Natural Selection has been the main but not exclusive means of modification' (Darwin 1996: 163f.).

Independent incarnation

The evolutionary process as outlined by Darwin (supplemented by continuing research on our own genetic structure) does not, then, allow us to suppose that there is any complete structural genetic demarcation between us and other animals. Indeed, much of current biotechnological research is based on the opposite premise. Yet an unease with this remains, and, although relatively few would cite religious reasons for it, it is one of the driving forces behind resistance to biotechnologies or at least, behind calls for regulatory curbs on them. At the theological heart of this unease are the implications for traditional Christian doctrines of the Incarnation which assert that one member of our species, Jesus of Nazareth, was 'independently created' by God, an independence which, in the doctrine of the 'Virgin Birth', requires that his conception was 'independent' of normal sexual intercourse; that in him alone 'God became man': a man not kin to fish, fowl or four-leggeds, but only to us. And Christian doctrine has based its claim to true revelation, and its ability to disseminate it in certain metaphorical networks, on this distinction. It is based, in short, on the claim that God chose to be incarnate in a human body, one which was marked out 'before all time' as being chosen for incarnation, and which therefore was born perfect, complete, in a way distinct from all other bodies. God became one of us, lived as one of our species at a particular moment, in a particular time, place and person who spoke to us, and like us, alone. Western culture, consciously or not, still draws the line here, an evolutionary 'break' evident in the western/global calendar and its 'Millennium' celebrations.

Teilhard de Chardin imagined that with this event, evolution itself became redundant, for what other goal could it have? It established another 'beginning' which offered us a guide to what we should be. Every Christian refers back to the time of Christ and to his person as a moment in history when we were given *the* pattern of what it means to be fully human, and measures her/his life and conduct against what is recorded of Christ's life and death. What he did and said, how he lived and above all, how he died, have become the definitive revelation of God. His recorded words, together with accounts of his lifestyle and his actions are taken as definitive, immutable bases on which traditional theology rests. Appeals to 'Scripture and tradition' are theological shorthand for this process (Primavesi 1991: 111–32).

I too distinguish Jesus' life, in so far as one can, in order to respect it, especially for its embodiment of the spiritual principles of truth, love, justice and freedom. And, indeed, for his recorded outbursts of emotion, whether in grief at the death of a friend, anger at injustice or compassion for suffering. I lament his recorded death as a victim of imperial militarism, representative of all victims of militarist regimes which still today inflict torture and death on those who threaten them. Descriptions of his life have been, and continue to be, a valuable lifeguide for many generations of Christians. As a unique human life (for every human life is unique in its *SelfScape* being coincident with a particular *SocialScape*, *EarthScape* and *PoieticScape*) it manifested the sacredness of all life. As does every life lived humanely.

This does not, however, absolve theologians now from the task of looking at the function throughout western history of some presuppositions about his human nature and in particular, how they affect our relationships with other species today. The presuppositions were intuited and partially expressed by a contemporary scientific correspondent of Darwin's, the botanist Asa Gray. He was a man of deep religious convictions, brave enough, when he lectured on evolutionary theory to the theological faculty at Yale, to voice some of the implications for us of Darwin's theories. If, he asked, we share a common nature with brutes [*sic*], are we not thereby lowered [*sic*] to their level? Gray reassured his audience by saying that man [*sic*] is special, because he alone has the power of abstract thought. But this power, he said, has itself evolved from powers still found in animals.

He then went on to ask: 'Why do people care so much about this issue? Why are we so resistant to the idea that we are "kin" to "lower" animals, and draw dividing lines between them and us?' This resonates with an overarching question addressed by a coevolutionary theology: Why have we made and why do we insist on certain 'orders of merit' in God's relations with us and with all other living creatures in our environments? Or, taking up his point about being 'lowered' to their level, why do we distinguish ourselves from them in order to down-grade them, to make them of lesser account?

Gray concluded that part of the answer lies in the consequences of our acknowledging that kinship. It would, necessarily, affect our behaviour towards them. It would be difficult to deny, he reasoned, that, in so far as they are similar to us, they have the same rights as we do. (It would take just over one hundred years before 'Legal Rights for Natural Objects' became an issue debated in the United States. See Stone: 1987.) But, he concluded sadly, we do not wish to give animals what he saw as a moral claim on us on account of what he called a 'meanness' in us, evidenced in our wish to divorce ourselves from the rest of creation. Against this, he argued that it would make us more humane if we realized that as they have a life in which we share, so they have rights we are bound to respect. This idea was not, of course, as James Rachels notes, entirely consistent with Gray's earlier assertion that we are 'immeasurably exalted' above the rest of creation (Rachels 1990: 82–6). But his argument is still relevant today.

It is interesting to note Jesus being credited with use of the reverse argument when he is taxed with wrongdoing because he heals a woman on the Sabbath. In what I see as a typical outburst of anger at injustice and compassion for suffering, he argues that if on the Sabbath one is allowed by law to untie an animal and lead it to water, then ought not 'a daughter of Abraham' bound by infirmity be loosed from it? All his adversaries, we are told, were put to shame. And while feminists will not be surprised at a woman being 'reduced' to the status of an animal, in the context of this chapter I count myself among 'the people who rejoiced' at this glorious thing (Luke 13: 10–17). For Jesus appears to make inter-species relationships normative for those between humans, or rather, refuses to separate them in any absolute sense.

Made in God's image

Rachels does not take Christian doctrines of incarnation as his grounds for critique but focusses on another problematic area in the western religious tradition, which he characterizes as a blend of Judaism and Christianity. This relies on, and invokes, a sharp contrast between human and non-human life based on the claim that our species alone is made 'in God's image'. This religious taxon supports the claim that our life, therefore, is to be regarded as sacred, or at least, as of special importance. Non-human life does not have the same degree of moral protection. Indeed, for some, it has no moral standing at all. Non-human animals are there for our use, to be worked, killed and eaten in any way we please. Like the rest of creation, they are presumed to be there for our benefit. Almost all western religious commandments (although, as mentioned above, there are exceptions in the Sabbath laws on the treatment of animals) refer to our treatment of other human beings, who are not to be killed, lied to, stolen from or otherwise mistreated. Their lives alone are sacred. Their property is protected not only in deed but in thought, since we are forbidden to covet it in the first place.

Most manuals of Christian ethics are based on analyses of and commentary on these commandments and until recently confined themselves almost exclusively to the regulation of inter-human relationships. In the 1940s, Aldo Leopold observed despairingly that philosophy and religion had not prepared people intellectually for the 'extension of the social conscience from people to land': for including nature in an extended morality. Since then however, the concept of an extended ethical obligation has emerged within Christianity, and within philosophy receives a significant amount of attention. Its emergence, and the difficulties attendant on it within both disciplines, is chronicled in Roderick Frazier Nash's history of environmental ethics as 'The Greening of Religion' and 'The Greening of Philosophy'. Both chapters are accompanied by informed comment and comprehensive bibliographies. (Nash 1989: 87–160. See also Midgley 1996: 1–14; 107–17 on the need to find different philosophical models for dealing with our relationships with the non-human world, and Ingold 1994; Elliot 1995 for wide-ranging discussion of the issues.)

The major difficulty for both disciplines is a sharp distinction between human and non-human life traceable to the claim (one not always recognized or acknowledged in philosophy) that we alone are created in the likeness of God. This, argues Rachels (and few could disagree with him), is the central idea of our moral tradition. Of course many people, in increasing numbers, no longer believe the religious story underlying the tradition, and consider their own thinking independent of it. (A case in point, not cited by Rachels, is the fierce attack on proponents of 'deep' ecology by Marxist theorists such as Murray Bookchin, and by secular philosophers such as Luc Ferry, on the grounds that they do not assign primacy to human life and culture.) Yet when examined, their arguments for human supremacy on the basis of the capacity for abstract thought or rationality (Gray), ultimately rely on these qualities being taken, throughout history, as 'divine' elements in humanity. In religious terms, they signify that humans alone are made in the image of God. Rachels traces this 'rationality thesis' from Aristotle through to Aquinas, who held that 'of all parts of the universe, intellectual creatures (us) hold the highest place, because they approach nearest to the divine likeness' (Rachels 1990: 86–103). Generally in western society when people (including Darwin) say they have given up religious belief, and give reasons for discarding it or arguing against it, it is Christianity, not Hinduism or Buddhism, that they reject.

This question of 'rationality' being distinguished as the most highly valued element in human nature, and what it implies, has already been mentioned, and will be again (see Prigogine's use of 'bounded rationality' in Chapter 2). At this stage, I will only note, with Rachels, that when a definite answer is sought as to what exactly defines rationality, there is no consensus on what is supposed to constitute our most distinguishing and distinguished characteristic (Rachels 1990: 132–47). What is even more interesting is how biased a question it is. If ever 'attribution' played a part in scientific and religious discourse, it is here. For whatever way the question is posed, or answered, it is always assumed that rationality in animals or other living beings must have the characteristics ascribed to it which we discern in ourselves. Or more precisely, in some of us. In spite of feminist theorists' best efforts, man is still presumed to be the measure of all things here. As too, in spite of feminist theologians' best efforts, the 'ideal' image of God remains predominantly the human male (Primavesi 1991: 137–57). So we see that 'God' has, in fact, been 'made' in man's image.

Coming to see our species, in common with all others, as still evolving, as mutable, deeply disturbs Christian consciousness and, as Rachel Carson acknowledged, is resisted for reasons of which we are scarcely aware. But they need to be expressed as a contribution to the evolutionary dynamics of Christian narratives and practices. Theologically, the mutability of our species subverts perceptions of creation as a momentary, *very good* act of God, that is, perfect and complete, with nothing missing and nothing to be added. This was already referred to as the classical concept of 'original creation'. From that perspective, the complete truth about us and God is to be sought in a previous time, about which the complete truth is necessarily hidden from us. In such a 'beginning', supposedly, we are to find the fullest realization of what it is to be masculine and feminine. The same, it is assumed, is true of the church. Its ideal state has again and again been identified with the early church of Jerusalem, the one presumed to be closest to Jesus Christ. This epistemological presupposition was stated in lapidary form by Tertullian: 'If it is certain that the earlier is the truer … it is equally certain that what has come down from the apostles is that which is held sacred among the churches of the apostles' (Schmitz-Moormann 1997: 16f.).

The 'end' of evolution

However as Schmitz-Moormann points out, 'nobody who studies the earliest stages of the universe could write an algorithm that would lead with certitude to the existence of humans'. The earlier does not necessarily contain the later, any more than it justifies it (a point which will be taken up again in the next chapter's discussion of sociobiology). New realities come into existence step-by-step, but no step seems absolutely necessary or clearly planned (Schmitz-Moormann 1997: 18). Sudden changes in the environment can trigger diversification and expansion in different species, and from one species into another. Catastrophic changes can extinguish species. Scientists generally point to either flood basalt eruptions, volcanic activity and/or meteor impact off the coast of Yucatan about 67 million years ago as causing the extinction of the dinosaur, the dominant life form at the time. For our species, its diversification and expansion (causes disputed/unknown) is commonly held to have begun with bipedalism, about 5–10 million years ago, continuing through the evolution of *homo erectus* about 1.5 million years ago and on through humans' expansion out of Africa (Leakey and Lewin 1992). Or you can push the evolutionary diversification back to the beginnings of bacterial life forms on earth in the Archaean period, about 3.7–2.5 billion years ago (Lovelock, Margulis, Fortey). But in neither case can you point to a particular moment, or place, when the process was, or is, completed. In neither case can we draw a line under any stage of evolution and say: 'Revelation of God, to our species, began then'; or, more to the point, finished then.

Whichever coevolutionary process we try to unravel, it leaves us with a conclusion already reached on other grounds: that any revelation addressed to humans must at least have been understandable to those living at the time, with the language, in the sense of a medium of revelation, defined by the knowledge of the time. There are words in biblical Hebrew and New Testament Greek we do not understand with certainty any more, and there are words now, such as postmodernism, black holes, computer or DNA which would have made no sense a hundred years ago. If theology is to express contemporary truth today, it will intersect somewhere with the metaphorical networks of science. As the 'eternal verities' are put in question by new knowledge, new truths are introduced into the universe. New theological descriptions must, then, also emerge.

If they emerge from a coevolutionary perspective, they disclose a world which is not a stable structure, unchanged from beginnings described by religious texts or reimagined by science. Rather, we exist within a dynamic becoming, with a very dim beginning and a very open future. This open future and its resultant uncertainty has, as Rachel Carson testified, created a widespread fear, and a common reaction is to look for certainty, especially in an 'ideal' state of affairs in the past which gives grounds for a definitive statement about the future. Both religious fundamentalism and scientific conservatism are symptomatic of a reluctance to acknowledge change, whether in our environments, in ourselves, in our doctrines or in our perspectives. Conservative theology, and conservative movements in general, align well with this reaction. But the reaction is itself a reaction to the reality of evolution, to a world which does not come to a standstill.

Putting it bluntly, Schmitz-Moormann says that the theology of the apostles is not necessarily the best possible theology for those who belong to the church of the apostles today (1997: 21–4). Yet the text known as the *Revelation* or *Apocalypse* of St John the apostle has become for many Christians, and for those influenced by western culture, the focus of their hopes, fears and expectations of what the end of the world will be like. Catherine Keller, in the aptly titled *Apocalypse Now and Then*, notes that fundamentalist Christians today are 'foundationally apocalyptic', and that at the end of the twentieth century, this movement was the fastest growing and arguably the most influential Christianity anywhere. Common to a contrary view, she says, it does not simply feed on uncertainty and fear. By finding in 'the horrors of history and the bankruptcy of modernity' the fulfilment of prophecies, it performs its *tour de force* by making these causes of fear into the source of hope. It reads 'prophecy' as 'specifically predicting current events: John had *us* in mind, not his people' (Keller 1996:

55). But a significant element in the fundamentalist hope is that they alone are saved out of these horrors.

Asa Gray found over one hundred years ago that the change of perception brought about by taking evolutionary theory seriously creates quite a shock. Today, widespread rejection by American Christians of evolutionary theory in favour of the biblical account of the 'beginning' of the world, as well as fundamentalist appeals to biblical teaching about the end of the world, simply show how shock-resistant Christianity has proved to be. An important element, in the shock and in the resistance to it, has been the rather inchoate realization that the authority of biblical texts and church teachings changes from absolute to relative. The reaction to this, understandably, is a tendency to fundamentalism and authoritarianism, dividing those who claim to have received the 'true' revelation and teaching from everyone else. Another element is what Bateson calls the economical aspect of the phenomenon of habit, one rooted in the evolutionary process itself, where a response becomes habitual and results in an economy of mental process whereby the habitual response can be immediately produced without expenditure of effort (Bateson 1991: 101).

But, to reiterate a point already made, if God is the Creator of an evolving universe, it is hard to argue for a revelation to us outside that process; or to hold that revelation could suddenly begin, or stop, at a certain point in time. Even if we confine a certain strand of revelation to the biblical narratives, the Bible as we now have it has evolved over 2–4,000 years; 2,000 years in its original languages and a further 2,000 in its translations. (For many evangelical Christians in Britain, that evolution stopped in 1611 when the King James Version was published.) There is, therefore, no possibility of Christian doctrines having been formulated once and for all. As the universe itself has only reached a provisional state, theology in 'the real world' must recognize that its formulations too are provisional. All of which makes resistance to a coevolutionary perspective within the churches quite understandable. But costly. For if the evolution of truth is not accepted for fear of the loss of authority, the churches are left in the curious position of prescriptively universalizing a particular authority bound to a particular time, place, people and expressive environment. And of authorizing a concept of God which is both locally determined and determinist.

Natural selection, or natural drift?

Theologians can learn from scientific formulations not only about 'life in the light of the truth as it now appears to us' (Carson), but also from the way in which scientists' narratives are also subject to the mutability of truth and provisionality of expression. Darwin's own idea of evolution through natural selection is being pushed to its limits, as Michael Behe shows, by discoveries in biochemistry. The astonishing complexity of subcellular organic structures has forced the question on from *whether* or not all this has evolved to *how* it could have evolved. Scientifically, the question of *how life works* was not one that

Darwin or his contemporaries could answer. To them, that peculiar little organism, the cell, was a black box, one which could not be opened without further technological improvements such as electron microscopy (Behe 1998: 8–15).

Darwin made sense of how life works by arguing systematically for evolution by natural selection working on variation above the cellular level. He described it using the metaphor of a breeder or gardener selecting some animals or plants to propagate, and not others, with variations favourable to survival preserved and others, injurious to survival, rejected. Apart from its scientific shortcomings, it implied, even against his own intent, a 'Selector', conventionally taken to be 'Nature' or God. This ambiguity led to an ongoing dispute over whether the power of selection and the intelligence it represents belongs to an all-knowing God or to impartial nature alone; whether it descends from above, arises from below, or is shared universally at every level of the scale (Dyson 1997: 186). The metaphor also allows, in some measure, for a view of our species as 'selected' by God, not only to survive, but to be 'chosen' while others are 'rejected'.

One hundred years or so later, Maturana and Varela, working at the level of molecular biology, have discarded Darwin's metaphor of 'selection' as 'the main but not exclusive means of modifications' within species, and use instead that of 'natural drift'. This highlights the environment as a means of species modification. They base their metaphor on the analogy of natural drifts of water drops on a hill, where the diverse paths taken by the water result from different individual ways of interacting with the irregularities of the land, the wind and so on. The peak and the initial direction of the water are equivalent to a common ancestral organism which gives rise to descendants with slight structural changes. The multiple repetition of those changes corresponds with the many lineages from those descendants. The hill is the entire surrounding environment of the living beings. It too changes through history, the changes being partly independent of the way the living beings develop and partly dependent on them. Varela stresses the fact that the environment of the organism is not a 'pregiven': organism and environment are mutually enfolded in multiple ways, and so what constitutes the world of a given organism is enacted by that organism's history of structural coupling (Maturana and Varela 1998: 107–17; Varela et al. 1993: 200–3).

'Natural drift' is a rather vague, non-agent term, in contrast to Darwin's 'natural selection'. It accentuates the fact that, in an autopoietic system, evolution is not a goal-seeking process. Its causes are accidental, in the classic sense of contingent rather than intended to produce a certain result, as the claim to our exaltation or another's degradation by God would imply. Bateson uses the term 'capricious' to describe what he calls 'the sort of dirty trick that nature plays upon the well-adapted organism'. For many generations she lets it rely on some characteristic in the environment. And then, that characteristic undergoes change. This is, he says, in a sense most unfair. But 'looked at in a wider perspective, this unfairness is the recurrent condition for evolutionary creativity' (Bateson 1991: 102–6).

Luhmann makes the same point in reference to the evolution of religious forms and systems (Luhmann 1990: 150). In regard to the evolution of theological narratives, the process is exemplified for him in the history of heterodoxy in Christianity. This does not show, from their own writings, that Pelagius or Luther (and later, Elizabeth Cady Stanton or Mary Daly) set themselves the goal of subverting contemporary orthodoxy. The exigencies of their personal, religious and social evolution opened certain paths to them which they might or might not have taken. Each of them, we may assume, set out to write theology in the light of the truth as it then appeared in their religious, cultural, social and political environments.

Theology still emerges from the exigencies of the theologian's *SocialScape* and *PoieticScape*, and, I would add, our *EarthScape*. Traditional views of ourselves as a species are perturbed by the realization that we cannot hold, against what science is revealing of the nature of the world, that we evolved in a unique way, and that our evolution became redundant when Jesus was independently created by God to redress the effects of an individual's sin and save us from the physiological necessity of death; that we alone are made in God's image; that we alone have been addressed by God and that to us alone (in Jesus) has God revealed how the world was made and will end. While relatively few people within western culture would say they hold these views as religious truths, they have profoundly affected not only our ability to accept the implications of evolutionary theory, but our view of ourselves in relation to other species. They are seen to have supported a thoroughgoing anthropocentrism which itself supports the view that everything in the world has been created for our use. All of which, as John Passmore remarks, 'encouraged the development of a particular way of looking at nature, not as something to respect, but rather as something to utilize. Nature is in no sense sacred: this was a point on which Christian theology and Greek cosmology agreed'. And '[w]estern ethics built on this premise have certainly done nothing to discourage, have done a great deal to encourage the ruthless exploitation of nature' (Passmore in Elliot 1995: 131–41).

While Passmore rejects any reversion (for so he sees it) to a primitive belief that Nature is sacred/divine because this can dangerously underestimate the fragility of so many natural processes and relationships, he argues for a scientific understanding of them which treats change, diversity and complexity with the seriousness they deserve. 'If we can bring ourselves fully to admit the independence of nature, the fact that things go on in their own complex ways, we are likely to feel more respect for the ways in which they go on' (1995: 141). Following the drift of evolution takes us, if we allow it, closer to a sense of kinship with all species, and so closer to a respectful and nonviolent lifestyle. We discern the 'inhumane' function of certain God-concepts which sanction violence toward other species and their habitats on the grounds that God's image is found in us alone. We discern the 'idolatrous' function of a divine image marked by violence, violence towards those who differ from us by race, religion, class, gender or species. Instead, we come to view them with the respect they deserve; we perceive that as we share a common life, their lives, in common with ours, are sacred and valued by God.

> For how can we possess dignity
> if we allow them no dignity? Who will recognize our beauty
> if we do not revel in their beauty? How can we hope
> to receive honor if we give no honor? How can we believe
> in grace if we cannot bestow grace?
>
> (Rogers 1997: 36)

5   Evolutionary description

> Darwin found the constant placing of man at the centre of explanation probably the most exasperating characteristic of providential and natural theological writing. ... The reflexive nature of such an explanation of the universe makes it impossible to outgo man's experience and to propose laws which have nothing to do with him. Moreover it diminishes the extent of possibilities and demeans powers of life which lie beyond man's cognisance. ... The sense of incongruity – of the insufficiency of man's reason as an instrument for understanding the material universe – was always with Darwin.
>
> (Gillian Beer 1983: 50f.)

Passmore's comments at the conclusion of the previous chapter are echoed and expanded in Gillian Beer's assessment of Darwin. His exasperation with androcentrism (for so it is) and its effects on whatever explanations of the universe we give or accept was well founded, and this chapter will explore not only some of those explanations which were and are so affected, but the effects of those explanations themselves. In other words, I shall look at the nature and function of evolutionary descriptions.

Earlier I used Eddington's metaphor of the ocean and the two-inch fishing net to highlight the problems of trying to describe the world around us. In spite of the problems, scientific and, rather more slowly, theological descriptions continue to evolve. Some of the scientific ones too 'call on evidence beyond the reach of our senses and overturn the observable world'. A case in point is quantum theory. Even though when first proposed, these descriptions 'tax, affront and exhilarate those who encounter them', in fifty years or so they are 'taken for granted, part of the apparently common-sense set of beliefs which instructs us that the earth revolves around the sun whatever our eyes may suggest' (Beer 1983: 3f.). That is the stage at which they become assumptions within the *SocialScape*, no less in need of examination and critique by scientists than by theologians.

I shall present an overview of some evolutionary descriptions which, in differing ways, have reflected and reflect the multivalency of evolutionary concepts and their interaction with the common sense of our culture at different times. It will become clear that this does not safeguard them from becoming assumptions which encourage, or at least condone violent tendencies within that culture. In fact, quite the contrary. They also illustrate Maturana and Varela's point (reiterated by Rogers) about different meanings being read into descriptions by their readers as well as by their authors, and in this too, scientists are not different from theologians. Gillian Beer observes that one of Darwin's preoccupations was to avoid the Platonic scheme which makes things insufficient substitutes for their own idea. He persistently opposed all attempts to distinguish meaning from matter. For him, meaning inheres in activity and in interrelations. It cannot be referred out or back to 'some unknown scheme of creation' (Beer 1983: 40f.). How far his scientific heirs and heiresses kept faith with him in this, as well as in his attempts to 'de-anthropocentrize' evolutionary explanation, will be considered in this chapter. The latter project suffers today, as in his time, from the fact that although the material world is not anthropocentric, human language is (a fact which affects theology also, of course). But, as Darwin saw, that places more, not less, of an onus on us, theologians and scientists alike, to choose our words carefully.

Scientific distinctions

Since Darwin, scientific distinctions made between life forms have left the Linnaean dichotomy plant/animal far behind, although, as Beer observes, it was not immediately obvious that his work was to revolutionize our understanding of the natural order. Now, however, even the supposedly iron-clad distinction between life and non-life becomes fuzzy for those who look back far enough in time, so that there are many competing descriptions of evolutionary relations on all levels (Ingold 1994: 64). The choice of any particular one is determined by personal perspective and the linguistic code of a particular scientific discipline which requires that it be expressed in terms subject to and effectually contained by peer review.

Darwin's descriptions, however, were very much literary texts accessible to readers without a scientific training. Today, as Beer points out and this book demonstrates, scientific ideas reach the general reader, or 'layman' (an interesting use of a standard theological distinction) through a process of extrapolation and translation, although some make their work more accessible than others. I can grasp the distinctions between, although I cannot give precise scientific definitions of, Margulis' 'five kingdoms of life': first, *monera* (all bacteria, that is, prokaryotes: cells without nuclear membranes); second, *protoctista* (eukaryotic organisms consisting of cells in which genetic material is contained within a distinct membrane-bounded nucleus). These organisms (not 'Adam') bequeathed to all subsequent kingdoms the physiological necessity of death. Numbers three, four and five, *fungi*, *animals* and *plants*, are also eukaryotes, a fact which, as we saw, can further blur distinctions between us and other living organisms (Margulis and Sagan 1995: 116; 176; 1997: 91–110).

She also differentiates bacteria according to their nutritional modes, that is, the ways in which they acquire energy, carbon and electrons for their internal chemical reactions. Other contemporary classification systems use nutritional modes to divide macroscopic entities into three classes: *plants*, or producers, which derive their food from inorganic sources using photosynthesis, and *animals*, or ingestors, which derive their food – preformed organic compounds – from other organisms. (The latter may also be subdivided into three classes: those who eat plants (*herbivores*); those who eat animals who eat plants (*carnivores*); and those who eat both (*omnivores*).) The third nutritional mode is that of *fungi*, or decomposers, which, unlike animals, do not incorporate food into their bodies, but 'secrete digestive enzymes into their environment to break down their food externally', absorbing the resulting small molecules from solution. Animals and their metabolic processes can then be catalogued as intermediate transforming agents between two polar opposite life forms: the composers, or organisms that 'build up', and the decomposers, or organisms which 'break down' (Ingold 1994: 63–5).

Classification systems which take nutritional modes as their base line, marked here as the intake of energy through various processes, give us some insight into and appreciation of their and our position in the drift of evolution. We too exist between energy and dissolution, life and death, as do all living forms. We belong to the class of ingestors dependent on other organisms to photosynthesize for us by using the sun's light/energy to transform matter and themselves into the nutrition our bodies need to survive. Understanding these complex processes, as Passmore noted, can lead to an increased respect for them and an awareness of our dependence on them.

In a human-centred 'consumerist' culture, however, reflections on these interactions have largely, up to now, ignored this dependence and concentrated instead on the ways in which our consumption of energy may be constantly maximized by being made more pleasurable and more conspicuous, and therefore more profitable (in monetary terms). The effects of this expansionist spiral of consumption on the global environment, and its relationship to justice, that is, to the common good of other individuals and organisms, is only now and only in some areas claiming attention.

Later chapters will explore the relationship between access to energy sources, consumerism and justice in some detail. The focus here is on the function of scientific distinctions in regard to relationships between ourselves and other life forms. Such distinctions can, if presented in a certain way, increase our respect for those others and our delight in their seemingly infinite variety. Ignorance of these distinctions, or certain descriptions of them, leaves us with a false sense of self-sufficiency or, theologically, with the assumption that these organisms were brought into being simply to provide us with what we need. This anthropocentricism (as Passmore and Beer note, based largely on ignorance) demeans the power of other life forms. They are deprived of their dignity, in its root sense of intrinsic worth. They are devalued by not being valued for what they are in themselves, but only for what they are for us. This is a version of a Platonic schema, implicitly at least sanctioned by Christianity, which places meaning outside matter. When this assumption shapes our perspective, the long, slow, awesome evolution of other life forms and their place in nature is discounted, and they themselves all the more easily destroyed.

Evolutionary narratives

Against Darwin's best intentions, a view of ourselves as somehow outside of, or proprietors of the living world owes much to evolutionary narratives themselves. In his descriptions of what he observed, he was, naturally, influenced by his cultural and expressive environment, and chose metaphors based on certain culturally dominant aspects of human interaction. A particularly powerful one was that of competition/cooperation. This anthropocentric metaphorical network has had enormous influence on subsequent evolutionary descriptions, to the extent that most of them have assumed that as this is, apparently, our dominant mode of interacting, then it applies to all life forms. Worse still, this particular binocular vision has, in an inordinate number of cases, been reduced yet further to the monocular one of competition alone.

Aware of the partiality of his own perspective, Darwin did his best to counteract it. In the section of *The Origin of Species* entitled 'The Struggle for Existence', he stated that it had been shown (by De Candolle and Lyell) that 'all organic beings are exposed to severe competition'. He then went on to stress that he used the term 'Struggle for Existence' [*sic*] in '*a large and metaphorical sense* [italics added], including dependence of one being on another, and including (which is more important) not only the life of the individual, but success in leaving progeny'. He used the metaphor of tree and mistletoe in which the mistletoe is dependent on the tree, but 'can only in a far-fetched sense be said to struggle with that tree. Several seedling mistletoes, growing close together on the same branch, may more truly be said to struggle with each other'. The existence of the same mistletoe, he points out, depends on birds, as its seeds are disseminated by them. It might then, he concludes, 'metaphorically be said to struggle with other fruit-bearing plants', in order to tempt birds to devour and disseminate its seeds rather than theirs. 'In these several senses, which pass into each other, I use for convenience sake the general term of struggle for existence' (Darwin 1996: 165).

On the whole, his attempt to keep the metaphorical is/*is not* balance between the aspects of cooperation (dependence) and competition (struggle) can be seen as a failure, in that the aspect of competition came to play a dominant, and therefore unbalanced, role. The reasons for this are complex, deriving from political and economic developments within western culture and allied political, economic and scientific responses to his work, some of which became part of other evolutionary narratives.

Starting with his contemporary, Karl Marx, each response reflected, unsurprisingly, a particular viewpoint. In Darwin's use of 'Malthusian' theory, Marx says, he projects a view of English society (with its division of labour, competition, and opening up of new markets) on to beasts and plants. This 'struggle for existence', summarizes, according to Marx, 'Hobbes's *bellum omnium contra omnes*', so that 'in Darwin the animal kingdom figures as civil society'. Beer commends Darwin for substituting 'struggle' for his original use of the Hobbesian phrase 'the war of nature'. This was an attempt on his part, she says, to move away from a human perspective by using a word which lacked the organized force of war and expressed instead 'the interpenetration of energies' (Beer 1983: 58; 1986: 215). Darwin himself took the trouble, as I said, to insist that 'the struggle for existence' was to be used in a large and metaphorical sense, and to articulate the varying senses in which he himself used the term, together with the degrees of appropriateness the term possesses (Darwin in Glick and Kohn 1996: 165). In spite of his efforts, however, and his other observations and descriptions of the world as one 'of infinite interconnections', or as an 'inextricable web of affinities', a picture of 'universal man', characterized by militant competitive individualism, came to monopolize evolutionary descriptions of human interactions. The baseline became a starting line for the human race, determining winners and losers.

This was (and still is) the position of those now called Social Darwinists. For them, as economist J. K. Galbraith remarks, economic society is an arena in which men meet to compete. The terms of their struggle are set by the market and those who win are rewarded with survival and, if they win brilliantly, with riches. Those who lose go to the lions. Or rather to their modern equivalent, to the noisome slums where the workers who create the riches dwell in poverty and degradation (Galbraith 1991: 48–51).

Evolutionary competition and capitalism

This model of militant competitive individualism has remained dominant in western culture apart from a short time span in the early 1950s when, in reaction to World War II, and as an attempt to combat racism, the possibility of a natural human predisposition to cooperation over competition was taken seriously. Unfortunately, as the Cold War gained momentum its inherent and declared competitiveness between the western and eastern power blocs became the prevailing model for nation-to-nation and then individual-to-individual relationships, especially when capitalism, with its stress on competition, became dominant in the western economy. Since then, Donna Haraway remarks, primary categories of Darwinian description, such as struggle, competition, and 'the survival of the fittest' have become normative in descriptions of human interaction. Mirror-imaging of these norms for non-human species behaviour have also become standard, so that in a self-reinforcing methodology, civil society figures as animal 'society', and vice versa. In the proposal for an experiment in primate studies, the anthropologist Sherwood Washburn argued for a study of primate evolution (in this instance, seen in terms of human functional categories 'walking, eating, mating, thinking', rather than chronology) primarily as a method of understanding human behaviour. The perceived logic of human interaction (competitive individualism) became the perspective from which primate behaviour was studied and described. This recursive methodology was then expressed in a universalizing discourse about a supposed 'universal man' [*sic*] known as 'Man the Hunter' (Haraway 1992: 197–228).

Under pressure from feminist critique, he was eventually partnered by 'Woman the Gatherer'. She too, however, evolved according to the conventions of the time into an embryonic venture capitalist. One of the most influential women in anthropology, Sarah Blaffer Hrdy, describes her evolution as one of a root conflict of interest that cuts across sexual difference, in which sexual pleasure and concealed ovulation can give 'the competitive edge to some females, in competition with other females, in their struggle to turn males, pursuing their own reproductive ends, into a resource or at least less of an enemy' (1992: 363). The market, Haraway points out, is the birthplace of a Darwinian natural economy, of the concept of natural selection as a competitive struggle of all against all for profit, with troubling parallels in political economy. Darwin himself acknowledged his debt to Thomas Malthus for highlighting scarcity as a motor of nature (Haraway 1991: 57–68). Marx declared that Darwin's book was important for him personally because it served him as 'a basis in natural selection for the class struggle in history'. Shortly after the publication of the *Origin*, Darwin wrote to his colleague Lyell noting with amusement that in a Manchester newspaper he was credited with proving 'might is right', and that therefore Napoleon and 'every cheating tradesman is also right'.

Another superficial reading which became commonplace was one in which, despite his careful distinctions between them, the theory of natural selection and the concept of the 'survival of the fittest' (which in fact came from Herbert Spencer) were taken as equivalent, and the latter in particular was invoked time and again to justify competitive economic and even political systems. The American industrialist Andrew Carnegie wrote that we must accept and welcome 'great inequality; the concentration of business, industrial and commercial, in the hands of the few, and the law of competition between these as being not only beneficial, but essential to the future progress of the race, because capitalism alone ensures the survival of the fittest'. Another capitalist giant, John D. Rockefeller, in a talk to his Sunday School class, proclaimed that the 'growth of large business is merely the survival of the fittest'. Citing the practice of sacrificing early buds in the commercial production of the American Beauty rose, he declared that this was not an evil tendency in business but merely 'the working-out of a law of nature and a law of God'. A more recent and most sinister application of this principle was Heinrich Himmler's claim that Darwinism supported purging Europe of the 'unfit' Jews (Rachels 1990: 2; 62f.; Beer 1983: 17; Galbraith 1991: 51).

Sociobiological reflections

I want to highlight here the fact that throughout this growing interest in explaining and justifying aspects of human behaviour in evolutionary terms, the role of the *EarthScape* dimension of the environment in evolutionary process all but disappeared. It was (and still is for some) reduced to a passive, non-agent commodity resource base. On this hidden base the anthropocentric evolutionary metaphorical heap was raised to a new level in 1975 in Edward O. Wilson's *Sociobiology: the New Synthesis*. He defined the science of sociobiology as 'the systematic study of the biological basis of all social behaviour'. This project, in its broad remit, could be seen to encompass a wide range of disciplines, including the work of Maturana and Varela. Wilson's concluding chapter, however, argued that some of the most troubling aspects of human social life (as evidenced in an American industrial city) are inescapable features of our human nature. One such feature, male dominance, was, therefore, unavoidable in human societies. As might be expected, such pronouncements were met with responses ranging from relieved acceptance to total rejection (Rachels 1990: 73–9).

Sarah Hrdy's sociobiological response kept the premise of dominance but changed the conclusion that it was necessarily male. She found her argument in the biological origins of male/female. 'Competition among the small cells for access to the largest ones favored smaller, faster, and more manoeuvrable cells, analogous to sperm. The hostages we might as well call ova … the ground rules [*sic*] for the evolution of two very different creatures – males and females – were laid down at this early date.' One group began amassing resources into themselves, while the other specialized in 'competing among themselves for access to these stockpiling organisms'. These manoeuvres (her term) are described as 'intra-sexual competition' for access to the means of reproduction, that is, the 'opposite sex'. Since females put more into reproduction, they become the so-called 'investing sex'. The investing sex becomes the limiting resource: the sign and embodiment of what is most desired and always scarce. If competition for these scarce resources drives the whole system (reverberations here from Darwin's 'Malthusian motor of scarcity'), competition for food determines much else. These competitive relations can include all kinds of coalitions and forms of cooperation, which are, however, described as 'proximate matters in the great ultimate game of genetic investment according to the principles of methodological individualism'. Hrdy concludes, in a depressing example of how the competition model is extended to other species, that 'competition among assertive, dominance-oriented females is an absolutely central principle of primate social life, built into their natural status as limiting resources whose eating habits are the pivot of sexual politics' (Haraway 1992: 350–67).

This self-reflexive conclusion offers a bleak picture of ourselves projected onto other species. It also ignores the interactive dynamics of every species with its *EarthScape*, the physical/chemical/material dimension of environment reduced here to a primary resource base for competing primates. It is implicitly determinist, in that it supposes that human and non-human behaviour is driven only by competition, with the condoning of violence by 'winners' against 'losers' which this implies. In a consumerist culture, those who control the markets in food and other energy-giving commodities are seen as winners (the wealthy), and those without access to them, as, necessarily, losers (the poor). The statistics of incomes on wealth indicators such as the Forbes 500 register, or reports from United Nations agencies such as the International Fund for Agricultural Development, show how many losers there are globally. And their numbers are rising. Because of this, there is some resistance to the determinisms of the market. 'Pricing policies, credit systems and social and productive services which neglect the poor ... are not natural, universal and inevitable facts – and neither is the poverty they give rise to' (Ryan and Whitmore 1997: 146). Yet the fact that the authors felt it necessary to reject this opinion shows how entrenched it is. Routinely, when rising unemployment, for instance, results from the increasing dividends for the wealthy, politicians justify it on the grounds that it is the result of competition. As though this, and its results, were a (super)natural law. So the explanation has become the justification. The 'invisible hand' of the market has become a new Platonic schema and, for some providentialist Christians, a surrogate 'hand of God' (Primavesi 1997: 140–6).

The issues raised briefly here will be discussed in some detail later. Staying with evolutionary narratives and their effects, Donna Haraway makes a salient point in her own response to this type of evolutionary description. Sociobiology, she says, is a science which describes human societies based on a premise of what Fox-Keller calls atomic individualism (Fox-Keller 1992b: 115). It is structurally akin to advanced capitalist theories of investment management, control systems for labour, and insurance policies based on population disciplines. Wilson, Haraway notes, needing 'an explanation for altruism' [*sic*] with its premise of the common good, found the solution by extending the notion of natural selection and population genetics to that of 'inclusive fitness: the sum of an individual's own fitness plus all its influence on fitness in relation to other than direct descendants'. Parental investment in genes and combinations of genes, even if dangerous to the parents, when viewed as strategies for maximizing reproductive profit made economic, and therefore biological sense.

This description of evolutionary process takes us onto the floor of the genetic Stock Exchange, where profit is measured in the currency of genes and individuals compete with different investment strategies (Haraway 1991: 57–68). What happens to those individuals or species whose genes are considered high-risk investments? Evelyn Fox-Keller notes that forty years ago, it was culture, not biology, that was seen to make us human. Culture was simultaneously the source and the object of our special human freedom to make choices. Today we are being told, and are apparently coming to believe, that what makes us human is our genes. I heard the director of the Human Genome Project in Cambridge confidently assert at a public lecture that 'everything that makes us what we are is written in our DNA'. No mention of our structural coupling with any dimension of our environment, whether physical, personal, social, or expressive. Genes, Fox-Keller remarks, became big business in the 1980s, and they are likely to become even bigger business in the decades to come (Fox-Keller 1992a: 281). 'Genes 'R' Us' is not only a growing metaphorical heap, but the brand name of a megastore in which gene technology and patents in genetic code, cell lines and DNA sequences are sold and bought as capital investment. Transnational pharmaceutical corporations and agribusinesses buy 'broad species' patents on a whole range of genetically modified crops and transgenic plants, and one, Monsanto, sells as a package herbicide-resistant soya seed and the herbicide, the latter guaranteed to kill every plant and seed except the soya. Any farmer who wishes to sow the seed must sign a contract with Monsanto. Stored in seed-'banks', guarded from competitors by security systems, its 'owners' have made Darwin's birds redundant.

I would like to draw attention to the militarist language routinely used by herbicide/pesticide corporations, a characteristic captured in the common perception of their production of a 'terminator' gene. This is hardly surprising, since these products were mainly developed as biological weapons in the Cold War, whether as defoliants, land poisons or anti-personnel weapons. The language itself has become so accepted that it is used even by those who want to challenge the assumption of the alienation of the organism from its environment (in every sense). This has, according to the geneticist R. C. Lewontin, made the organism nothing but a battleground between outside forces and inside forces. It implies that we must do the best we can to find our way through the minefield of life using whatever equipment our genes have provided us with to get us to the other side in one piece. What is so extraordinary about this, he says, is that it completely contradicts what we know about organisms, their behaviour and environment and the rich set of relations between them. Organisms, he says, do not experience environments. They create them out of the bits and pieces of the physical and biological world (Lewontin 1993: 108–9).

Theological reflections

Standing back, as it were, from the evolution of Darwinian descriptions, I want to highlight a key element in them which emerged in the preceding chapter as well as in this one. This is the question of how well Darwin or his successors succeeded in preserving what I see as one of his primary aims: asserting the dignity of all life forms in the face of the human-centred order of his time. It seems clear to me that with the convergence of capitalist economics and sociobiological theory, the worth of any living being, including the human, has been greatly reduced. Instead of allowing for, and ideally stressing their intrinsic value, they have been reduced to their commodity/market/investment value. This has been most noticeable in regard to attitudes towards non-human life, but, as we saw, is implicit and increasingly explicit in relationships with human beings also. Workers are now routinely referred to as 'human resources', or 'units of production'.

This convergence and its reductionism is seen by some as a result of Darwinism, and rightly too, on some evidence in the preceding chapter. But was capitalist ideology not equally responsible, equally reductionist in its attitude to living beings, human and non-human? It depends on your perspective. James

Rachels believes that Darwin, in his efforts to assert the dignity of all life forms, fatally undermined human dignity. The idea of human dignity, he says, is the moral doctrine which says that animals and humans are in different moral categories, and that humans 'merit a level of moral concern wholly different from that accorded to animals' (Rachels 1990: 171). This idea implies that our moral concern for humans would lead us inevitably to behave differently towards animals, that is, in ways which do not respect their dignity, or indeed allow for their having any. But does this have to be the case? Could it not, as Asa Gray hoped, lead us to behave more 'humanely' towards them, that is, in a way which would enhance our own dignity by respecting theirs? Do we not, as Pattiann Rogers avers, 'need to know that we come from such stock so continuously and tenaciously and religiously devoted to life'? If we are related to all other life forms as descendants of the firstborn cell, then does their life too not share dignity with ours? We know that we share a common evolutionary history written in our genes, a common present filled with contingency and hope, and a common future.

This understanding of dignity can only be enhanced by theology from a coevolutionary perspective, which would, ultimately, see God and the five kingdoms of life as sharing that history, that present and that future. And if we did accord other life forms that dignity, what would it mean? One of the clearest theological contemporary statements on human dignity, the Vatican II document *Dignitatis Humanae Personae* (literally, *The Dignity of the Human Person*), translated as the Declaration on Religious Freedom, makes an important connection between according dignity to another being and respecting their freedom. The text is, in the manner of its time and provenance, relentlessly human-centred, yet makes clear that according dignity and respect to other people, and, by extension, to other forms of life, centres on developing noncoercive relationships.

It begins by stressing the connection between a growing sense of the dignity of each person and the obligation this lays on us of recognizing and empowering each one's freedom to act without coercion. This demand for freedom in human society, the document stresses, is founded on the quest for values proper to the human spirit, with first among them, the right to free exercise of religion, a freedom which relies on immunity from coercion. This freedom is in accordance with our dignity as persons, which at once impels us and imposes a moral obligation on us to seek the truth and order our lives in accordance with it (Abbott 1966: 678f.).

These systematic norms assume the interdependence of respect for the dignity of all persons and living in noncoercive relationships which safeguard others' freedom, in particular freedom to seek the truth and live according to that truth. It is a short but crucial step to respond to Aldo Leopold's plea and extend those norms to our relationships with all living beings. This step was taken publicly by Gandhi, exemplified in his life and expressed memorably in his observation that nonviolence means 'the largest love, the greatest charity' (Naess 1974: 50).

6 Poietic process

Live metaphors inspiring innovative thought and metaphors extinguished into the formalities of literalness are constant witnesses to the metabolic nature of our culture. ... In a synoptic view we could regard as metaphorical the variety of messages which are exchanged between different aspects of our living structure, each endowed with its own code and specific organization. In this view we could come to think of metaphoric links as extending from our biological metabolism on to the life of our minds.

(Gemma Fiumara 1995: 26–8)

The brief reference to militarist language which concluded the previous chapter also serves to introduce this final chapter of reflection on scientific evolutionary theory. I want to concentrate now on one etymological component of autopoiesis implicit in the concept itself: 'poiesis' as poetic process. This refers to the imaginative component in our structural coupling with our environment, where the imagination acts as the 'bond of action and reaction between my world and my thought in myself alone'. Simone Weil used this extraordinary phrase in her reflections on science and perception in Descartes, for whom the concept of imagination was pivotal. It is there, he said, that the idea of everything that can be related to the body must be found. Weil typifies the imagination as 'a knot of action and reaction that attaches me to the world'. It represents, or rather constitutes the grasp that she has on the world, 'the correspondence that exists between a thought of mine and a change outside me' (Weil 1987: 50, 69f).

It will, I hope, be immediately obvious where this is leading. Our *PoieticScape* couples us with our environment through the creative action and reaction of our imagination, and in this chapter I shall concentrate on the creative process we call metaphor which links a thought of mine with a change in the world outside my personal (skin) boundary. Ricoeur considers this double reference in poetic process, to things as they are and to things as possibly other than they are, to reality and to other possible realities, as the paradoxical function of metaphor in poetry. Its dual fidelity brings together what Fiumara calls our biological metabolism and the life of our minds. In this way, 'poiesis' or our *PoieticScape* bridges *EarthScape*, *SocialScape* and *SelfScape*, and can be taken as 'lively expression which expresses existence as alive' (Ricoeur 1986: 38–43).

The scientists Ilya Prigogine and Isabelle Stengers appropriate this 'poetic' quality for scientific enquiry. In our society, they say, with its wide spectrum of cognitive techniques, science occupies a peculiar position, 'that of a poetical interrogation of nature, in the etymological sense that the poet is a "maker" – active, manipulating, and exploring' (Prigogine and Stengers 1985: 301). Maturana and Varela do not themselves stress this etymological sense of poiesis in self-making, but they touch on it indirectly with their emphasis on the nature of description and their insistence on the importance of the emotions. They also endorse Fiumara's concept of metaphoric process as a vital linkage between our biological mechanism and the life of our minds when they say that communi–cation, in this case human language, arises through third-order structural coupling, or social life, and takes place in a domain of social behaviours. When these behaviours become stable through generations, we call them cultural, that is, 'the whole body of ontogenically acquired communicative interactions that give a certain continuity to the history of the group, beyond the particular history of the participating individuals' (Maturana and Varela 1998: 193–201).

For them, a key feature of this interaction between *SocialScape* and *PoieticScape* is the effect of language on us, in that it radically modifies human behavioural domains and makes new phenomena possible. It enables us to describe ourselves and our circumstances through the linguistic distinction of linguistic distinctions, an exercise evident throughout this book as well as theirs. 'We human beings are human beings only in language. Because we have language, there is no limit to what we can describe, imagine, and relate' (1998: 206–11).

Metaphoric process within society has then, paradoxically, the capacity for stability and continuity *and* for innovation and change. The former tendency resists change for the sake of security and stability (loyalty to the King James' version of the Bible within certain strata of English society can stand as exemplar) while the latter responds to stimulus from an evolving culture by radically innovative descriptions. 'Essential to a linguistic domain is the co-ontogenic structural drift that occurs as members of a social system live together. Language is an ongoing process that only exists as languaging, not as isolated items of behaviour' (1998: 209f.).

Languaging as a metaphoric process operates as an affective and effective force for stability and change in the human societies from which it emerges. The drive to stability is evident in some familiar component retained in the metaphor, providing enough orientation to allow the hearer/reader to follow its meaning into new territory. Examples of this within western Christian culture are 'new' metaphors for God, such as lover, mother, friend, which retain the aspect of God as 'person' fundamental to traditional metaphors. The tension between stability and change serves both as a means of mutual educa-tion/persuasion/enjoyment and as a creative activity which makes things present and visible to us which we would not otherwise perceive. This latter not only discloses something new; it creates it. 'The engines of evolution are driven by the recombination of genes; human creativity is driven by the recombination of ideas; literature is driven by the recombination of books' (Dyson 1997: xi). Through the generative power of linguistic couplings and recombinations, metaphor produces and reproduces possible realities, non-existent possibilities. By 'metaphorizing' unicorns and utopias into existence, our thoughts, imagination and emotions take us beyond the actual, over the boundary line between the possible and impossible which cannot be rationalized even as rational hope. The development of alternative, possible perspectives enables us to rethink radically what family is, what environment is, what religion is. Most importantly, metaphorizing can inspire us, in our behaviour, to confirm or contest the present situation.

Metaphoric process and emergent perceptions

As our thoughts, imagination, emotions and expressions metabolize through physical and linguistic coupling, they evolve. They change according to their internal dynamic and in response to perturbations from their environment, moving away from or towards literalism. A pertinent example is the evolution of what Myerson and Rydin call 'the environet', a rhetorical web of communication composed of topics marked by 'environment words' such as resources and energy; population; biodiversity; species; pollution; global warming; Gaia; sustainability (Myerson and Rydin 1996). This metaphoric evolution, as Schmitz-Moormann reminds us, affects both scientific and theological descriptions. It also, as Ricoeur points out, 'makes us see things'. It 'carries us along with it', presenting the abstract in concrete terms, making the subvisible visible. Doing so, it changes our perspective, not only on abstract concepts but also on 'inanimate' things by showing them 'as if' acting. The power of making things visible, alive, actual, awakens imagination and emotion in the readers or listeners. It enables them to 'see' and be persuaded of the truth of whatever viewpoint is being presented, and so to 'see', as Volk says, that 'truth resides in the very fact of multiple viewpoints'.

Ricoeur describes the process by which paradoxical metaphor conveys new ideas. He quotes Aristotle: 'To metaphorize well is to imply an intuitive perception of the similarity in dissimilars.' By bringing together terms which first surprise and then bewilder the reader/hearer, leaving her in search of new insights, it then reveals the relationship hidden beneath the paradox (Ricoeur 1986: 23). It reveals an identity while at the same time denying it; thus opening the possibility of claiming an identity which has been ignored, or denied; or of denying one which is now seen as imprecise or harmful.

The claim to identity or non-identity with animals, can, as we have seen, offer an intuitive perception of our relationship with them which, affirmed or denied, can radically alter our self-perception. Our reasoning about this relationship cannot be done from any point of view other than our personal perspective, metaphorically projected and propositionally elaborated. Such metaphorical projections, and arguments on their behalf, are not arbitrary, but are significantly determined by our biological metabolism and emotional vicissitudes. They are also, as Luhmann reminds us, determined by whether or not they are meaningful within our society. There seems to be a consensus, for instance (one I find increasingly irritating), that football hooligans are 'animals' in a clearly pejorative use of the word. A popular vocabulary of 'bestiality' is used to project on to animals all that is violent and predatory in human nature while at the same time, as we saw in the previous chapter, academic anthropology reads animal behaviour through the lens of capitalist free market theory. One hundred years ago, before supersonic missiles and satellites were part of our world, metaphorical projections of ourselves as star trekkers or of the inhabitants of other planets as 'invaders' would have had no meaning. And how many churchgoers now agree that God is our King? Examining metaphors, one has to come to terms with the evolving biological conditions within the societies from which our meanings derive, and with the practices with which they are implicated (Fiumara 1995: 28).

Metaphorical imagination

Poietic processes not only generate metaphors in the one who conceives them. Within the *SocialScape* they generate a response from the hearer/reader which Pattiann Rogers brought to our attention. In her book, *Poetic Justice*, Martha Nussbaum names this internal dynamic 'fancy' (in the literary sense), or imagination. We need, she says, to be able to imagine what it is like to live the life of another person who might, in other circumstances, be oneself or one of one's loved ones. She commends Dickens for valuable insights into the power of imagination in politics, insights not unconnected with the metaphorical and linguistic richness of his own writing. The very structure of the interaction between the text and its imagined reader invites the reader to see how the mutable features of society and circumstance bear on the realization of shared hopes and desires – and also, in fact, on their very structure. This metaphoric interaction she defines (taking us back to Ricoeur's analysis) as being able to imagine non-existent possibilities; to see one thing as another and one thing in another; to endow a perceived form with a complex life (Nussbaum 1995: 7–52).

These poetic processes, as Simone Weil realized, take us beyond our bodily constraints; beyond the bounds of present reality. The poet Adrienne Rich, writing about Emily Dickinson's language, says that it concretizes the world at large, the self, and the forces within the self. Those forces are rescued from formlessness, made lucid and integrated in the act of writing the poems. But there is more. The poet is endowed to speak for those who do not have the gift of language, or to see for those who, for whatever reason, are less conscious of what they are living through (Rich 1980: 181). All this can, of course, be said of music too.

These processes do not, it must be stressed, displace the workings of political and economic facts (as I shall point out in the next chapter when discussing inequalities in personal or economic power), or of the kind of reasoned argument used by scientists and philosophers. Nussbaum insists that her intention is not to disparage reason or the scientific search for truth. (I scarcely need to make this disclaimer.) What she and I are saying is that any particular scientific or rational approach that claims to stand alone for truth misrepresents the complexity and inherent unpredictability of human beings and human life. So any scientific, economic or social theory which reduces our multidimensional interactions to one of competitive individualism must be challenged. Its claims must be exposed as misrepresentation by drawing attention to the gap between a theory (of justice, of truth, of freedom, of society, of economics or of religion) and the living expression of that theory. This reminder of the gap between theory and practice helps us avoid the extremes of either a 'no-ownership' or a 'sole ownership' perspective by making the boundaries of our own perspective more or less permeable to the perspectives of others. It enables us to endorse, even without sharing, another's perspective, and where possible to validate it as a contribution to the truth of multiple viewpoints.

Imagination and emotion

According to Nussbaum, the reader/listener with such a metaphorical imagination is one whose emotions and imagination are highly active, promoting identification and sympathy in him. This cuts through the self-protective stratagems which keep our knowledge of other people and their environments at a distance, requiring us instead to see and respond to many things that may be painful and difficult to confront. A good example of this, for readers in the economic North, would be our ability to engage with and respond to reports of the effects of our consumerist lifestyle on the countries in the economic South. In order to service their debts to Northern banks, they must earn cash by supplying us with luxury foods, the cropping of which destroys their *EarthScapes* and *SocialScapes*. This economic system, called ESAP (Economic Structural Adjustment Policy) by financial institutions, is renamed in Africa as ASAP (Acute Suffering for African Peoples). The majority of us without first-hand experience of this suffering can only respond to this through our imagination, and then act (in our shopping practices) on our identification with those suffering from our excesses.

In language which gives a new resonance to charity as action, Nussbaum holds that there is a charity in this ability and willingness to engage with and go beyond the personal. It is a charity which prepares us for greater charities in life, for an acceptance of generous fancies which project our own sentiments, needs and inner activities onto the forms we perceive about us. This charitable imagination is the necessary basis for good government. With it, she concludes, reason is beneficent, steered by a generous view of its object; without its charity, reason is cold and cruel (Nussbaum 1995: 43). This description of the relationship between reason and imagination could be read as a redescription of what it means to love one's neighbour as oneself. It can also be taken as a condition of possibility for a nonviolent lifestyle, or as another way of understanding Gandhian nonviolence as 'the largest love, the greatest charity'.

She gives an example of the emergence of this greater charity. In one of her lectures on literature to law students, she asked one, a Mr Riley, why Dickens attached so much importance to nursery rhymes, and how he (Riley) felt when, as a child, he sang 'Twinkle, twinkle, little star'. Mr Riley began by describing his image of a sky blazing with stars and bands of bright colour. She and the other students listened spellbound as he related, in a low-key, matter-of-fact tone how this wonderful sight somehow led him to look in a new way at his cocker spaniel. He would look into the dog's eyes and wonder what the dog was really feeling and thinking, and whether it might be feeling sad. It seemed right to him, he said, to wonder about the dog's experience and to think of the dog as having both love for him and the capacity to feel pleasure and pain. All this, in turn, led him to new ways of thinking about his parents and about other children.

As the previous chapter showed, metaphors are not neutral. The star at Mr Riley's birth of fancy was, she remarks, 'a diamond', not a missile. The metaphor nourished a generous construction of the seen. The child who takes delight in stories and nursery rhymes is getting the idea that not everything in life has a use. It is learning a mode of engagement with the world that is capable of cherishing things for their own sake. And this the child takes into its relationships with others. It is not only the ability to endow a form with life that makes the metaphorical imagination morally valuable; it is the ability to view what one has constructed in fancy as serving no end beyond itself, as good and delightful for itself alone (Nussbaum 1995: 4–12, 38–42). It is a perception of intrinsic worth in others, which, ideally, moves us to behave justly toward them.

Distinction and differentiation in religious description

Suspended within and supported by metaphorical networks, the kind of differentiations made by Mr Riley between the star and the spaniel, between the self and the star, between autopoietic entity and environment, are crucial for our understanding of what holds us together; of our unity in difference. From a scientific perspective, it is the Gaian system which supports our common life. From an individual perspective, the poetic imagination connects us, as ourselves, as autonomous organisms, with whatever dimension of environment is being described. But it can transcend this boundary too and connect us with the Gaian system, even though we can, literally, only imagine it in its magnitude. Parents, siblings, dogs and stars are all, in this way, seen as related to me. Do I see them as delightful? Or as threatening? As having intrinsic value in themselves? As awesome and incredibly complex?

These questions also resonate from every religious description of our coevolutionary history. Religion, according to Luhmann's definition, qualifies unreservedly as a communication system, that is, as one which functions by representing 'meaning' in a complex world. It offers a particular representation of the complexity of the world which provides access to shared topics for communication. It places all concrete items against a horizon of further possibilities and finally, against the world of all possibilities. Within the world created by the operations of this system, there is a surplus of possibilities which nobody will be able to follow up all at once. Every next step has to be selected out of other possibilities. Within this world, therefore, every concrete item appears as *contingent*, as something that could be different. There is then, no other way of identifying religious forms than that they refer to the ultimate paradox: the *necessity of contingency* (Luhmann 1990: 147–9).

Contingency, briefly here, is used by Luhmann in a logical sense rather than in its primary theological sense of dependence on God. For reasons which will become apparent I shall for the moment stay with the logical definition of contingency as the negation of impossibility *and* the negation of necessity. Just reflecting on that paradox can give one a headache. If persevered with, however, it offers an intuitive grasp of 'how things are'. One way of tackling it is to go deeper and deeper into the question: 'Why do I, and not some other life form, exist in this space?' One finds that ultimately, the paradox discloses the fact that there is no 'why', no 'necessity'. Unless, of course, you cheat and answer the question with 'God knows', or some such formula. But this, the poet e. e. cummings would say, is one of those beautiful answers which asks a more beautiful question.

I shall return to this type of cause/effect question in the last chapter, but here I want to stay with Luhmann's analysis of what society, and religion in particular does when presented with this 'ultimate paradox'. Society copes, he says, by developing forms of discourse which *deparadoxize the world*. (This can be attributed to the capacity and need for stability in languaging.) In very early religions the sacred remains immediately paradoxical, evoking images of enchantment and terror, attraction and repulsion, good and evil *at the same time* (italics added). Religion, however (and here he takes Christianity as the religion of western culture), has successfully used binary codes, within its own self-referential system, to resolve the paradox. These codes are totalizing constructions having a claim to universality and possessing no ontological limit. Everything that falls within their domain of relevance is assigned to the one value or the other. The God who 'knows' good and evil is reduced to a God who is good, opposed by a Satan who is evil. As codes are valid only within their domain of application, religion as a communicative system can totalize this coding in a way which reduces everything to two opposed possibilities. All evil connotations are abstracted from the word 'God', until the word itself comes to stand for what is 'good'. 'God is a good God from Whom evil has mysteriously slipped away or (for Whom it) serves mysterious ends' (Luhmann 1989: 95. Mark C. Taylor has done a similar critique of 'coding' in *Erring: A Postmodern A/Theology*, but I stay with Luhmann here because he has an autopoietic perspective on the problem, and because he focusses on paradox as the seminal issue).

With regard to its coding, the system operates as a closed system; every value like 'true' and 'false' refers to its respective counter-value alone and never to other, external (scientific/political/economic) values. No matter how responsive the system may be structurally, and no matter how sensitive its own frequencies, its capacity for reaction rests on the polarity of its code and is sharply limited by this. Job, for instance, saw that what appears necessary to the system, that is, good and bad behaviour as expounded by his 'friends', is in fact contingent on their perspectives. He, however, glimpsed the paradox of a God who gives and, at the same time, takes away. And that there is, ultimately, no 'why' for how God is seen to behave.

The coding of religion ultimately resides, Luhmann concludes, in the distinction of *immanence* and *transcendence*. Transcendence is no longer understood in terms of another world or as a separate and unattainably high or low region of the world, but 'as a kind of second meaning', that is, as a complete, all-encompassing second version of the world, whose meaning is what cannot be transcended. (This, not surprisingly, is reminiscent of Darwin's 'Platonic schema'.) The same 'second version' coding obtains, as we shall see, in the Augustinian binary code heaven/earth. This code has many different semantic versions, but what matters is its effectiveness. By absolutizing the difference between heaven and earth, God is excluded from the world. In an allied move in the code, the difference between sacred and profane effects the desacralization of nature in order to specify religious rites alone as sacred. In early modernity, this desacralization of nature merely changed its reference system. It was no longer primarily religious, but became a scientific or economic requirement, and religion, Luhmann remarks wryly, could not intervene in the process because it had to preach the same sermon.

Luhmann comes to the bleak conclusion that problems about the world, and in particular, environmental problems, cannot be solved by using this binary code of immanent/transcendent because ultimately, the code serves as the 'justification' of God as 'good', with that 'goodness' situated beyond the world, beyond the visible, messy, problematic complexity of coevolutionary processes. Therefore, he says, religion will only be able to offer protest against deforestation, air pollution or nuclear danger which is dependent on an antecedent social awareness. Or, as is evident in the rise of fundamentalist literalism, it provides the penultimate answer 'God' to ultimate questions about human existence (Luhmann 1986: 32–43; 94–9).

When this happens, religion, he says, becomes endangered by its own success as a successful way to handle paradoxes. Within the Christian religion, 'God' can be spoken of as the centralized paradox which at the same time deparadoxizes the world. Christianity has done this through a process of articulating its binary codes as a set of religious distinctions. Whatever we may think of the Christian belief system, he says, it brought about an important structural change – some would say an evolutionary change – compared to earlier religions. 'Never before had religion been so articulate.' Never before had it set up its own distinctions between believers and non-believers, abstracting from all other distinctions such as our people/other people, citizens/strangers or freemen/slaves. Never before was it so completely on its own in regulating inclusion and exclusion. Never before had religion in this sense been a network of decision premises, or its professionals been so skilled in handling distinctions. The old difference between sacred and profane, applied to places, occasions, persons etc., was replaced with a difference that could be handled as a purely internal difference within the system itself, representing, as it were, the differences between those included in (the saved) and those excluded from (the damned) the religious system. This was accessible to all kinds of clerical and private manipulation, since one's inclusion or exclusion could be, and was, presented as the most important question in one's life.

A supposedly divine sanction for these distinctions has engendered divisions and endemic violence within Christianity. The effects remain potent today in both religious and secularized forms, and this alone would be a serious reason for concurring with Luhmann's analysis of Christianity as a religion 'unified' by distinctions. There is, however, another reason for taking him seriously. This long process of doctrinal evolution had, he says, another effect on our interactions with nature. By distinguishing nature as the realm of the profane, the possibility of communication with the sacred is reduced to two forms; revelation and prayer. Revelation is seen as intentional communication by God to us, open only to those within the system, who are free to accept or not to accept the message. The consequences of doing so, or not, are implicit in the revelation, that is, it distinguishes the saved from the damned. The specification of the forms of communication between God and human beings as either certain texts or certain pronouncements leaves the relationship between us and nature as non-revelatory: as scientific, economic or aesthetic. Or rather, these latter are distinguished from the former as non-revelatory. All this stupendous and unique construction of theological doctrine was possible only on the basis of structural differentiation (Luhmann 1990: 146–53).

Contingency and hope

Luhmann's radical assessment gives a coherent account of the structural religious basis within Christian linguistic codes for what I have been referring to simply as 'distinguishing in order to de-grade or de-value', as opposed to distinguishing in order to respect, with an emphasis on the binary codes animal/human and sacred/profane. It also serves to illustrate how such religious linguistic codes can be used to justify degradation (in every respect) of what we call the natural world. It leaves us with few illusions as to where we may look for help in approaching the problems following on this degradation which will be considered in the rest of this book. However, two things may help. The first is that his analysis, while it is consistent, cogent and precise, does suffer from a handicap he himself brings to our attention: the tendency to totalize. 'Theology' for him is a theoretical construct, and not an activity engaged in by theologians with perspectives formed by time, place, circumstance and gender. This means that his analysis, which must be taken seriously because it says so much about the evolution of western literate culture, needs redressing with other perspectives, and, in particular, perspectives which allow for paradoxical descriptions of structural coupling in coevolutionary process. While some theologians may adhere to many, if not all the types of religious structural differentiation he refers to, there are other theologians, and believers in God (the two are not always the same) who take more account of the potential charity of our metaphorical imagination, of our capacities for compassion and for acting out of a sense of God's presence which is beyond articulation.

In particular, I would want to stress the capacity for imagining non-existent possibilities, which is as good a translation as one could wish for of the traditional religious formula that faith is the assurance of things hoped for, the conviction of things not seen. This is not a vain hope, or a fantasy as usually understood. It belongs to Nussbaum's metaphorical, charitable imagination which has the capacity to metaphorize alternatives to the present reality and so inspires us to contest that reality in the hope that a new one will emerge. It is here that the paradoxical bridge in imaginative process is at its strongest and most open to actively creating the future. When Martin Luther King said he had a dream, he described a place where, in the imagination of his hearers, they could live differently. Doing so, he energized their lives in ways which are still bringing structural change to American society.

Hope, says the Marxist philosopher Ernst Bloch, is a place as inhabited as the best civilized land and as unexplored as the Antarctic. Bloch's metaphor implies that it is not a place one sets out from. Rather, one charts a course towards it. The future dimension, he said, contains what is feared or what is hoped for: as regards human intention, that is, when it is not thwarted, it contains only what is hoped for. Hope has its positive correlate, he says, in 'the still unclosed determinateness of existence' (Bloch 1995: 4f.). This paradoxical formulation corresponds to the predictable unpredictability of contingency. The future dimension would then be one in which differentiation and distinction were used to generate respect for diversity, rather than to reduce the complexity of existence by creating divisions between us and other life forms. Such an attitude would also, one hopes, dilute the determinist element in Christian apocalyptic rhetoric.

This takes me to the second point I want to make which is, again, implicit in Luhmann's critique. It concerns the concept of contingency. The complexity of interactions in our world is such that their outcomes, their effect-explosions, can never be adequately computed, represented or predicted by us. This realization lay at the heart of Darwin's dissatisfaction with the insufficiency of human reason as an instrument for understanding the universe. For the element of contingency means that that which is not necessary on the basis of what is past – an event or an entity which might or might not happen or exist – can and may emerge into existence. Scientists have used the term to describe the ingenuity of life which, with unforeseen results, makes the most of symbiotic interactions.

The unforeseen results could be an unexpected animal form. Or the road protest movement in Britain.

Theologians and philosophers have connected contingency with freedom, whether God's freedom, the world's freedom, or our own freedom to act in unexpected ways. Pannenberg insists on the independence of the world from God, on its freedom to exist and evolve as a subject of God's love not as an extension of God's self-love. (I use 'subject' here where Pannenberg uses 'object'.) The same is true of us (Pannenberg 1993: 12, 71–114). This freedom is the condition of possibility for free beings to evolve, their freedom being bound up with the contingency of the world. 'The freedom of the (human) will consists of the impossibility of knowing actions that still lie in the future' (Wittgenstein 1961: 39).

Merleau-Ponty, while he does not use the term contingency, describes its reality when he asks: 'What is freedom? To be born is both to be born of the world and to be born into the world. The world is already constituted, but also never completely constituted; in the first case we are acted upon, in the second open to an infinite number of possibilities.' But this analysis is still abstract, he says, 'for we exist in both ways *at once*. There is, therefore, never determinism, and never absolute choice'. (Merleau-Ponty 1962: 453. This description of contingent being will be important for the later discussion of structural sin.)

Freedom to act in a world which is not completely constituted gives space for hope in how it might be differently constituted. The theologian Michael Welker, while he too does not use the term contingency itself, nevertheless helps us grasp its theological meaning when (after Luhmann) he employs concepts of emergent change in speaking of God's Spirit as a force field of divine power. These concepts imply that unpredictability is characteristic of God's freedom to act. The Spirit, and the Spirit's action, he says, is experienced as unpredictable, unforeseeable emergent processes which cannot be calculated or controlled (Welker 1994: 28, 142f., 242f.). This *reparadoxizes* the concept of God as Spirit, for, true to its unpredictability, God's Spirit may or may not act in ways we understand or desire.

Lévinas' concept of *essoufflement de l'esprit*, the possibility of the Spirit holding its breath, holding back, also supports the important notion that God is free *not to act* (italics added; Lévinas 1978: 16. In his reference to Plato, Lévinas is directing attention to what is 'beyond essence', and therefore potentially beyond action in the Spirit. But I do not think this invalidates using this metaphor of 'holding back' as indicative of the notion of contingency.) This is important as a defence against a *deus ex machina* (never determinism, never absolute choice), which would deparadoxize the Spirit of God. The freedom of the Spirit not to act challenges us to take responsibility for what happens around us. We too are free to act, or, when necessary, to refrain from acting. We are called to act, or not, in such a way that we can live with the consequences for our environment of what we do, or refrain from doing.

For me, this argument from contingency contributes to a redescription of God as the Spirit of paradoxical hope – paradoxical because it is exposed to the risk of failure. We experience the force of this Spirit within a coevolutionary society which is, to adapt Prigogine and Stengers' formulation slightly, an immensely complex system involving a potentially enormous number of bifurcations in the natural drift of its evolution. We know that such systems are highly sensitive to change, to fluctuations. This, they say, leads both to hope and to threat: 'hope, since even small fluctuations may grow and change the overall structure. As a result, individual activity is not doomed to insignificance. On the other hand, this is also a threat, since in our universe, the security of stable, permanent rules seems gone forever' (Prigogine and Stengers 1985: 312).

Prigogine and Stengers call this situation one of 'qualified hope', and explain it by reference to a Talmudic text which reparadoxizes the God of Genesis. This God exclaims: 'Let's hope it works!' when, after twenty-six failed attempts, the present world emerges out of the chaotic heart of the preceding debris. This qualified hope has accompanied all the subsequent coevolutionary history of the world, a history 'branded with the mark of radical uncertainty' (1985: 313). As is its God.

7 Justice and judgment

> Justice consists in seeing that no harm is done to anyone. Whenever anyone cries inwardly: 'Why am I being hurt?' harm is being done to that person. The cry raises quite different problems, for which the spirit of truth, justice and love is indispensable.
>
> (Simone Weil 1957: 39)

The sculptures in the south portal of Chartres Cathedral are a graphic depiction of the Last Judgment, usually interpreted as Christ's coming at the end of the world to judge us all. This apocalyptic vision is a common theme in religious art, a popular form of it being one where the saved and the damned are depicted as sheep and goats. Luhmann's Christian binary codes are a reliable guide to reading the figures' identity, with those on the 'right' side of Christ (the saved) being opposed to the 'sinister' figures on his left (the damned). In the Chartres sculptures there is a group placed in front of him whose equivocal presence has particular relevance for a coevolutionary theology. They are the dead, summoned to appear so that they may see the consequences of their actions and of the choices they made in life. Their reaction to this disclosure, in one version of the event, emphasizes their autonomy even beyond death. As they see the effects of their life choices, they themselves judge on which side of Christ they will stand forever. And as we stand before them, and him, the continuum between present choice and future judgment draws us too, the viewers, inexorably into the scene.

This powerful description of judgment, as present choice (exercised in limited freedom) which is inescapably bound to future consequences, presupposes a concept of justice as nonharming. It connects contemporary nonviolent/violent lifestyles with their effects on the life support systems of future generations. From this perspective, refraining from, or engaging in violence now, against oneself or against others, has effects which overflow the spatio-temporal boundaries of one's lifetime. This domino effect is, sadly, well documented in child abuse cases. A coevolutionary perspective focusses also on the future effects on the global *EarthScape* of present action, or inaction. The structural coupling between us and our environments, as part of the natural drift of evolution on the planet as a whole, entails a future partially shaped by the consequences of what we do today. The present English landscape, for instance, has been almost entirely shaped by human activity. Graham Harvey, in his aptly titled book *The Killing of the Countryside*, documents what has happened to that landscape and its non-human inhabitants since the advent of modern intensive farming.

Justice is done, and will be judged to have been well done, where no harm, no violence has been done. Or, more realistically perhaps, where one has tried, to the best of one's ability, to be just and to do justice to every living being. This gives grounds for hope as well as fear, for it emphasizes our freedom – limited freedom it is true, but freedom none the less – to do no harm to others, or at least to minimize that harm. It involves each of us in the process of justice-making rather than leaving it to those individuals or groups usually charged with the dispensing of justice as generally understood. Hope in this context is not a wish for, or a dream of justice. It *is* the struggle for justice, living in the expectation that today's struggle will bring something better tomorrow. Hope relies on a perception of ourselves as members of communities engaged in the evolution of ideas, values and shared environments. It depends on the ability to address fearlessly, intelligently and imaginatively, powerful and unjust political, religious, financial and economic processes within those communities. Judgment on us as justice-making individuals or as societies will include the efforts we make to improve the world we shall leave to those individuals, societies and species which will come after us. In terms of Weil's definitions, and of the preceding chapters, judgment will be made on the basis of our sustaining nonviolent lifestyles, for which the spirit of truth, justice and love is indispensable.

Distinguishing justice

This radical description of justice can be clarified by looking at an important contemporary theory which also takes account of its intragenerational aspect. In 1972 John Rawls proposed a 'contractarian' theory of justice, that is, one whose basis is mutual agreement between members of a society in which behaviour is the product of a social contract. Concerning justice between generations, he uses his concept of 'justice as fairness' to list three rights which all generations can claim from their predecessors: first, to an appropriate rate of capital saving, second, to the conservation of natural resources and the natural environment, and third, to a reasonable genetic policy. According to this 'just saving principle', every generation is expected to hand on to its immediate posterity a somewhat better situation than it has inherited. Anything less would be unfair to them; anything more, unfair to the present generation. Eventually, he applies this principle along what he calls 'family lines', in which parental concern is the only 'rational self-interest' which can be relied on to transcend generations, and by doing so, support obligations corresponding to the rights of the immediate one or two generations following (Agius 1998: 5f.).

While endorsing the attempt made by Rawls to include future generations in the remit of his theory, there are serious shortcomings in this concept of justice which almost empty it of its content as 'fairness'. They lie principally in the notion of rights itself. It seems at least ungrateful, at worst regressive, to criticize this notion at a time when we can celebrate fifty years of its beneficial effects following on from the United Nations Declaration on Human Rights and its adoption in various legal conventions by a majority of nations. Nevertheless, there are problems with it, some of them articulated by Simone Weil as long ago as 1943.

The notion of rights, Weil points out, is linked with the notion of apportioning, of exchange, of quantity. It concentrates, in my terms, on commodity value. It has, she says, something commercial about it, something evocative of legal process and argument. Also, the tone in which 'rights' are asserted is that of contention, 'and when this tone is adopted, force must be there somewhere to back it up, or else it lays itself open to ridicule. Rights by their nature depend on force' (Weil 1957: 23f.). We have, she comments (referring to the French and American Revolutions), inherited the notion of rights from the Romans, who, like Hitler, understood that power is not fully effective unless clothed in a few ideas, and used the idea of rights for this purpose. It suits it admirably. Examining Roman law, we find that 'property was defined by the *jus utendi et abutendi*, by the right to use and abuse. And in fact the majority of the things which the property owner had the right to use and abuse at will were human beings' (Weil 1957: 25; McClellan 1990: 279).

This critique exposes another problem with Rawls' theory, which is the assumption that 'contractarian' relationships apply, or can be applied universally. They may apply, notionally at least, to an economic, educated, predominantly male, politically aware and powerful elite in the G8 countries, but they do not apply to any population as a whole, even within those countries, and certainly not globally. The reason, quite simply, is inequality of power. If we rely exclusively on the notion of rights as contractarian, we may find there are situations where the imbalance of power is so great that the notion clearly does not apply. The ability of one partner in the contract to exercise force over the other makes a nonsense of it. Weil gives an example. If, she says, someone tries to browbeat a farmer into selling his eggs at a moderate price, the farmer can say: 'I have the right to keep my eggs if I don't get a good enough price.' But if a young girl is being forced into a brothel she will not talk about her rights. In such a situation, the word sounds ludicrously inadequate (Weil 1957: 26f.).

What would Weil have to say today when the farmer tells her that his contract is with a supermarket chain which has the power to bankrupt him if he doesn't lower his prices? Can he now talk about his rights without sounding ridiculous? And if he lives in Malawi, who does he talk to? Countries in what is called the developing world no longer have any real control over their currencies, commodity prices and markets. Much of Africa and Latin America has had two 'lost' decades in which declining commodity prices and the external debt trap have bled their countries of resources and reduced them to the status of beggars. Under World Bank and International Monetary Fund (IMF) policies, Structural Adjustment Programmes (SAPs) are, theoretically, economic packages agreed after negotiations between the Bank, the IMF and the government that needs to borrow money – a good example, one might think, of Rawls' 'contractarian' relationship. But the negotiations are between very unequal parties. Third World governments have few internal resources and nowhere else to turn.

This means they are forced to accept economic packages conditional on the removal of trade barriers. What the rich countries call 'barriers' are in fact defence mechanisms (such as tariffs, or regulations and conditions on the entry and operations of foreign companies, or rules controlling the inflow and outflow of funds) set up by local communities to protect themselves. Their removal allows cheap imports from transnational corporations, and can force the closure of national companies with higher costs. These are often aggravated by devaluation of the national currency, which means the local industries cannot afford to import raw materials. SAPs can also have a dangerous effect on a country's ability to feed itself. Farmers have to grow cash crops for export to earn foreign currency, which means less food is grown for home consumption. Despite the fact that Zimbabwe is a drought-prone country, grain reserves were sold off under ESAP, and in 1992, during the worst drought for fifty years, Zimbabwe exported maize while its people went hungry (Madeley *et al.* 1994: 19–35).

Rawls' 'just saving principle', of leaving natural resources and the environment in a good condition for future generations, looks ludicrous here. SAPs generally have a damaging environmental impact, with deforestation and soil degradation becoming very serious problems in Ghana, Guyana, Bolivia and the Philippines (Madeley *et al.* 1994: 36f.). Every survey of biodiversity, natural resources and fresh water supplies gives an increasingly sombre picture. (See *State of the World 1999: A Worldwatch Institute Report of Progress Toward a Sustainable Society*, eds Lester Brown, Christopher Flavin and Hilary French, Norton, New York.) Such surveys demonstrate that inequalities of power between the parties in these economic contracts, whether at the individual, corporate or national level, make the rights model and its just saving principle at best redundant.

Mary Midgley draws attention to some further shortcomings in the notion of Social Contract, a conceptual tool used by prophets of the Enlightenment to put political obligation on the governed rather than the government, on the assumption that the authority of government represents the will of the people and serves their interest. After fierce disputes and much bloodshed, this startling idea was widely accepted, to the extent that 'questions about it largely ceased to be noticed and vanished under the floorboards of many Western institutions'. The authority of contract is now treated as obvious. Yet difficulties with it are on the increase. In a pertinent comment, she asks what happens to the claims of children, of the inarticulate and the insane, and of people as yet unborn? 'What about something that, till recently, our moralists hardly mentioned at all, namely the non-human, non-speaking world – the needs of animals and plants, of the ocean and the Antarctic and the rainforests?' There is a whole range of questions here which we find strangely hard to deal with, because, she says, our culture has been so obsessed with models centring on contract. 'Again, even within the set of possible contractors, we might ask who is entitled to a voice on what?' (Midgley 1996: 6f.). This resonates with an important theme in the UNCED Rio documents, which is their stated concern for four classes of people most at risk from environmental degradation, and most powerless to do anything about it – women, children, indigenous peoples and the poor. Women, as well as being specifically categorized, are disproportionately represented in these groups.

At the very least we need to deepen human rights discourse by integrating a gender perspective into them , as well as mechanisms for redressing the violence done to communities and collectives. Existing human rights discourse has no concept of collective property, such as is found in indigenous societies, and so when 'development' destroys the biophysical environment of such communities, or displaces them from their lands, there are no legal means available to them to resist the plundering of their cultures, their land and the resources it holds. A judicial paradigm which understands human rights as the rights of the powerful must give way to one which sees violations through the eyes of the powerless victims of development, of progress, of technical fixes; of those whose cultures have been ransacked and whose peoples, whether in Irian Jaya, Ogoniland or the cloud forests of Colombia, have been ruined (Kumar-D'Souza 1996: 29–55).

Judgment now

It is, I believe, self-evidently the case that while Rawlsian 'rational self-interest' may be the only acceptable motivation in a culture of competitive individualism which needs an explanation for altruism, it is at best a reductionist description of human relationships, even for those who see themselves as 'investing' in their children. More important however, for a concept of judgment allied to justice, is the fact that Rawls' theory of justice is distinguished, to a large extent, by an expectation of continuing growth, of things 'getting better' for each succeeding generation. It presupposes that the resources for growth, and for continuing development, are available; that thanks to science and reason, together with the spread and improvement of education, we shall be able to hand on a better situation than we inherited. The future of generations to come is, then, automatically taken care of by devoting as much energy as possible to improving the life circumstances of present generations. The presupposition behind this expectation is, of course, that the natural resources of the planet, or more precisely of the biophysical environment of human society, will sustain this improvement.

This presupposition has been a constant in western patterns of political discourse and in party manifestos, where 'a computer in every home' or 'universal access to the Internet' are present variations on the theme. Projected numbers of university graduates are routinely assessed upward, as well as those of car and house ownership. Up to now such indicators have been unquestioningly accepted as marks of progress. A Copernican-like change in perspective, which would see that the earth does not revolve around the economic projects of global capitalism, is barely discernible in the public eye. It can still appear merely pessimistic, or at least counter-cultural, to protest that the protection of future generations requires not the expansion of the consumerist culture, with its concurrent expansion of markets and profits, but its gradual demise.

One move in this direction is to do what I have done briefly in this chapter, and will do in some detail later, which is to make the 'invisible hand' of the market visible. Part of my remit is to make clear how often this has functioned as the surrogate hand of God, an idea partially at least underpinned by an evolutionary idea of history as human fulfilment; as a divinely guided destiny played out on the world stage with the physical environment as unchanging backdrop to the human drama. Rather like the stone facade of Chartres.

Now, however, there is a forest of scaffolding around the facade/stage – and the figures/players. The age, composition and weathering process of the stone is being investigated as a matter of urgency. Its fragility, rather than its strength, is the subject of debate, research and decisions about access and use. Can the facade support so many figures? If not, which ones will be kept, and which discarded? Or, more frightening still, will the stone itself, as it slowly crumbles into dust, decide which will be jettisoned? For as they fall, they will reveal that they too are made of dust.

Justice now

The fragility of living things is a compelling argument for a concept of justice as nonviolence. So too is a belief in their essential oneness. Putting the belief into practice requires the kind of revolutionary perspective possessed by Barbara McClintock. She looked at living organisms and distinguished them as subjects to be respected (see epigraph to Chapter 2). Coevolutionary justice sees them in the same way: as subjects in their own right. This means that as subjects, we accord them their intrinsic value, that is, respect them for what they are in themselves rather than solely for their commodity or instrumental value to us.

In a market economy instrumental and commodity value tend to become more and more indistinguishable, so that people themselves are increasingly valued only in utility terms – human 'resources' measured as output, as units of production calculated in units of time, or as units of consumption taken as indicators of economic growth. Our bodies themselves, rather than their relationships or activities, are commodified as 'market players', as genetic patents, as sperm, egg and blood banks, as 'soft targets', as tissue or transplant units and wombs for hire. These are just some of the publicly recognized, graded values given to us in a 'utility' culture, even though it is still not clear that utility, or any concept like utility, is a fundamental determinant of the behaviour of any known organism (Bateson 1991: 95).

It is hardly surprising then that in the industrialized nations living organisms other than the human have been almost totally commodified. In 1960, John Kennedy used a report in his presidential campaign entitled *Resources for the People*. It advocated positive leadership in protection and conservation of the country's natural resources. We ought not, the report cautions, deplete or ruin these resources irreversibly for the sake of future generations. The earth is 'a warehouse stocked with chemical and physical resources to fulfil the health, industrial, defence, recreational and aesthetic needs of human consumers'. Are we as a nation, the report asked, doing all we can to ensure the wise utilization of our resources? (Hynes 1989: 140f.)

Two years later, Rachel Carson had finished examining the same evidence and, says Hynes, pushed its significance beyond the view that something is only worth respecting and saving if we can use it for an economic resource, for sport or personal pleasure. Her efforts awakened a social and political environmentalism in the United States which led to a bill signed by Nixon on 1 January 1970, known as the Environmental Policy Act. This made the integrity of the environment a central value and a primary consideration in decisions about public projects. Its purposes were, paraphrasing its own language, to encourage harmony between humans and nature, to prevent or eliminate damage to the biosphere and human well-being, and to enrich our understanding of ecological systems and natural resources. '*It contained some understanding of the value of nature for its own sake, not only for its usefulness to human projects*' (italics added; Hynes 1989: 141f.).

In spite of this rosy dawn, in the cold light of day the Act has been substantially amended in favour of human interests. Not only that. It has been used also against some of those interests in favour of others, showing blatant disregard for the health and living conditions of some of the poorest communities in the States. Their cause has been taken up by the Environmental Justice movement, which aims to redress disparities in the distribution of environmental hazards by ensuring equal treatment for all individuals, groups or communities regardless of race, ethnicity or economic status. This has given a new impetus to 'environmentalism', seen now as an 'environmental equity' movement (Dowie 1995). In Europe, social and political environmentalism was also aroused in the 1970s, most notably in the founding of the Green Party in (then) West Germany and by international organizations such as Greenpeace and Friends of the Earth.

Yet today in Britain farm animals are classified as 'agricultural goods'; the farm land surrounding them is assessed in terms of competitive yields, labour and marketing costs and the whole subsumed under the name 'industrial agriculture'. Chemically supported high-yield agriculture has reduced crop growing to a series of simple choices between 'competing chemical products'. These crops grow and are harvested in what Harvey describes as 'a landscape of the dead' (Harvey 1997: 35f.). In a passage reminiscent of Carson, he writes that the most striking characteristic of this landscape is its silence. There is no sound in this land; no buzzing of bees, no rasping of crickets, no birdsong.

Saddest of all, there is no joyous ripple from Shelley's 'blythe spirit', no 'silver chain of sound' from George Meredith's *Lark Ascending*. The skylarks have gone from this modern field. Here the heavens are as devoid of life as the waving wheat beneath them. Down below the ripening ears, on the bare earth, no bugs or insects are visible among the forest of stems. Nothing lives here. The pesticides have seen to that.

(Harvey 1997: 35–49)

Is this what future generations will inherit? And if so, can we say, or believe, that we are handing on to them a better environment than the one we inherited?

Coevolutionary judgment

In the opening quotation from Weil, she alludes to 'quite different problems' raised by the cry 'Why am I being hurt?' Her point of contrast is the other cry, which we hear so often: 'Why has somebody else got more than I have?' This cry refers to rights. It evokes a spirit of contention and inhibits any possible impulse of charity. It invokes a repressive justice which uses fear as a deterrent. We must learn to distinguish this cry from the other, she says, and try to do everything possible, as gently as possible, to hush it. This can be done with the help of a code of justice, regular tribunals and police, for words like *right* and *democracy* are valid in their own region, which is that of institutions.

They are secondary however, to our response to the primary cry for justice, that of pain. 'If you say to someone who has ears to hear: "What you are doing to me is not just", you may touch and awaken at its source the spirit of attention and love' (Weil 1957: 38, 26). With these words Weil asserts the importance for a just society of the *SocialScape* and the *PoieticScape*: the social, imaginative, interpersonal, emotional and corrective dimensions of our responses to other living beings. They are integral to the connective relationships which form our *EarthScape* and through which we interact with that of others. They are as much part of us, through our structural coupling, as our constitutive relationships with food, water and fresh air: dimensions of the *relational, total-field image* of ourselves proposed by Arne Naess, in which the intrinsic relations between the *SelfScape* and the other dimensions belong to the definition of what we are, so that without those relations, we are no longer the same person – or indeed, a living organism. An organism, he says, is a knot in a field of intricate relations (Naess 1989: 28). Coevolutionary justice consists in paying attention to as many knots as possible.

Weil's important contribution to our perspective here is her insistence on the role of emotion in a just response. Love and justice, summed up for her in the notion of 'a spirit of attention', includes those imaginative powers which enable us, as Nussbaum says, to put ourselves in another's place. They enable us to hear the cry of affliction, often silenced, one which is, in intent if not in practice, excluded from a rights model of justice. This assumes that one can calculate, apportion, divide and dispense 'objectively', that is, by treating others as objects.

Weil gives a graphic image of this process. 'Just as a vagabond, accused of stealing a carrot from a field, stands before the judge, who, seated comfortably, engages in elegant queries, comments and witticisms while the accused cannot even stammer a word, so truth stands before an intelligence solely concerned with elegant manipulation of opinion' (Weil 1957: 32).

Standing with her before the figures at Chartres, we are moved by their mute suppliance, by their coming to present judgment on the scaffold. We are aware that past generations have stood here also and seen little if no change in the figures and facade. We know, too, that they, no less than we, were 'knotted' into a field of intricate relations with their environment, and that these relations, which have maintained the figures up to now, have been and are dynamic. Every breath taken by past generations, every action and reaction of the physical environment has triggered some change, created some perturbation. Past generations assumed that their children and grandchildren would stand before these figures and find them as beautiful, as majestic and seemingly immutable as they did. They assumed that the only damage that could be done to them would be by direct blow against them, from hand, shot or hammer.

But now? How many generations in the future will be able to see them in their beauty and majesty? Are those who see them crumble moved by the sight, moved to respond in a spirit of love and attention to the environment they, and we share? 'Because affliction and truth need the same kind of attention before they can be heard, the spirit of justice and the spirit of truth are nothing other than a certain kind of attention, which is pure love' (Weil 1957: 36).

8 Justice North and South

My skin
is a window of vulnerability
without moisture, without touching
I must die

The window of vulnerability
is being walled up
my land
cannot live

(Dorothee Sölle 1990b: vii)

A concept of justice as loving attention, as nonviolence or nonharming, perceives and responds to the vulnerability of all living things. We are vulnerable because of the permeability of our personal boundaries (our 'skin') in relation to the environments we inhabit and share, and because our continued existence depends on that same permeability. It permits us to be taught and touched, inspired and fed, delighted and energized; or sadly, ignored and starved. In common with all autopoietic entities, we touch and depend on other aggregations of cells for our intakes of energy, and depend also on what is not always immediately tangible: the dynamic equilibrium of the environment and the constancy of atmospheric conditions favourable for life. It is this permeability and shared dependence which make us vulnerable, and, at the same time, capable of harming ourselves and/or others.

This chapter focusses on one particular mode of interaction with our environments: our extraction and absorption of energy from them. This is an obvious way in which we touch them and affect the lives of those who share them with us. In today's consumerist culture, overextraction and overconsumption of energy can be seen to harm the most vulnerable members of society and other life forms on the planet. The harm lies not only in the gross inequalities between one group's access to energy sources compared with that of another, but also in the fact that the extraction and processing of raw materials has been advanced to a stage where the scale and pace of their extraction far outstrips the scale and pace of their replacement. The resources themselves, and the environmental effects of their disappearance, are lost to view in industrial processing, discounted in marketing the end product. Blatant examples are oil extraction in Nigeria and its effects on Ogoniland (Watts 1998: 243–264), and industrial forestry and clearcutting in the temperate rainforests of North America (Devall 1993). The marketing of their products, through images of limitless growth, choice and demand, effectively cloaks the fact that if we are too successful in extracting energy from our environments, we destroy them, ourselves and other living beings in the process.

The use of the term 'energy' here needs some clarification, although oil, its extraction and use, would be commonly accepted as synonymous with it. In Chapter 1, when summarizing Maturana and Varela's description of autopoiesis as systemic organization of living organisms, their vocabulary of 'dynamic production processes', 'transformation of components', 'maintaining structural integrity and organization by using solar energy', 'metabolic activity' and 'networks of chemical and energetic transformations', conveyed a sense of power at work in the self-'making'. Their metaphorical heaps brought together clusters of scientific terms conveying an image of transformative activity, of energy exchanged between the organisms and something absorbed from the environment by the organisms into themselves, and vice versa. The descriptions were of continuous exchange, between the environment and the organism, between the components of the organism, and between the results of that exchange ('excessive life chemistry' or Margulis's 'making of messes') and the environment. This transformative cycling and recycling of components within and between organism and environment, sustained through energy transfer, constitutes their structural coupling. Its mutuality, continuity and cessation sustain what we call nutrition, love, life and death.

Using words like 'coupling' in descriptions of energy (with overtones not only of bodily intimacy and separate identities but of railway lines and engines), blurs the outline of the metaphorical energy heap. This happens because, as Joan Solomon points out in her study of general knowledge about energy in schools and in society, the word 'energy' has extraordinary pliability. It is used frequently with a large number of different meanings capable of stimulating a variety of images, all loosely related. Its cultural salience is, she says, crucial for its power to seize the imagination. But inevitably this process blunts the meaning of the word at the same time as sharpening its value as a universal image (Solomon 1992: 16). I want to capitalize on its power to seize the imagination, but without blunting its primary meaning in this chapter, which is an intake or output of the power needed to sustain life and well-being. This power can be transmitted through fuel, food, water, heat, fire, light, activity, calorie intake, chemical transfer, bodily fluids, fusion or fission and so on. Such terms are themselves multivalent.

As far as we know, no organism or species has ever achieved a fraction of our success in extracting, transforming, processing, transferring and, in our case, storing, packaging and marketing energy from our environments. It is also a fact that, as I pointed out in the previous chapter, this extraction has demonstrably depleted the reserves of energy available not only to the planet's present inhabitants, but also to those coming after us. They too will depend on climatic equilibrium and on other organisms, both plant and animal, to transform matter and themselves into whatever form of energy humans need to survive. But this survival is now threatened by overextraction and overconsumption, both integral to the reigning free market economic expectation of continuous growth in output requiring ever more input into the system. Willi Brandt, introducing the 1978 Report on the world economy and international development issues, *North-South: A Programme for Survival*, asked: 'Are we to leave our successors a scorched planet of advancing deserts, impoverished landscapes and ailing environments?' Twenty years later, what answer can we give?

Energy and access to its sources

The Brandt Report, as it is commonly known, took as its setting what it called 'the North–South divide', acknowledged to be a simplified view of the world but with enough reality to be able to define the 'North' (including, south of the equator, industrialized Australia and New Zealand and now, twenty years on, Pacific Rim countries such as Singapore, Malaysia and South Korea) as 'rich and developed', that is, 'market-economy industrialized', and the 'South' (including oil-exporters south of the equator with higher *per capita* incomes than some of the geographically northern countries) as 'poor and developing'. In spite of its shortcomings, this economic rather than geographical distinction remains largely true in a world which is still 'a fragile and interlocking system, whether for its people, its ecology or its resources'. The raw materials for the industries in the North still come, to a large extent, from the South; financial markets are still ruled by New York, London, Tokyo and, to a lesser extent, Hong Kong. The distinction still has force because the economic dominance of the North, and the resulting dependence of the South, continues. As does the demonstrable fact that 'economic forces left entirely to themselves tend to produce growing inequality' (Sampson 1980: 19, 30f.).

The inequality was spelt out in 1978 in terms of disparate wealth distribution and its effects. The North had a quarter of the world's population and four-fifths of its income; the South, including China, had three-quarters of the world's population but one-fifth of global income. The average individual in the North could expect to live for more than seventy years, would rarely be hungry, and would be educated at least up to secondary level. In the South, the life expectancy of the majority was closer to fifty: one out of every four children died before the age of five; one-fifth or more of all people suffered from hunger and fifty per cent were illiterate (Sampson 1980: 32).

Twenty years later, the studies, statistics and classifications proliferate, but the inequalities between North and South remain constant or have become in some cases even worse. According to the 1996 Report of the United Nations Development Programme, the life expectancy of a child born in Sierra Leone is 39.2 years, that of a Japanese child 79.6, that of a North American child 76.1

and of a British one, 76.3 years. In the South, a pertinent statistic is the daily calorie supply *per capita*, which ranges from 3,223 in Barbados to 1,505 in Somalia. The calories available are not equally distributed either, so even within the economic North an increasing number suffer malnutrition and/or acute hunger. Russia and other countries in the former Soviet Union are a case in point. Another vital disparity is that in Hong Kong in 1996, 100 per cent of the population had access to clean water: in China 67 per cent; in Haiti 28 per cent; in the Central African Republic 18 per cent; in Afghanistan 12 per cent.

These quantitative measures of energy sources and access to them largely focus on the individual's coupling with the *EarthScape* as a resource base. Other studies take into account our social coupling, our input to and from the *SocialScape*. In *The Quality of Life*, a collection of essays edited by Martha Nussbaum and Amartya Sen, Erik Allardt, for instance, gives both subjective and objective weighting to indicators of access to resources. He distinguishes between objective measures of external conditions, such as clean water or soil quality, and personal, subjective evaluation by the individuals concerned. Taken together they indicate the satisfaction of basic human needs and the resulting quality of biological, physical and social life. These needs signal conditions without which human beings are unable to survive or to avoid misery, including the overall need to avoid alienation from society and from non-human nature. The needs are classified as *having* (economic resources: income, housing, working conditions, health and education); *loving* (those attachments which satisfy the need to relate to other people and form social identities); and *being* (integration into society and living in harmony with the non-human world). This expanded perspective allows for the complexity of relationships implicit in social justice, including our relationship with nature (Allardt 1993: 88–94). It also allows for an expansion in the concept of value by specifying loving and being as intrinsic to the quality of human life.

Quality and inequality

Emphasizing the concept of 'quality' within a discussion of in/e/quality diffuses a purely quantitative measure of resources, not by ignoring it, but by connecting it to other needs and 'knots', social, personal and natural. Quality enlarges the relational field and encourages a generous definition of the 'energy inputs' needed to sustain the relationships. Such an enlargement lies behind the title of an essay by G. A. Cohen: *Equality of What? On Welfare, Goods, and Capabilities.* His title itself refers back to an earlier lecture by Sen entitled *Equality of What?* Both essays, and the one by Sen which follows Cohen's in this volume, enquire as to what aspects of a person's condition should count in a *fundamental* way for egalitarians. Both essayists go back to Rawls' theory of justice as a watershed in the discussion of *what people should have equal amounts of* (italics added). For Rawls, this revolved around 'primary goods' and their distribution. His notion was expanded by Sen to include the opportunity for, or capability of an individual to acquire those goods and to use them to his or her own benefit (Cohen 1993: 9–50).

This necessarily brief reference to such a complex and in-depth discussion cannot do justice to its carefully nuanced arguments. However, reference to it, together with the essay by Cohen quoted above, opens the question of which aspects of a person's condition should count in a *fundamental* way when assessing equality or inequality, and leaves it open by a refusal to accept the narrow Rawlsian proposal of limiting those aspects to what people should *have*. Even with Sen's shift to what it is possible for people to have and to use given their ability and level of social advantage, the focus remains on inter-human relationships. Allardt's inclusion of integration/alienation in regard to nature is a necessary step further.

From a coevolutionary perspective, the inclusion of objective and subjective aspects of human relationships with our *EarthScapes* is essential. The narrower focus on human financial and social inequalities is not discounted or relativized, but set in context. This is particularly true of those economic goods which we have, or not, such as housing, income, and food. Then the question becomes: what aspects of a person's environment contribute in a *fundamental* way to his/her capacity to satisfy basic needs? And further to this, what access does s/he have to them? And, as a consequence, what kind of access to them is available for other species? Which can be summarized by asking what, within our global *EarthScape*, should people have equal amounts of?

The short answer, in terms of this chapter, is access to energy sources in accordance with the natural limits of those sources. (This is a reminder that in autopoietic process, our autonomy/freedom in self-making is limited by the resources available for the making.) The rather longer answer in this chapter explores these limits through two complementary concepts: (a) the ecological footprint and (b) environmental space. The former quantifies the amount of energy accessed and used at present by people North and South (understood economically). The latter helps us to understand the limits to the total amount of energy and non-renewable resources available globally and locally, and so establishes a benchmark amount for individual use. In both cases, the notion of limits to resources, and therefore limits to economic growth and consumption, is axiomatic.

The ecological footprint

The concept of the ecological footprint has been developed by Mathis Wackernagel and William Rees. They consciously work from the perspective of the earth's ecosystems, stressing their inability to sustain current levels of economic activity and material consumption, let alone increased levels. Then they ask how these can be lowered. Their answer, which echoes much already said in this book, is to rethink our relationships with each other and with the rest of nature. Most writers on the subject of sustainable living, they say, treat the 'environment' as 'something *out there*, separate and detached from people and their works'. So, when economic activity causes unexpected damage to some environmental value, this is called a 'negative externality' (or an 'objective' factor), emphasizing the environment's place on the periphery of modern consciousness. They argue instead that any human enterprise cannot be separated from the natural world, even in our minds, because 'in terms of energy and material flows, there is simply no "out there" '. This premise is so simple, they say, that it is generally overlooked or dismissed as too obvious to be relevant (Wackernagel and Rees 1996: 1–5).

As a way of changing perspective, the authors go on to develop 'ecological footprint analysis', an accounting tool that enables them, and us, to estimate the resource consumption and waste assimilation requirements of a defined human population or economy in terms of a corresponding productive land area. It should be possible (and they show that it is) to produce a reasonable estimate of the land/water area required by any city (and any individual within any conurbation) to sustain itself. This 'is its *de facto* "ecological footprint" on the Earth' (Wackernagel and Rees 1996: 11).

For modern industrial cities the area required is of orders of magnitude larger than the area physically occupied. London consumes 120 times the resources available within its own land area. So its ecological footprint is 120 times greater than its geographical boundaries. [Applied to countries, the same analysis shows that Holland, for instance, consumes the resources of over 15 times more land than lies within the country's own political boundaries (Wackernagel and Rees 1996: 88–93)]. In this respect, the authors say, the city is similar to a cow in its pasture. Its economy needs to 'eat' resources, and eventually, 'all this intake becomes waste and has to leave the organism the economy again.' The pasture has to be big enough to support that economy, that is, produce all its feed and absorb all its waste. This 'industrial metabolism' determines the size of the city's ecological footprint, that is, of its inhabitants and their activities. With this established, the ecologically productive land available to each person (the average person's footprint) can be worked out, and, with the help of comparative studies of consumption, that of individuals North and South (Wackernagel and Rees 1996: 12, 93–118).

When this is done, a striking inequality appears in land appropriation *per capita* relative to ecologically productive land. The present ecological footprint of a typical North American represents three times his/her share of the earth's resources. It also appears that our footprints keep growing while our *per capita* 'earthshares' shrink. Since the beginning of this century the 'available' *per capita* ecological space on earth has decreased (through wars, industrialization, overpopulation and land/water degradation) from between 5 and 6 hectares per person to only 1.5 hectares. The inequality between earthshares North and South grows proportionately.

Wackernagel and Rees offer their model as a useful tool to help us plan for sustainable use of resources, aware that further refinement of the concept is desirable and necessary. Its great benefit is its linking of ecological deterioration and material inequity, and enabling these to be linked to individual and institutional decision-making about consumption, economic growth and energy use. It also highlights a fact which has already been mentioned, which is that modern cities and industrial regions are dependent for survival and growth on a vast and increasingly global hinterland of ecological landscapes in the South. The 'banana footprint' in the UK, for example, is about 48,300 hectares of land elsewhere (Wackernagel and Rees 1996: 28f., 92.) A visit to any supermarket in the North, and a quick glance at 'country of origin' labelling for this and other tropical fruit, brings home the scale of this global hinterland. A longer look at the label raises deeper questions, some of which will be discussed in the next chapter, about the quality of life and environment for those who grow and pack the fruit (Primavesi 1996: 91–101).

Environmental space

Another allied tool for measuring resource use is the concept of 'environmental space'. This stands for the total amount of energy and non-renewable resources which can be used globally or regionally. Based on a quantitative and qualitative assessment of sustainable resource use, it was worked out in 1992 by a team of researchers for the Dutch Friends of the Earth and has become the basis for the Sustainable Europe Campaign and the Sustainable Societies Programme of Friends of the Earth International.

It rests on three principles. First, that environmental space is limited, and that its limits are sufficiently quantifiable to provide valuable policy guidance. Second, that there is a need for equitable global development, which means that all countries should have equal access to the world's resources, and equal responsibility for their management. Third, that production and consumption should serve to enhance the quality of life rather than degrade it. Vital aspects of living, such as the need for health, work, family and community, as well as cultural and spiritual life, are to be balanced against the short-term benefits of material consumption (Carley and Spapens 1998: 8f.).

There are obvious connections here with the Brandt Report, the social justice and quality of life debate, and the realities of overextraction and overconsumption by the North highlighted in the ecological footprint approach. The environmental space programme also includes a stated concern for the rights of future generations. All of these approaches, implicitly and explicitly, demonstrate the common vulnerability of organisms and their environments. They also show the harm inflicted on vulnerable people and environments by the dominant consumerist culture and by the refusal of those who control it to acknowledge the harm, as well as by their determination to cloak any limits to growth.

The refusal to set limits to human desire for commodities is effected primarily through advertising, which stimulates desire for them while apparently guaranteeing the fulfilment of that desire. This is actually a refusal to acknowledge that in the long run, 'our economies and our quality of life are dependent on the environment – not the other way around' (Carley and Spapens 1998:

57). It is the global environment (and here the term is used primarily in the sense of *EarthScape*, or biophysical environment) which ultimately provides us with a home, with sources of energy and materials, with services such as carbon absorption and climate regulation, and with 'sinks' for waste energy and waste materials. Recognizing this, Carley and Spapens propose three basic principles of environmental space which, if adopted universally, would enable us, as a species, to preserve that space to the benefit of all who inhabit it.

The first is a commitment to living within the earth's biophysical limits by mid twenty-first century.

The second is a commitment to global equity of access to resources, *within those limits*. 'As long as rich countries continue to consume a high amount of renewable and non-renewable resources *per capita*, developing countries can also morally command the right to do so, if they too ignore the limits. As a result, the planet will be locked in a vicious and downward cycle of environmental and, ultimately, socio-economic degradation.' Unless, that is, we in the North are prepared to make radical changes in our management of the human economy and therefore in our unsustainable lifestyles (Carley and Spapens 1998: 57–67). The present economic 'recovery' programme in Japan, for instance, is reportedly based on the interlocking strategies of encouraging people to 'spend' and 'consume'.

The third principle is a commitment to total quality of life within national cultures. This is seen as a positive step, as 'an exciting opportunity to increase quality of life in our communities'. One way of doing this is to build on the growing recognition that 'economic prosperity is necessary, but hardly sufficient, for total quality of life' (Carley and Spapens 1998: 72). This finding harks back to the debate between Sen and others, and it also sounds a positive note in what is, in reality, a call to voluntary austerity in the North. It also reinforces the importance of the *PoieticScape*, of our capacity for creative action and reaction to our environments. Indeed, the whole scope of the project relies on our ability to express that larger charity of the imagination which can move us to deny ourselves for others' sake.

Carley and Spapens themselves respond to the question of how the concept of environmental space differs from that of the ecological footprint, a difference which my necessarily summary treatment of both may have obscured. The footprint is a less complex tool, since it reduces all forms of production and consumption to a hypothetical measurement of hectares required to generate those forms compared to the actual physical space occupied by the city or region under analysis. Environmental space is more complex because it analyses various key resource sectors at national level, and because it encompasses energy and non-renewable resource consumption. Both concepts, however, arise from the same concern for excessive production and consumption in the North and for development prospects in the South. Both foster discussion and debate on sustainable production and consumption within sound biophysical limits, and link North and South in a common framework of responsibility and action (Carley and Spapens 1998: 70).

North/South and theology

The discussion in this chapter has focussed largely on the economic relationship between North and South based on the distinctions made in the Brandt Report. What has this to do with theology as usually understood? Why should descriptions of autopoietic process, and of ourselves as autopoietic entities dependent ultimately on the well-being of the global *EarthScape*, be a basis for theological reflection? These descriptions are, as the discussion above shows, taken as synonymous with 'environmental' issues, and there are environmentalists who would be astonished (even, as I have discovered, slightly resentful) to find theologians wandering onto this territory. Equally, there would be many theologians who would strenuously resist any invitation to venture there, or any suggestion that they should do so.

This attitude harks back to the point I made earlier about the separation in Christian theology between knowledge of God mediated through the natural world and that mediated through chosen Christian texts and teaching (p. 35 above). Those who count only the latter as valid in the revelation of God's will and purposes reject the possibility of having the earth disclosed to us by science as 'full of divine riches' (Psalms 104: 24). In general, even theologians who are not rigidly neo-orthodox rely on religious narratives and, rather less, on spiritual experience as guides for interpreting their own and others' lives. The traditional language of these narratives, with their talk of soul, redemption, grace, eschatology, transcendence and confession (in all meanings of the word) makes little sense to people brought up in a *SocialScape/PoieticScape* informed by Darwinian, Freudian, Einsteinian, systemic and genetic concepts. It is also the case that as an academic discipline, most theology has been concerned with writing, reflecting on and articulating the meaning of the 'right' answers to questions about God, the world and human nature posed in a pre-Enlightenment, pre-evolutionary context and reliant on a shared worldview very different from ours. This has taught us that everything in the universe, including ourselves, is made up of particles such as protons, electrons and neutrons – entities whose very existence is defined in purely mathematical terms and which physicists now assert are the basis of life, including human life. 'Rather than see ourselves in relation to mythical heroes, gods, and religious laws, we in the West now see ourselves in relation to atoms, stars and scientific laws' (Wertheim 1997: 5f.). And, I would add hopefully, in relation to our global *EarthScape*.

This transition from a spiritual to a physical cosmos is not, Wertheim says, simply logical, but 'an enormous shift in the psychic bedrock of the western subconscious'. It is above all a shift in our awareness of relationality – of ourselves as related to atoms and stars, to bacteria and mountains, to North and South in a multiplicity of modes. Today's *questions* arise in that context and problems are seen from that perspective. The *answers* are, and will be, sought and found with the help of analyses from the material sciences, literally those which deal with the material activity and relationships of living entities. The answers come increasingly from multidisciplinary work, as do the environmental studies mentioned above, which bring together a 'green' (environmental) analysis of material interchanges between people and nature and a 'red' (socialist) analysis of capitalist production relationships, competition and world markets (O'Connor 1994: 163–171).

This conjunction of red/green is an additional problem for Christian theology. The mutual and professed antagonism between Christianity and Marxism created one of Luhmann's classic Christian binary codes, still potent in western culture, in which 'communist' is opposed to 'Christian' as 'evil' to 'good'. The Vatican excommunicated communists for being communists. It did not excommunicate Nazis for being Nazis. It is hardly surprising, then, that it was, and is a minority of theologians in Europe who openly take account of Marxism. They believe, as Dorothee Sölle believes, that a theological education which awakens no sense of need for an economic theory betrays its own goal. After 'nearly a century of hate, fear, self-deception, denial and lies' theologians entered into dialogue with Marxists: not in conference halls, but in Fascist prison cells and concentration camps where Christians and Marxists met and shared suffering and hope, cigarettes and news (Sölle 1990b: 26).

One precondition for this dialogue, she says, is the historical experience that neither religion nor socialism can be suppressed by pure force. In the dialogue itself, Christians not only became acquainted with socioeconomic analyses, but began to understand their own contribution to the various forms of oppression. In some groups therefore, 'the learning process led to a feeling of shame which, according to Marx, is a revolutionary sentiment. Christians, especially in the Third World, joined liberation movements or at least took part in groups that fought against brutal violations of human rights'. Thinking back on those days, Sölle sums up her own experience by saying that her encounter with Marxism deepened her Christian understanding of the historical and social dimensions of human existence. Through it, she learned to take material existence, rather than disembodied heavenly being, more seriously, in the two-fold sense of body and society. She learned that capitalism is served not only by death squads, the mining of harbours or napalm bombs, but also by an obliging theology that neutralizes victims, silences hunger and oppression, and individualizes hope. Such a pre-Marxist understanding of theology is, she declares, in no sense neutral. It is a theology of death (Sölle 1990b: 27–30).

The next chapter will describe the theologies which emerged and continue to emerge from a post-Marxist understanding of theology. Routinely classified as 'liberation' theologies, theologies of freedom, they take socioeconomic and ecological analyses as a basis for reflection and action. Above all, they ask different *questions*, which can be summed up as the overriding question of this chapter: Is access to energy sources/freedom from hunger a theological question? Or to put it another way: How does the concept 'God' function in the light of some of the gross inequalities described in this chapter?

Liberation and ecology

Before going on to liberation theologies as such, a brief look at the concept of liberation ecology will help put them in context. Liberation ecology, according to Michael Watts and Richard Peet, sees the environment itself 'as an active constituent of imagination', and therefore discourses in social and environmental movements 'assume regional forms that are, as it were, thematically organized by natural contexts' (Peet and Watts 1996: 36f.). This emphasis on context as a constituent of imagination is another way of saying that the *PoieticScape* includes an aspect of environment which can and does influence societies and individuals. How we refer to, imagine or describe our relationships with particular environments affects them and us. Castoriadis calls this web of biophysical and descriptive relationships 'the social imaginary', that is, the way in which 'societies create themselves as quasi-totalities held together by institutions, social imaginary significations, and systems of meaning and representation which organize their natural worlds and establish ways people are socialized' (Peet and Watts 1996: 267).

Imagination, whether as visual images or invention and creativity, does not reside or work solely inside our heads. It is, as we saw in Chapter 6, a bond between ourselves and the world, generated and nurtured between us and all aspects of our environments and by the landscapes we inhabit. This means that there is an essential diversity in *PoieticScapes* and in the discourses they generate and use. A banana plantation worker struggling for justice in Central America will use different images to describe his life from a fisherman in Alaska trying to cope with the destruction of his livelihood by oil pollution and overfishing. Both descriptions will differ from that given by a Chinese farmer who grew up in a Maoist collective and now has to adapt to working within a short-term, individualistic economic framework. All share the experience of practical struggles over livelihood and survival, but their descriptions contend with each other in ways which do not allow for us who hear or read them to privilege or universalize one over the other. Each derives its truth, its legitimacy, from its context. The *SelfScapes, SocialScapes* and *EarthScapes* of these *PoieticScapes* inform their making. They belong to 'environmental imaginaries, whole complexes of imaginaries with which people think, discuss, and contend threats to their livelihoods'. This makes them necessarily fluid rather than 'an already formed structure of ideas' (Peet and Watts 1996: 37).

If we acknowledge, as we must, the existence of these multiply dimensioned *PoieticScapes* and their contesting claims to truth, then, say liberation ecologists, we must subvert, contest and reform certain environmental practices, institutions and academic systems. We must free ourselves from the pervasive Northern notion that there is 'a' social, economic, scientific or environmental formula or solution for every situation. I heard an amusing example of this 'contesting' from a Swedish ecologist/theologian, Ingemar Hedstrom. He worked in Ecuador and Costa Rica for many years, and told us that one day he and a group of 'experts' were inspecting crops and found one field where a large strip of planted soil failed to show more than the faintest tinge of green shoots.

The experts discussed various possible causes for the failure and proposed different agrochemical solutions. The peasant accompanying them finally managed to make his excited interjections understood. That strip, he explained, had been planted three months later than the rest of the field.

The subversion, contesting and reforming of Northern 'imperialism' in all its forms is dubbed liberatory because it frees ecology, in the broadest sense, from the North's claims to know, speak and practise truth valid for everyone, especially through the medium of technoscience. This is most evident at the moment in the resistance of farmers in the economic South to the patenting of 'suicide gene' sequences by Northern agrochemical corporations. The farmers see this as drawing them into 'bioserfdom'. Instead, liberation ecologies argue that by their very existence, each society carries a *PoieticScape* tightly coupled with its *SocialScape/EarthScape*, a way of imagining Nature which includes visions of those forms of social and individual practice which are ethically proper and morally right with regard to Nature. Through this 'situated knowledge', liberation ecology sees nature, environment and place as *sources* of thinking, reasoning and imagining: the social is, in this quite specific sense, naturally constructed. Liberation ecology shares with Marx the belief that reasoning provides a basis for political action. Liberation ecologies provide a particular kind of reasoning: a sort of mapping of social, political and economic relations to nature and a guide to the strategic interventions which can be based on them (Peet and Watts 1996: 260–3).

Donna Haraway describes this liberatory *PoieticScape* as 'the dreams and achievements of contingent freedoms, situated knowledges, and relief of suffering' which contest the powers and discourses of Northern hegemonies and the Scientific Revolution, and focus on the intensified misery of billions of men and women organically rooted in the 'freedoms' of transnational capitalism and technoscience. She coined the term 'situated knowledge' to describe a way of knowing rooted in imaginative connection and hard-won, practical coalition. (This is another way of describing the power of metaphorical imagination outlined in Chapter 6.) The situatedness does not mean parochialism, but specificity and structures of accountability 'to each other and to the worldly hope for freedom and justice' (Haraway 1997: 3, 11, 199f.). This resonates with the embodied, expressive, social and imaginative aspects of our individual structural coupling with specific environments. The struggle for justice, for freedom, for love and for truth is the resistance of one kind of situated knowledge to the universalist takeover claims of another. One is then able to help the other reform its perspective through an exchange of perspectives, of knowledge, of energy, of feeling and of power. The dialogue between Christians and Marxists is a potent example. In the next chapter we shall see what effect such situated knowledge has had on theologians in the South, and on their theological descriptions.

9 Freedom for theology

> The goal is a theology and politics of liberation fuelled not by protest alone but by an inspiration to reimagine and to refashion existing social systems and institutions.
>
> (Sharon Welch 1997: 127)

The Brandt Report recognized that its findings would call for structural changes North and South in economic relationships and in international institutions. Liberation theologians, like liberation ecologists, found, and continue to find, a similar North–South reciprocal relationship when they discover, as Dorothee Sölle did, that certain 'Northern' theological *PoieticScapes* are in the service of death, not life. This discovery has been made by those in the North who move South to live and work, a move which brings them face to face with the death inflicted on those in the South, and on their environments, by the 'free' market mechanisms imposed on them by the North.

They move into a *SocialScape*, *PoieticScape* and *EarthScape* neither experienced nor imagined in the North. There, God is the God of the freemen and the economy that of the 'free' markets. But this 'freedom' is seen in the South for what it is – an illusion. It is an illusion for those in the North who repeat the mantra of 'freedom' on the understanding that it encourages personal freedom, creates jobs and prosperity and shores up democracy. For in fact all markets are managed – not so much by governments as by transnational corporations, banks and trading companies mainly located in North America, Japan and western Europe – not to stimulate personal or communal development, but to maximize profit for their shareholders. In order to get the free trade agreements of NAFTA, GATT and WTO approved by Congress, the Bush and Clinton administrations made deals with a variety of corporate interests – textiles, financial services, agriculture, telecommunications, steel etc. – which created a favourable climate for maximum returns on US private investment (Ryan and Whitmore 1997: 150).

In the South, the illusion of freedom is soon dispelled when its obverse, economic slavery, is imposed on the majority of the population by Northern capitalist structures. Freedom for those in the South would mean freedom from this slavery and the suffering it causes. Imagining this freedom, and refashioning existing theological, social, economic and political institutions to bring it about, has come to define the theological task for many Southern theologians. The resultant theologies, deliberately or not, subvert and contest those of many Northern theologians, and by doing so, in some cases, and in some measure, have helped reform them.

Situated knowledge North and South

Yale theologian Cornel West acknowledges this in his introduction to the American translation of Franz Hinkelammert's Marxist-Christian description of North–South political economics, *The Ideological Weapons of Death: A Theological Critique of Capitalism*. West describes this liberation theology as 'a worldly theology, one which not only opens our eyes to the social misery of the world but also teaches us to understand it better and to transform it'. Academic theology in the North, he says, 'remains preoccupied with doctrinal precision and epistemological pretension'. Therefore it either refuses to get its hands dirty with the ugly and messy affairs of contemporary politics, or pontificates at a comfortable distance about the shortcomings of theoretical formulations and practical proposals in liberation theologies. Yet, he says, for those Christians deeply enmeshed in and united with the poor in the South, 'theology is first and foremost concerned with urgent issues of life and death, especially the circumstances that dictate who lives and who dies' (Hinkelammert 1986: v).

The situated knowledge of theologians structurally coupled with the *EarthScape*, *SocialScape* and *PoieticScape* of the poor in the South is not, then, used primarily to discuss theological ideas, or to rationalize suffering in the name of a God who 'desires sacrifices'. Instead they highlight human account-ability for that suffering, giving a specific account of the devastating effects of the capitalist 'empire' of the North on the lives and environments of the communities they minister to in the South (Hinkelammert 1997: 25–48). Theologians situated there are more likely too to be alert to their own institutions' role in or collusion with contemporary forms of economic and social oppression, whether in ignoring the effects of church investment policies, of church ownership structures or of church employment practices.

When the Commissioners of the Church of England lost £800 million in property and stock market speculation the clergy pension fund was threatened. But it has now recovered thanks to increasingly generous support from parishioners and more prudent investment. In the South, the devastating effects on the poor of interest rate movements and raw material price increases are all too visible in increased malnutrition, unemployment and the inability of parents to house or clothe their children. So when theologians there speak of the poor they are not discussing theological concepts of charity or poverty of spirit. They are talking about dependent, weak, helpless, anonymous, contemned and humiliated people. When they say 'dependent', they are not arguing about the theological concept of contingency, or about how our dependence on God may or may not affect our free will. They call attention to the fact that the survival of workers in the South 'depends' on decisions made by capitalists about investment and production processes. And they are also saying that 'one part of humanity has been forced to serve the consumption of the other part', so introducing an imbalance that will, sooner or later, destroy both. Global capitalist structures directly and indirectly support the onslaught against nature in the 'dependent' countries in order to provide consumer goods at the lowest possible price. The result is that the 'dependent' part of the world is forced to live with an ever smaller share of natural resources in absolute or relative terms (Segundo 1988: 13). No argument about free will here.

Both types of dependency were horrifically illustrated in the aftermath of Hurricane Mitch in 1998. The North American banana company Chiquita owns extensive plantations in Honduras. (It is worth reminding ourselves that no bananas grow in North America or Europe.) These plantations were in many cases established on deforested hill slopes which, in the torrential rain accompanying the hurricane, disintegrated into mudslides engulfing the workers' villages and families. In the days following the disaster, when the extent of destruction in the plantations became clear, Chiquita announced that it was laying off 7,000 banana workers. The 'banana footprint' of the North is not only muddy, but bloody.

Liberation theologians denounce such decisions from within the Christian North, aware that despite its changing historical roles, the Christian church and its theology has consistently buttressed the expansion of empire, whether military or economic. The majority of church members in the North (some of them possibly members of the board of Chiquita) have, at some time, blessed and benefited from colonialism, neo-colonialism, economic colonization, extreme stratification of wealth, centuries of genocide of Amerindians, blacks and Jews, the subordination of women, the persecution of the sexual other and the social exclusion of the pagan (Batstone *et al.* 1997: 13; Balasuriya 1984). Small wonder then, that liberation theologian Juan Segundo asks: 'Why do we feel so uneasy today when we hear someone say: I am going to realize the kingdom of God on earth? And why do we feel more uneasy insofar as the speaker possesses more power?' (Segundo 1988: 16).

Orthodoxy's consistent defence against this fifth column has been its characterization of liberation theology as Marxist. Dom Helder Camara recognized this strategy: 'When I give food to the poor, they call me a saint. When I ask why the poor have no food, they call me a communist.' Such religious McCarthyism both relies on and reinforces a powerful binary code which sustains a Christian Cold War ideology. 'The [capitalist] empire interpreted itself as the Christian (western) world, a reign of god facing a reign of atheist evil. ... *To believe in God and to fight on capitalism's side against enemies seemed to be the same* (Hinkelammert 1997: 35; italics added).

This lapidary statement about the function of God-concepts within capitalism, and within theologies, is at the same time a claim for the truth of liberation theologians' perception of that function as integral to a theology of death. They contest, subvert and seek to reform the claim to absolute Christian truth made for such a theology by Northern academic or ecclesiastical institutions, and do not hesitate to describe its God, seen from the Southern perspective, as a god of death. In the struggle between capital and labour, this 'god' named 'Mammon' functions as 'Moloch', before whom lives are sacrificed.

I shall discuss later, in some detail, Hinkelammert's analysis of capitalism and his subversive account of its hidden use of God-concepts. The point I want to make here about the situated knowledge of liberation theologians is that it demands, implicitly at least, recognition for the truth of multiple perspectives. Part of its subversive force lies then in its challenge to the imposition, by any authority, of one perspective as universally normative or valid. This imposition of an authoritative norm was defined and ratified theologically in the church rule formulated in early Christian centuries as 'that which has been believed everywhere, always and by all' (Bettenson 1963: 84). This 'Vincentian canon' (named after its author, Vincent of Lerins), simply by postulating such a norm simultaneously established its possibility, validity and acceptance.

For liberation theologians, the viewpoint of the poor, of the enslaved, of the oppressed, of those who, by their life circumstances, are excluded from positions of power, has its own validity and authority. At the very least, their reading of the Bible (where they can read it) has a claim to be considered truthful; as disclosing something valid about the nature of God. But their perspectives, and their readings, differ radically from those of Christians in the consumerist North. Their theological *PoieticScape*, their descriptions of who God is for them, differs accordingly.

The disclosure of this difference, Hinkelammert remarks, threatens the religious homogeneity of capitalism. In response to the threat, he points to the fact that from the sixties onward theological centres of a completely new character have emerged. They range from The American Enterprise Institute and the Institute for Religion and Democracy in North America to the theological reflections of the secretary of the International Monetary Fund, Michael Camdessus. Theological rebuttals and reactions from the North include Vatican documents such as Cardinal Ratzinger's 1984 *Instruction on the Theology of Liberation* and various disciplinary actions against individual theologians such as Leonardo Boff, Ivone Gebara and Tissa Balasuriya.

Camdessus' theological reflections are particularly pertinent, since they reveal the homogenous nature of Northern capitalism and 'orthodox' Christian reflection. Hinkelammert critiques Camdessus' keynote address at the National Congress of French Impresarios at Lille in March, 1992, the gist of which was repeated in an address to businessmen in Mexico. Camdessus' primary target was liberation theology's stated 'option for the poor'. He coopted this in such a way that preferential opting for the poor and preferential opting for the IMF were identified with each other, opening up a tempting vision for Christian orthodoxy (self-defined) in which one can opt for the poor without entering into any conflict with the powerful structures that destroy their lives. (This routinely defensive, laissez-faire approach appears openly offensive (in every sense) in the aftermath of Hurricane Mitch.) A call for writing off the debt burden of the devastated Central American debtor states has been met by responses in which, as Hinkelammert presciently commented, the option for the poor becomes 'an option for the IMF and its structural adjustment programmes' (Hinkelammert 1997: 42–4f.).

The option for the poor

What then, does the option for the poor mean to those who formulated it and try to live out its demands within the Southern context? An extensive treatment of this pivotal principle can be found in the works referenced in this chapter. I shall for the most part discuss the descriptions given by Sobrino, Segundo, Gutierrez and the Boff brothers.

The phrase/formula/concept 'the preferential option for the poor' was adopted and endorsed in the late 1960s and early 1970s as an expression of commitment to the poor and oppressed (Gutierrez 1996: 26). It expresses the situated knowledge of the theologians, that is, their particular perspective on what it means to bear witness, in the midst of ever-encroaching death, to a God of life: to the God of Jesus who said: 'I am come that you may have life, and have it more abundantly.' Their overriding question is: 'How can this witness be given in a context where the life of the masses is routinely threatened and destroyed?' The life they testify to is 'life' unqualified, at its most elementary. It is not 'eternal' life, or 'spiritual' life, or 'divine' life, or 'Christian' life. It is what it means to be alive. (In this book, what it means to be an autopoietic entity structurally coupled with and consistently energized by its environment.) This is the level at which witness to a God of life begins. Sobrino quotes one of the forefathers of liberation theology, the fifteenth-century missionary Bartholomé de Las Casas, who declared that a living infidel is a sacrament of the God of love, while a murdered Indian, even if baptized, is a sacrament only of idols. It is not possible to bear witness to a God of life by colluding with death; by neglecting the elementary levels of life.

This restoration of importance to a neglected level of existence (neglected, that is, in traditional theologies) may seem, says Sobrino, a minimal achievement, but in the context of Central and Latin America it is radical. 'What sin is', he says, 'reveals itself in historical form through the death that human beings inflict on each other. Unjust structures bring death near and inflict it daily.' He characterizes these as 'the presently prevailing structures – a capitalism of dependence and national security, whatever their forms'. Both these factors – the destruction of life for the masses and structural injustice as its cause – are central to understanding 'the option for the poor'. For in this situation, there is no question of a third-party attitude: of any silent collusion with the structures of death (Sobrino 1985: 164–9). Neutrality, Segundo comments, is not an option (Segundo 1985: 117).

In a recent essay entitled *Option for the Poor*, Gustavo Gutierrez says that it is not 'optional' in one sense, since we owe love to every human being without exception. Nor does a commitment to the poor and oppressed ultimately rely on any social analysis, or on our compassion, or in the direct experience we may have of poverty. All these are valid reasons, and play an important role in the commitment. But for Gutierrez, and here he speaks as a Christian, his commitment is rooted deep in the gratuity of God's love. He too quotes de Las Casas, who committed himself to the poor 'because the least one, the most forgotten one, is altogether fresh and vivid in the memory of God'. It is of this 'memory', Gutierrez says, that the Bible speaks to us. Such a perception of the poor 'prefers' them not because they are necessarily better than others from a moral or religious standpoint, but because God is God. No one lays conditions on God. Or on God's love. Gutierrez examines the gospels and finds the gratuity of God's love contrasted with a narrow notion of justice, and concludes that 'only a church in solidarity with the actual poor, a church that denounces poverty as an evil, is in any position to proclaim God's freely bestowed love' (Gutierrez 1996: 27–34). I shall come back to this notion of gratuitous, unconditional love in the final chapter, but would draw attention here to the fact that liberation theology, in its loving attention to the poor, is at the same time proclaiming God's liberty to love freely.

It is from this theological perspective that liberation theologians denounce the socioeconomic slavery endemic in their situation, simultaneously asserting the intrinsic value of every enslaved person. Without its exhibiting the overt oppression of physical slavery, they see the capitalist empire operating today as the bondage of the poor by the rich; as reducing them to commodity value only. Later in this chapter I shall enlarge on the mechanisms for and effects of this devaluation as analyzed by Hinkelammert and recorded by Simone Weil. In such a system, the poor, their families, their animals, their work, their lands are there to be used, and therefore, abused. Their labour and resources are appropriated without just reward or return, the end products marketed with maximum profit: not for them, but for those in the North who control the markets. This control is not, usually, exercised through whip and gun, but through 'the invisible hand' of market forces. Although sometimes, as in military regimes in Brazil, Colombia and Nigeria, this invisible hand wields visible weapons. The system essentially denies the intrinsic value of the enslaved people, and by reducing them to nothing, renders them totally vulnerable.

Gutierrez quotes the painful and sadly relevant biblical description of the wretchedness of the poor which is at the same time a bitter indictment against the powerful who oppress them. In the book of Job, the wicked move boundary marks, carry off flocks and shepherd, drive away the orphan's donkey and, as security, seize the widow's ox. The needy search from dawn for food, go harvesting in some scoundrel's field and pilfer in the wicked's vineyards. They go naked and starve; two little walls shelter them at high noon. Parched with thirst, they have to tread the winepress, and spend the night with no covering against the cold. The orphan child is torn from the breast and the child of the poor exacted as security (Job 24: 2–12).

Gutierrez says that this passage shows that poverty is not something fated, but something caused by 'the wicked'. They are the ones who say to God: 'Go away!' They deny God and are the enemies of the poor: attitudes which, for him, are but two faces of the same coin (Gutierrez 1991: 150f.). Justice, he says, is established by enabling the poor to liberate themselves from this wickedness, and so from suffering.

The function of 'God' in liberation theologies

Liberation theologians like Gutierrez work with a concept of freedom and justice which essentially asserts, in the name of God, that each and every person has intrinsic value, regardless of class, gender, income or race. 'God' then functions for them, and for the poor, as a liberating, empowering word. I want to clarify now exactly what I mean by the 'function' of God-concepts. 'Function' here is a 'part' word, that is, it implies a whole relationship within which the part works or is used. There is no 'function' as such in a concept alone, or in any substantive such as aesthetics, or religion, or theology. The function is inherent in the relation between the person using the concept and the position they take in regard to whatever or whoever is under discussion. 'Function is inherent in relation and not in things. An ax does not have a use. The use of an ax is related to its position between a person and a tree.' If, Bateson says, you want to ask about the function of aesthetics, for instance, then you must also ask, 'well, between what and what, within what whole are you attributing function to what parts?' (Bateson 1991: 304)

What God 'is', is by definition indescribable, but we describe God anyway, and the terms we use are necessarily derived from those relationships defined here as structural coupling within multidimensional environments. A 'couple' always implies a relationship. This affords an infinite range of possibilities for describing our 'couplings', and for describing God, but no matter what possibility I choose it will refer ultimately to my own experience of a defining and defined relationship. I will then speak metaphorically about God. The problems some women/men have with calling God 'father' or 'mother' arise when we forget that these are metaphors, exercises in metaphorical imagination which bridge the gap (without closing it) between what we experience in the world and what we say about God. Because they function as bridges for me, my images of God 'function' as representing all that I hold most sacred and valuable, whether or not I can express what that is. They function as a validation of the distinctions I make in my relationships with others.

'God' then, does not have a use, a function, outside a relational field encompassed by the horizon of my environment. 'God' may indeed be seen as defining that horizon, as an absolute mystery which recedes as I approach (Rahner 1978: 59–65). Within that relational field 'God' is seen and described *by me*, in terms understood (or not) in my *SocialScape/PoieticScape*, as related in some way to whatever or whoever it is I am interacting with; as related in whatever way makes sense within the whole network of relationships to which I see myself belonging at that time. The function of my God-concepts inheres in that network of relationships which includes those I have with God and with other living beings. I use the image of/name for/concept 'God' within that relational field. It is there the word 'God' means something, or not, to me. 'You get nowhere if you just say "God". Those three letters – they are just a code, an unknown quantity, a stopgap. You have to make a long journey from "God", a meaningless, boring, empty cliché, to "our God", "my God", "God of the living", a meaningful, personal name full of echoes of God's history' (Oosterhuis 1968: 6).

Liberation theologians live in and share the relational field occupied by the poor, whatever criteria are used to define that poverty: whether it is their capacity to have, to love or simply to be, to exist. Within the *PoieticScape* of the poor, a meaningful, personal name for God is 'God of the poor'. Whoever the theologian, or whatever language he uses to describe this relationship with God, it validates his relationship with the poor. And the poor, and their struggles to escape poverty are validated by the theological expression of their own relationship with God. Wherever liberation theology is practised, the word 'God' functions, *and is seen to function*, as a 'liberating' word within a whole network of economic, social, political, theological and ecological relationships. God is aligned with the poor in their struggle and against those who oppress them. No neutral theological position is possible within this relational field.

Of course outside it, other theological positions are possible. The resultant clash, as I said, has been and is a great source of tension between theological and ecclesiastical institutions and liberation theologians. And as I said also, it is the case that the tension arises, at a fundamental and sometimes unconscious level, from the latters' claim for authority for the truth of their situated knowledge. It is intensified when this truth is seen to be coloured by material-ism/Marxism and therefore, from authority's perspective, not only as subversive but perverse.

The tension became confrontation in the 1984 Vatican document from Cardinal Ratzinger, *Instruction on the Theology of Liberation*, and the response to it by Juan Luis Segundo in 1985, *Theology and the Church*. Segundo goes to the heart of the matter when he refers to a previous Ratzinger article which 'seemed to come from a European who reads European phenomena and tendencies into a non-European context'. This is his way of saying that the churches and theological academies have, until now, assumed that there is one authoritative perspective from which God is seen and described: the perspective of those who hold academic or ecclesiastical power in the North. These 'freemen', living in 'free' market economies, their freedom assured by gender, education, social and economic resources and divine mandate, now find themselves challenged by the 'slaves' represented by Segundo.

The challenge lies in the conflict between the option for the poor and the logic of capitalist structures. This is read by orthodox theology as 'Marxist class struggle'. Marx, says Hinkelammert, is for the free world what Trotsky is for Stalinists: the non-person in which evil is supposedly incarnated. The denuncia-tion of liberation theology as Marxist is sufficient to condemn it. There is (apparently) no need to discuss or argue whether or not the option for the poor can or should overcome the logic of capitalist structures. In Chile, therefore, orthodox theology and the Chilean Episcopal Conference buttressed the pro-capitalist forces which overthrew Allende's Marxist/socialist government, condemning and demonizing it in the strongest terms (Hinkelammert 1997: 30f.). During Pinochet's detention in England, Church authorities (both in Chile and in the Vatican) have appealed for his release on the grounds of his destruction of 'Marxist/socialist' forces.

Liberation theology then, for those inside the Vatican, became a Trojan horse. So in his *Instruction* of 1984, while acknowledging that the theologies of liberation deserve credit for restoring great biblical texts in defence of the poor to a place of honour, Cardinal Ratzinger goes on to say that those same theologies lead to a 'disastrous confusion between the *poor* of the Gospel and the *proletariat* of Marx'. But, asks Segundo, if the poor are the victims of oppression, why would the 'proletariat' not belong to this category? Only because Marx defended them and therefore, they may be called, very improperly, the 'proletariat of Marx?' (Segundo 1985: 121) There is an implicit theological apartheid evident in the Vatican's inability to 'translate' the poor into the proletariat.

An important position Segundo takes in his densely argued response, even though he sees that it leaves him vulnerable to attack, is that the option for the poor derives from a partisan experience, leads to partisan practice and is expressed in partisan language. Therefore God is described in partisan terms: as a God who liberates the poor from the oppression of the rich. Therefore these theologians describe God in ways which place God on the side of the poor against the rich. In this situation, neutrality is not seen as an option for God either.

This does not, however, according to Segundo, necessarily mean (as Ratzinger and others hold) that 'God' functions to legitimate violence against the rich, or that the partisanship is destined to perpetuate itself in violence. 'The class enemy does not cease to be a human being whom we must love – and love effectively. But this does not mean that he or she ceases to be a class enemy – just as those who rejected him did not cease to be the enemies of Jesus.' There is, Segundo says, no analysis that can make that opposition disappear and so allow us to love more easily. 'How to love efficaciously in the midst of struggle and choice is and always will be a challenge to one's Christian creativity. Because one must opt; one must choose sides' (Segundo 1985: 117).

The function of 'God' in capitalist societies

How does the concept of God function then, on the 'other' side? What does the word 'God' mean in the capitalist relational field? Endorsing Hinkelammert's Marxist analysis of that field, Cornel West describes it as one in which the hidden effects of commodity relations in people's everyday lives make relations between people appear as relations between things (Hinkelammert 1986: v). This applies also, as we saw, to relations between people and their biophysical environments. How does God function to make both types of relation appear as commodity relations?

West remarks that too often Christians have little or no grasp of the complex conditions under which commodities are produced, the ways in which money is acquired and the means by which capital is expanded. Positing these complex relations as objects of theological reflection is almost unheard of in contemporary Northern theology. Yet, 'if theologians are to come to terms with the life-and-death issues of our time, there is no escape from reflecting upon and gaining an understanding of these complex relations' (Hinkelammert 1986: vi).

In the fourteen years since West wrote this, Christians, in common with everyone else, have been having a crash course in some of these issues under the heading 'sustainable development'. They have also seen what has happened since the collapse of the Soviet Union into a 'free' market uncurbed by any social consciousness. The preceding couple of chapters raised some of these issues. Environmental theologies, however, for the most part, have left the study of commodity relations to the economists, and concepts such as the ecological footprint and environmental space are not generally taken as subjects for theological reflection. Liberation theologians in the South, however, directly affected by their situation in complex commodity relations, have had to consider, from the perspective of the poor, the function God has in the lives of the rich. They see the visible effects of commodity relationships on the poor correlated to the 'invisible hand' of the market, and this 'invisible hand' as a surrogate deity. Making its 'invisibility' visible, that is, showing it to be a human hand, is the task Hinkelammert sets himself. Otherwise, no one can be held accountable, a state of affairs which more or less defines structural or systemic injustice.

Using Marx's analysis of fetishism to expose the *spirit* of the institutions which organize Northern society, he shows that that spirit works in two apparently opposing ways. First, the language of commodity relations is used to make it seem as though the relationships between human beings and the effects of the division of labour on human life are two totally independent and unconnected issues. As I understand it, this means that commodity relations (between commodity and its producer, between the one who determines its market price and sells it and the one who buys it, and between all of these and those who fix its share price and gamble on it on the commodities market) rely on an impenetrable, because unstated division between the commodity produced and the situation of the individual who produces it, and between that individual and those others who, once it is produced, relate to it as though that individual does not exist. Commodity markets depend on her/his invisibility. It is part of the 'rules of the game', taken for granted by everyone – including the worker. So the relation between the commodity's 'future' and the worker's future also remains invisible.

Writing or reading this in the North evokes derision or disbelief, since the media show us factories in which, alongside gleaming robots, glowing computers and microchip programmed machines, workers are not only visible, but usually, visibly content. In fact, their greatest fear is losing their place there. An increasing number of these workplaces, however, are assembly plants, putting together a range of components sourced elsewhere; or packaging plants, where raw or processed food and materials brought in from elsewhere are packaged for resale. These components and raw materials are all that is visible. This is especially true of cash crops from debtor nations such as vegetables, fruit or clothes. They are harvested or produced by increasing numbers of invisible people in the South, in China or in former Soviet bloc countries where 'labour is cheap'. That should read: 'where people are cheap'. As stock market indices in the North soar to new heights, the invisible poor at the bottom of the commodity pyramid are crushed under their weight.

One Marxist theorist in the North who decided to test his theories about the effects of this invisibility on workers was Simone Weil. Between 1934 and 1935 she took leave of absence from teaching and got three jobs as an unskilled factory worker living on her earnings. She kept a journal of her experiences which makes harrowing reading, not least in its echoes of the language used by liberation theologians today to describe the lives of the poor. The fact that she was far from unskilled intellectually did not invalidate the test, since she was below par physically and without technical skill or manual dexterity. This added to her financial difficulties as it meant her hourly wage (paid on the number of 'pieces' drilled or cut) was reduced when, as often happened, the pieces were substandard. Even when she managed the required number, it could be reduced below the agreed rate at the foreman's whim. One Monday she records a 'feeling of having been a free being for 24 hours (Sunday) and of having to readapt to slavery'. Terror takes hold of her when she realizes how dependent she is on external circumstances, for without that day of rest, when 'a few memories and shreds of ideas return to me, and I remember that I am *also* a thinking being, I would become a beast of burden, docile and resigned'. She notes later: 'Slavery has made me entirely lose the feeling of having any rights. It appears as a favour to me when I have a few moments in which I have nothing to bear in the way of human brutality.'

The work load leaves her no time or energy for personal relationships, either on the production line or outside the factory. Only when she is laid off looking for work and meets two unemployed men does she have 'all morning, extraordinarily free and easy conversation, on a plane above the miseries of existence that are the dominant preoccupation of slaves, especially women'. Coming out after her first day of working again, when she found it impossible to produce the required number of pieces and did not know if they would take her on again, she noted: 'in spite of my fatigue, I am so in need of fresh air that I go on foot as far as the Seine; there I sit on the bank, on a stone, gloomy, exhausted, my heart gripped by impotent rage, feeling drained of all my vital substance; I wonder if, in the event that I were condemned to live this life, I would be able to cross the Seine every day without someday throwing myself in.'

Her final reflections on what she has gained by the experience include the feeling that she does not possess any right whatever, of any kind, and her admonition to herself not to lose this feeling, for without it, she would lose her understanding of what caused it. She came near, she said, to being broken. 'I almost was – my courage, the feeling that I had value as a person were nearly broken during a period I would be humiliated to remember, were it not that strictly speaking I have retained no memory of it. I got up in the morning with anguish; I went to the factory with dread; I worked like a slave.' The feeling of self-respect, she says, built up by society, is '*destroyed*'. She finally gets a clear idea of her own importance. She belongs to 'the class of those who *do not count* – in any situation – in anyone's eyes – and who will not count, ever, no matter what happens' (Weil 1987: 151–225).

This dire conclusion leaves us in no doubt about the second 'invisible' effect of commodity relations. They affect the lives of the workers so profoundly that they themselves, as persons, disappear; not only in the eyes of those who employ them, but in their own. They see themselves as slaves, as the property of the factory owners; as slaves to their machines and to the commodities they produce. They do not count. Only the commodities do.

Hinkelammert notes this stage in commodity relations by quoting Marx's definition of commodities as 'physical-metaphysical' objects. This highlights the fact that on the one hand, commodities are objects, but on the other hand, they have a dimension of being themselves subjects, players in the economic process. It is in that role that 'they arrogate to themselves decisions over life and death, and leave human beings subject to their whims'. It is this subjectivity of commodities, this 'commodity-as-subject', which eventually robs the human subject of her/his freedom. Commodities-as-subjects set up relationships among themselves, described in 'bewitching' images which present them, in the *PoieticScape* of capitalism, as important surrogate players. 'Artificial nitrate battles natural nitrate and defeats it. Oil fights with coal, and wood with plastic. Coffee dances on the world markets while iron and steel get married' (Hinkelammert 1986: 6f). Trains challenge trucks and factory-made bread closes down family bakeries. The relationships are ruled by bulls and bears, before whom all slump or soar. And so on.

The commodity producers themselves come to be dominated by the social relationships established by the commodities. When they 'do battle', so do their owners and producers. Human beings are attracted to each other depending on the 'attractions' of commodities, and vice versa. This is not, says Hinkelammert, just an analogy. Commodities begin to move although no one can be seen to have this intention. This is a key point in the process of fetishism: when the commodity is seen as a person. The apparent life enjoyed by commodities, which is in fact human life projected onto them, deprives human beings of their freedom, and ultimately, their life. For the obverse of the 'personification' of commodities (and money and capital) is the 'commodification' of persons. Both transformations are wrought by the 'invisible' hand of the market. The resulting *SocialScape* is a form of social consciousness characterized by a loss of human freedom, a society in which persons have delegated decision-making power over life and death to a commodity mechanism for whose results they have relinquished responsibility (Hinkelammert 1986: 20).

Implicit in the commodity relations process is a system of valuing and devaluing which, by reducing human beings to commodity value alone, denies them any possiblity of having their intrinsic value as human beings acknowledged. Whether this is described, as by Simone Weil, as the feeling that one counts, or by Sen, as the constituent elements of the person's being seen from the perspective of her own personal welfare (Sen 1993: 36); or by Allardt, as the capacity to have, to love and to be (Allardt 1993: 88); or by Gutierrez (1991) as knowing one is loved unconditionally by God, it receives no sustenance, support nor reinforcement in a society where one's humanity is rendered invisible. Being assigned commodity value alone is a working definition of slavery.

There is a further twist in commodity relations which has particular relevance for coevolutionary theology. In risking capital in order to gain, production must grow. The ecological footprint must extend further and further so less environmental space is left available in the South. In the North, capitalists must make an act of faith in the ability of workers to consume the products of their own and others' labour. The whole system depends on a cycle of spend, consume (products and resources), spend. The compulsion to spend is another facet of the loss of freedom.

But in order to spend one must have money. Money is a commodity. It stands out above the rest, however, because it serves as their common denominator, one into which they must be converted in order to have their value confirmed. Commodity value and money value relate to each other as exchange values. Money serves as 'a depository of value: it allows for storing value in a form in which it is of no other use to anyone'. But this capacity is not inherent in it. It is only society's action which can turn money into a universal equivalent, and by doing so, rob individuals, once again, of their freedom. For it is 'the gateway to commodities, through which their value is confirmed'. Marx likens this function to that of the beast in the book of Revelation, which caused humanity to lose its freedom because 'it did not allow a man to buy or sell anything unless he was first marked with the name of the beast or with the number that stood for its name' (Revelation 13: 17).

As money becomes capital, the sense of belonging to capital is experienced more intensely where capital buys labour for large-scale industry. Here the confrontation is not with the capitalist, but with the machinery itself. Although it is only a tool, it becomes something different – a mechanism of production, whose organs are human beings. The worker who belongs to capital undergoes the experience of being converted into a part of some machinery. It is now the machinery which exercises the right to decide over the worker's life or death. Capital guarantees the life only of those workers necessary for its own life process. This, comments Hinkelammert, is 'a reversal of the image wherein God, as the self-moved Prime Mover, gives life to the human being with the touch of a finger' (Hinkelammert 1986: 29f.). It makes the God of life, as understood by the poor, invisible.

Liberating theology

This trenchant description of the function of 'God' in capitalist societies may seem a caricature, a set of rhetorical devices on the writers' part. Yet a glance through the financial pages of any newspaper finds the rhetoric of profitability and downsizing invoked and unchallenged as the rules of the game whenever factories are closed in the North and production is moved to the South. (In November 1998, Marks and Spencer announced, without apology, indeed as a rational decision, that because of falling profits they must buy more of their stock from outside Britain. In 1999, Pecks, the largest sock manufacturer in Britain, announced that it is moving production to Rumania and China.) This gambit in commodity relations makes their effects doubly invisible to consumers in the North. But they become all too visible to those liberation theologians in the South who, like Simone Weil, are able to record and analyze its effects on the majority of workers there. They make visible the civil religion of capitalism: faith in money value as the immanent spirit of commodities; faith in the pre-established order of the relationships of production. In liberation theologies working with people who believe in the God of the poor, this is perceived as faith in idols (Hinkelammert 1986: 1–45).

This is the contested ground between liberation and orthodox theologies, as the discourse flowing from the 'option for the poor' confronts and makes visible, as idolatry, the systemic 'theology' of capitalism. In an important collection of essays entitled *The Idols of Death and the God of Life*, Hinkelammert discusses at length the 'economic roots of idolatry' under the heading of 'entrepreneurial metaphysics'. He names the idols as commodities, money, marketing and capital, a relational field in which they are pseudo-divine beings, objects of devotion (Hinkelammert 1983: 165f.) This description necessarily excludes, or at least relegates, 'the rich' from pole position, and challenges the normative universalist perspective of Christianity from which both rich and poor are, supposedly, seen as equally the subject of salvation by God, or Christ. From this perspective, any attempt to claim truth for the perspective of the poor is treated, at best, as unorthodox, and at worst, as grounds for dismissal from the ecclesiastical or academic body politic. When this theological disapproval aligns with right-wing political/military power, as it did in Chile, South Africa and Central America, it can result in extreme suffering for the theologian, as Ernesto Cardenal, Smangaliso Mkhatshwa, Frank Chikane, Chilean 'Christians for Socialism' and others have found.

The Swedish theologian Per Frostin who worked in Africa identifies five interrelated emphases in the paradigm of liberation theology which subvert and contest the orthodox perspective:

1   The choice of *social relations/social sciences* rather than *ideas* as the main crossroad in theology.
2   The perception of God as a God who is 'on the side of' the poor and therefore in conflict with those who oppress them: the poor being defined as those who are most oppressed by capitalist technocracy. This God is defined in opposition to the idols generated by Mammon.
3   Arising from both 1 and 2, a conflictual perception of social reality, in particular between those designated from 'above' or from 'below', and an emphasis on the way in which one's theology is shaped according to one's context: either 'above' or 'below'.
4   Arising from 1, the use of the social sciences to define poverty: that is, not solely as an economic statistic but in terms of oppressive power structures. This indicates that theological method will be influenced, but not dominated by Marxism.
5   Dialectics between practice and theology makes practice, that is, commitment to liberation, 'the first act'. Doing theology is then a hermeneutical circle where action forces the theologian to look at theory and theory forces the theologian to look at action again.

(Frostin 1988: 1–26)

Extensive as this agenda might appear, liberation theologians themselves see the need to expand its remit. Sobrino acknowledges on their behalf that liberation theologians need 'to consider in depth the various kinds of oppression, not only the socioeconomic versions, but also those perpetrated in the areas of culture, ethnicity, religion, women, children and nature' (Sobrino in Sobrino and Ellacuria 1996: ix). This inclusion is already occurring as some theologians take account of and contribute to the policy documents coming from the official United Nations Conference on Environment and Development (UNCED), and later UN conferences in Cairo and Beijing (*Earth Summit* 1992: ed. Joyce Quarrie, Regency Press, London). These documents, as I said already, highlight four classes of people most at risk from socioeconomic slavery and environmental degradation: the poor, indigenous people, women and children. These four classes are seen to be, and are, those most powerless to do anything about their situation. It also becomes clear that they are the classes of the poor graphically depicted in the book of Job and made visible today by liberation theologians who share their situation. The fact that women belong to three out of the four groups will be explored in Chapter 11.

10 Freedom from competition

[A]ll organisms, absolutely all, are the result of an association of several individual organisms, which came together in the distant past, are united by physical proximity, have pooled their genes and have given rise to complex organisms with increasing powers. … Symbioses are continuous interactions, with actual physical contact between two or more organisms. … Symbiogenesis [is] the name given to the evolutionary process that entails permanent physical contact between two or more symbionts such that a new individual emerges. … [It] was undoubtedly a major spur to evolution as it opened up the possibility that organisms from distinct evolutionary pathways would be able to share metabolic strategies and so avoid the need to repeat a complex evolutionary history.

(Lynn Margulis 1996: 167–8, 11)

Before going on to discuss other forms of liberation theology, I want to connect Hinkelammert's critique of commodity relations in the preceding chapter with the reflections on Darwinian evolutionary theory in Chapter 5. I do this in order to 'situate' liberation theology within as broad a framework as possible, one which takes into account a richer view of our materially-based interactions with other organisms than that offered by Darwinism or neo-Darwinism. This latter, with its emphasis on the gene and natural selection, largely ignores the role of the environment, and of other organisms, in the essential processes of energy input and renewal and other metabolic survival strategies. Enlarging the discussion in this way, as Darwin himself would have done if he had had the technical resources, enables the discussion of human/commodity relations to move beyond the reductionist, free market model of them (as based only on utility and competition) to a symbiogenetic one, where the different associations between organisms, and between them and their environments, cannot be so narrowly defined. Using this model, the physical associations of different organisms for a significant part of their life cycles can be observed and described as sharing or pooling resources, or as engaged in mutually beneficial interactions and cooperation, not only within organisms of the same class but between different classes. This resists the tendency to reductionism by enlarging the metaphoric imagination.

From a coevolutionary perspective, it gives us another way of focussing on and describing the *nature* of our structural coupling with our environments, other, that is, than the dominant description of it as primarily competitive. We are invited by Margulis, for example, to see it as one in which organisms from different life 'kingdoms' are united by physical contact for more or less protracted periods of time. This leaves the nature of that contact open to other possibilities, including those where genetic resources can be pooled and new organisms, such as lichens, may and do emerge. Some lichen communities in Antarctica's Victoria Land living two or three millimetres beneath the rock are a symbiotic mix of fungi, algae and bacteria. The algae grow under the protective cover of fungi in this icy hell, clinging to sheer rock which ultimately they break down into soil which can be penetrated by roots of plants and fungal networks (Margulis 1998: 108–9). From such unions, she says, we too have emerged, and from this perspective, 'we are all symbionts', the product of a more or less protracted, close, physical coupling.

How best do we describe these biological dynamics? Wouldn't unitive, or generative, or loving, or practical, or enjoyable, or protective, or shared, or ecstatic be apt descriptions, sometimes anyway? How does a joint commitment to the symbiont arise, as it does in many cases, unless the partners are capable of what we would call, in our own case, empathy and close emotional bonding? And if such descriptions of the nature of our bonding are authentic, then a *PoieticScape* which linguistically couples two apparently antithetic disciplines like science and theology might itself be seen, metaphorically speaking, as a symbiont.

Competition rules

Scientists, Margulis says, describe what they can see. If Darwin, she conjectures, had seen present-day videos of microbial interactions his view and descriptions of the natural world would undoubtedly have been very different. As it is, we know that his conclusions were based on a particular view of human and animal individuality vividly imagined by him in metaphors of 'descent through natural selection' and the 'struggle for life'. They have been given the status of 'natural laws' in western culture, accepted as 'given', elaborated on as basic elements of the universe in both the natural and social realms, and, as was noted in earlier chapters, as though there is no fundamental difference between those realms (Sapp 1996: 154f.).

Once Darwin's poetic/metaphoric imaginings were given the status of 'natural' laws, they were then understood as defining the *nature* of our structural coupling with our environments, indeed, as defining *our* nature. The role of the evolution of the environment, and of the feedback between life and the environment which tends to stabilize and destabilize habitable conditions and so affect natural selection, was and is discounted. The complexity of autopoietic interactions between organisms and their environments is lost, as are the emergent possibilities contingent on that complexity. Also lost is the paradoxical view of ourselves as having limited freedom defined by our boundaries with the biophysical environment, and being at the same time dependent on energy-exchanges mediated through those boundaries and subject to perturbations from our environments and from other organisms in proximity to us. Absent too is the potential for variation in responses to our environments, occurring in accord with the nature of the perturbation and with the structural integrity of our individual selves. As the metaphorical imagination expands, however, to include all these transformative interactions (assumed to be excluded by the 'rules' of the evolutionary game) the evolutionary *possibility* of our interacting peacefully, fruitfully and happily with other organisms cannot be ruled out.

Darwin, in spite of his insistence that the term 'struggle for life' be used in a 'large and metaphorical sense', chiefly used the term in a narrow sense when describing individuals' interactions. As we saw earlier, following publication of *The Origin* a mass of 'facts' and examples (ranging from the production of the American Beauty rose to the Standard Oil Company) were gathered for the purpose of illustrating a real competition for life. The concept became narrower still when Herbert Spencer and later Social Darwinists made the 'pitiless' struggle a biological, sociological and economic principle to which we too must submit (Galbraith 1991: 50f.; Sapp 1996: 157).

The previous chapter demonstrated how complete this submission has become in a global economy dominated by capitalist competitive rules. In line with Marx's concept of fetishism, 'competition' is personified as a surrogate ruler who in turn personifies markets and commodities as 'players'; who pits one market against another in stock indices, one commodity against another in price wars, one school/hospital/university against another in league tables, one political party against another in opinion polls, one investor/politician/parent/pupil against another. And ultimately, all of us against the biophysical environment as we use and abuse it as a commodity base. We live in a culture where competition determines so many of our interactions because of our acceptance of its rules as 'natural' for us. This means that we accept as a governing principle in our biological dynamics that if one player wins something, another must lose it, and that society is divided into winners and losers, the latter always in the majority.

No part of our lives is unaffected by this perspective. The command to love our neighbour as ourselves was first enunciated in Leviticus 19: 18. Repeated by the Jewish lawyer in his encounter with Jesus recorded in Luke 10: 27, it became a 'given' in Christianity also. In the rabbinic commentary on Leviticus, the Sifra, the problems raised by the rule are discussed as follows:

> Two men are in the desert with a little water in possession of one of them. If the one drinks it, he will reach civilisation; but if the two of them share it, both will die. Ben Petura said, let the two of them drink, though both will die. Rabbi Akiba held that, in such a case, your own life has precedence.
>
> (See Llewelyn 1991: 33)

The rabbinic editor holds that Ben Petura's view is more heroic. Another view, implicit in much Christian teaching, is that we ought to love others more than ourselves, and therefore, the one with the water is required to give it to the one without it, and so to die for him. But is this not self-contradictory? For in enjoining us to live or die for others, the one without the water is obliged to refuse it.

I shall return to this exemplary tale at the end of this chapter. But it is my experience that generally speaking, when I recount it, it is dealt with according to the rules of who wins (the water, life, eternal reward) and who loses (the water, life, eternal reward). In Christian religious discussion there is the added nuance that the loser in this life may be presented as a winner in the next. In the gospels (Mark 8: 35; Matthew 10: 39; Luke 17: 33; John 12: 25), the aphorism is repeated in different settings, with the Johannine version making the clearest statement: 'He who loves his life loses it, and he who hates his life in this world will keep it for eternal life.'

Its contemporary relevance (water, essential for life, as an increasingly scarce resource) gives the rabbinic story an added edge, and, outside a religious setting, the problem it presents and the rules by which it is governed are approached rather differently. The bigger, stronger, fitter, more ruthless guy *takes* the water – and wins. The CIA have anticipated this approach, and mapped the prospect of conflict in the 214 major river systems on which 40 per cent of the world's population depends for water. These environmental 'flash points' signal possible 'Water Wars', the ultimate in competition for control of resources (Prins 1995: 18). Obvious examples are the rivers Jordan, Ganges, Nile and the Tigris–Euphrates. When downstream countries are relatively less powerful than water-controlling upstream countries, war may be unlikely, but social and economic instability and suffering can be enormous in the countries last in line to receive the river's water. Syria and Iraq are vulnerable to Turkey's massive Eastern Anatolian project of a series of dams on the headwaters of the Tigris and Euphrates as long as Turkey remains the dominant economic and military power. Most vulnerable of all are the stateless Kurds, whose traditional homeland encompasses the rivers' headwaters.

In Southeast Asia, the Mekong River nourishes millions of lives from Southern China through Burma, Laos, Thailand, Cambodia to the Vietnam delta. One project being considered by Laos in 1996, advised by the World Bank and the Asian Development Bank, was building 58 dams on Mekong tributaries for which US$25 billion in foreign capital would have to be raised. Another project is a cascade of fifteen hydropower projects on the Mekong in China which would affect the Great Lake in Cambodia, the country's major fishery resource. The scale of these projects means that their human and ecological consequences are enormous and life threatening. But the vast investment sums needed means that decisions about them are made by relatively few people (in governments and international investment institutions) living far from the river plains, for whom water is only a commodity to be bought and sold at the highest possible price. Slowly, very slowly, through the efforts of relatively small groups of activists, we are being made aware of the cost to the losers in this particular investment game.

I can still feel the shock of hearing, after the privatization of the water industry in Britain, that poor households had had their water supply cut off. The voters here, no more than the fishermen in Cambodia, were not consulted about this. I was not alone in being shocked, and the general outrage was such that some sort of safety net in the form of social service benefit was provided. But the families eligible for this usually have their water metered, and so pay more for it than those who pay through direct debit from their bank account. Once again the poor lose. In societies where the physical, public infrastructures are seen solely as a source of income, either through taxes, grants or shares, then those infrastructures are distorted from their common purpose of providing benefits to all citizens.

Ursula Franklin makes a distinction between divisible and indivisible benefits and divisible and indivisible costs which illustrates my point. If, she says, you have a garden and friends help you grow a good crop of tomatoes, you can share them among those who helped. What you have is a divisible benefit and the right to divide it. Whoever didn't help may not get anything. However, if you work hard to fight pollution by, for example, changing the practices of a battery-recycling plant down the street, those who helped get the benefits, but those who didn't also get them. These are indivisible. Normally, she says, in western culture one considers it the obligation of governments funded through a tax system 'to attend to those aspects of society which provide indivisible benefits – justice and peace, as well as clean air, sanitation, drinkable water, safe roads, equal access to education'. In other words, there is a notion that citizens surrendered some of their individual autonomy, and their money, for the protection, provision and advancement of 'the common good', that is, indivisible benefits.

Now however, the public infrastructures that have made possible the technology which provides those indivisible benefits have become more and more frequently providers of divisible benefits or dividends alone. The public purse provides, or has provided the wherewithal from which the private sector derives the divisible benefits. And at the same time as 'the realm from which the indivisible benefits are derived' (usually called 'the environment') has deteriorated, there has been a corresponding eclipsing of governments' obligation to safeguard and protect that realm (Franklin 1990: 69f).

Ultimately, we are talking here about the planetary *EarthScape*. In the Middle East, Southeast Asia and Europe, about treating the Tigris–Euphrates, the Mekong and the Thames as divisible benefits. The rabbi's tale needs answering in terms of whether water is a divisible or an indivisible benefit. Are the rules of competition the only way, or the right way, to decide?

Poiesis and mimesis

The concept of 'rules' (whether imposed by commandment, the market or by nature) functions as a cohesive factor in our *SocialScape*, and helps us express our perceived roles in ways which are commonly accepted. The rules of 'competition' have been accepted largely through what Bateson calls 'economy of habit', in that they save us the mental energy required to express ourselves differently. This phenomenon functions at several levels in our self-making. An important factor in the *poiesis* is an acceptance of our routine interactions as mimetic, as copying or conforming to or acting out a set of relationships which is 'natural' for us as organisms of a particular kind. *Mimesis* itself, as an imitative or representational activity, belongs to the poetic aspect of human nature, to *poiesis* as creative process. Ricoeur stresses the active and creative bond between them when he concludes: '*Mimesis* is *poiesis*, and *poiesis* is *mimesis*.' Nevertheless, following Aristotle, he is at pains to distinguish the particular role of mimesis in poetic activity. Whether in an epic poem, a tragedy, a work of art or a narrative text, mimesis is 'the ordering', the plot, coding or layout (as in 'beginning, middle and end'), which, in general, denotes the unity and order of action. This ordering clarifies the action, makes transparent for us whatever relationships are at stake, or are possible, and convinces us, at some conscious or unconscious level, that it is the process of living out this ordering which makes our particular kind of being-in-the-world 'human being'. We see, not just our essential biological features, but a representation of the life process itself; of the nature of relationships which can make us great and noble, or not. 'It is faithful to things as they are *and* it depicts them as higher and greater than they are.' It represents what is, what might be, and, in some instances, what ought to be (Ricoeur 1986: 39f.).

This contingent ordering is expressed within the metaphorical sphere, where things are discerned as what they are, and at the same time, as what they are not – but what they could be for us. It is here that the nature and function of metaphor in evolutionary description becomes clear. It opens our minds and imaginations to different possibilities in and for our self-making. But once the metaphor is literalized, fossilized into what is, into a rule to which we conform (because we believe we should conform to it in all respects), then we have lost its paradoxical force, and with it, our freedom to assert our essential dissimilarities from the description imposed on us. In an amusing example from the collection of pseudo Chinese wisdom called *The Wallet of Kai Lung*, it is related that 'a person of limited intelligence, on being assured that he would one day enjoy an adequate competence if he closely followed the habits of the industrious bee, spent the greater part of his life anointing his thighs with the yellow powder which he laboriously collected from the flowers of the field' (Bramah 1936: 106).

The drive to conform to a perceived order is intensified when the rule is apparently traced back to God or Nature as its ultimate authority. We cannot then, it seems, free ourselves from slavishly imitating such rules or principles. The authority is often implicitly invoked, but in Darwin sometimes explicitly, and so persuasively that even though in this instance he is writing about natural selection, the assumption of authority carries over to the next chapter and its exposition of 'the struggle for existence'.

> I have called this principle, by which each slight variation, if useful, is pre-served, by the term of Natural Selection, in order to mark its relation to man's power of selection. We have seen that man by selection can certainly produce great results, and can adapt organic beings to his own uses, through the accumulation of slight but useful variations, given to him by the hand of Nature. But Natural Selection, as we shall hereafter see, is a power incessantly ready for action, and is as immeasurably superior to man's feeble efforts, as the works of Nature are to those of Art.
>
> (Darwin 1985: 115)

Aristotle, and everyone else interested in the mimetic component of poiesis, assumes that its usual meaning, of imitation, also holds true. They assume that what is described will be acted out, copied, replicated in some fashion in the activity of those who see, hear, feel or read the mimetic representation. This mimetic faculty, which Walter Benjamin defines as our gift for seeing resem-blances and our capacity to produce similarities, has a long history. Nature creates similarities, and the perception of these natural correspondences stimulates and awakens the mimetic faculty in us. But, he warns, it must be borne in mind that neither mimetic powers nor mimetic objects remain the same over thousands of years. The gift of producing similarities, and therefore also the gift of recognizing them, changes with historical developments. In modern times, the coherence of words or sentences is the bearer through which, like a flash, similarity appears, and its production, like its perception, is, in many cases, limited to flashes (Benjamin 1997: 160–3)

In such flashes of perception, the viewer/hearer/reader recognizes, con-sciously or not, that the order of action represented in a particular description corresponds, or could correspond, in whole or in part, to the order of his/her own life and relationships. The biblical injunction after recounting a parable, to 'go and do likewise', and the rabbis' struggle to decide on the proper course of action for the two men in the desert, or for anyone else in an analogous position, rests on this assumption. As do numerous appeals to 'natural law' in Christian churches whose teaching has been influenced by Aristotelianism (as mediated by Thomas Aquinas) in such matters as slavery, the earth's orbit around the sun, the independent evolution of species and the subordination of women. But as the correspondence, whether actually or potentially valid, is established, for Ricoeur and for the argument of this book, within one vast auto/poietic sphere of metaphorical reference, it does not demand a slavish imitation, but a productive, constructive, individual and dynamic response from the viewer/hearer/reader. The flash of perception in which similarity appears, and appears possible, coexists, paradoxically, with the perception of, and possibility of, dissimilarity (see Chapter 3). This paradoxical moment gives us the freedom to respond to the perception of similarity in accord with our structural integrity, our limited freedom. It makes space for contingency, for different kinds of action, for creating something either in tune with, or dissimilar to, or emergent from and possibly an improvement on what is represented as 'natural order'.

In a Platonic schema, the representation of order is distanced twice over from its original reference, as things are seen to imitate ideas, and works of art to imitate things. Darwin, even though he intended to avoid a Platonic schema, invoked Nature as the 'original' artist whose works we seek to imitate. Furthermore, in his diagrammatic and verbal configuring of a tree as representing the principles of natural selection and extinction, he refers back to a biblical understanding of the diagram as 'the great Tree of Life' (Darwin 1985: 159–72). This intensification of authority through appeal to a powerful religious symbol informed the *PoieticScape* in western culture then, and still does, to a limited extent, even though many of the primary symbols have become cultural rather than religious references. Linnaeus had no doubt that scientific taxonomy had a sacred secular function, and referred to himself as a second Adam who could give 'true representation, true names' to species in his taxonomic order, thus reforming or restoring the 'pure' names bestowed by God and lost by the first Adam's sin. His role was to ensure 'a true and faithful order of nature' by seeing it clearly and naming it accurately (Haraway 1992: 9).

Aristotle's mimesis, on the contrary, seems more in tune with our secular/scientific culture. It has one single space in which the representation works: the sphere of human action. Within it, however, Ricoeur distinguishes at least three modes of metaphorical reference. We may refer the mimetic representation back to a familiar pre-understanding of the order of action; we may refer to it as a poetic composition; and finally, we may make our own reference, in a new configuration of this poetic refiguring, to the pre-understood order of action (Ricoeur 1984: xi, 31f. He elaborates these meanings in three densely argued volumes entitled *Time and Narrative*).

I noted a good example of this interactive mimetic comprehension in a lecture by Tim Ingold on the modern understanding of genetic inheritance through descent. He referred his own sketch of the order of inheritance back to genealogies of descent and to modern computer 'genetic bar codes'. So we had three interactive modes of reference: his own diagram, the standard computer genetic printout and the family tree of inheritance which records individual bearers of a particular genotype. His sketchy diagram (three triangles joined by a vertical line!) configured the order which was refigured both in computer printouts and in the family tree. In each instance, the order of inheritance was represented in a way which made its mimetic element perceptible to his audience, even though for some, the computer printout would supply the pre-understanding, and for others, the family tree.

Ingold was at pains to point out that none of the representations was in any way comprehensive, or gave a full account of the extremely complex interrelationships between the bearers of the genes. In fact, quite the reverse. Nor did he invoke the authority of biblical genealogies to claim that the computer printout was programmed by God, rather than a research team. His mimesis stayed within the Aristotelian referential sphere of human action, of human flashes of insight into the mysterious nature of genes and their interactions. Nor did he presume that the way in which the order was displayed governed all possible human responses to it. We do not have to behave like a Victorian or biblical patriarch or like a thick or thin slice of genetic code. Or like a 'free' market capitalist.

Yet this seems to have happened with Darwin's configuring of the nature of human existence, based on his particular pre-understanding of the nature of human interactions. He and his contemporaries, notably Malthus and Thomas Huxley, represented them compellingly in terms of competitive struggle for scarce resources, until this description, this configuring, became identified with the order of Nature. 'Competition' rapidly became a 'natural law' for social and economic progress. One of Darwin's most influential defenders and commentators, Thomas Huxley, made this absolutist claim in an article entitled *Struggle for Existence and its bearing upon Man*. Evolution in the animal world, he wrote, is on about the same level as the gladiators' show. 'The creatures are fairly well-treated, and set to fight; whereby the strongest, the swiftest, and the cunningest live to fight another day.' The same rules, he contended, hold for our evolution. The weakest and stupidest go to the wall, while the toughest and shrewdest, best fitted to cope with their circumstances, survive. Life, he says, is a free fight, and the normal state of existence, 'beyond the limited and temporary relations of the family, the Hobbesian war of each against all' (Sapp 1996: 157).

Today the language of competition, of some winning/some losing in the pitiless struggle for existence, shapes the contemporary Northern *PoieticScape* to the point where, remarks sociolinguist Deborah Tannen, public discourse is characterized by a kind of programmed contentiousness. Almost any issue, problem or public person is approached in an adversarial manner (Tannen 1998: 10). The adversarial approach also lies behind the concept of rights in a Rawlsian theory of justice. Rawls presumes that we are in competition with one another for goods and resources, and therefore that the task for society is to provide a framework which would insure against this by distributing these goods as fairly as possible. The basic tenet, of competing rights, is taken as 'given'. As is the implicit view of human nature motivated by greed and self-interest alone which makes competition inevitable. And it is here in secular society that we find religious doctrines, such as that of original sin, functioning at a subliminal level as a validation of this anthropology.

Liberation from competition

To see Darwinian rules of the game as 'divine', as imposed by a God who sees us as inherently flawed, incapable by nature of generosity or change for the better, preemptively curbs our freedom to 'make' ourselves otherwise. It denies us, and our perceptions, the freedom to evolve, to change through time. It assumes that our individuality as differentiated organisms is completely overridden by 'natural' laws. Its loss of the paradoxical relationship of the similarity of dissimilars curtails our freedom to behave in non-competitive, non-adversarial or non-violent ways, since any attempt to do so is easily dismissed as non-conformity to the human norm. The only way then left open to deal with the exponential violent effects of unbridled competition is to provide powerful government (the Hobbesian solution) or, in a post-Enlightenment era, to formulate and to enforce social contracts protective of individual rights. (There is now a minister in the British government to oversee 'competition'.) But these contracts, as was already pointed out, concentrate on universal norms of distributive justice (whatever the environment, equality between, or needs of, the individuals concerned) and, most importantly for market economies, on the right to own property and receive increasing divisible benefits without interference. But, as my rights to property and goods are acknowledged to compete with those of others, we stay within an adversarial relational environment. The acceptance of competition as the natural mode of interaction between individuals in society both assumes and reinforces the view that violence is endemic within us, as within our environments.

However, even as competition and progress-through-struggle became dominant themes of both natural and social science in the nineteenth century, and have continued, almost unabated, into the twentieth, an undercurrent of political and intellectual opposition has developed as well. (It is now, as the limitations and environmental effects of undiluted capitalism become more and more evident, very gradually developing into a groundswell.) Towards the end of the last century, trade unions, 'Friendly' and 'Mutual Aid' or credit societies were formed in reaction to a culture where the 'peaceful' competition of the free market was seen as a step forward in human progress, as a laudable replacement for the violent competition of war (as, sadly, William James saw 'war against Nature'). Mutualism arose in direct opposition to such a description of evolutionary progress, based as it was on a pitiless struggle for individual profit. In his book *Mutual Aid*, the Russian anarchist Prince Peter Kropotkin, reacting to Huxley's description of life as a gladiatorial contest, appealed to the same writ (the Book of Nature) to make the opposite point: 'Don't compete! Competition is always injurious to the species, and you have plenty of resources to avoid it!' That, he says, is the watchword which comes to us 'from the bush, the forest, the river, the ocean. Therefore combine – practise mutual aid!'

If humans were inherently cooperative, as Kropotkin believed them to be, then cooperative behaviour itself was an important progressive element in human evolution. The meaning and extent of the struggle for life had, he argued, been exaggerated, indeed, 'raised to the height of a biological principle which man must submit to as well'. At the same time, the importance of sociability and social instincts in animals for the well-being of the species and community had been underrated (Sapp 1996: 154–7). (The fact that Kropotkin can only be labelled an anarchist if competition is taken as the rule/r of evolutionary progress says much about the latter's supposedly normative status.

The sad and present fact that so many mutual societies in Britain have given up their mutual status and become shareholding institutions shows how the acquisition of divisible benefits has become the only game in town.)

In this century, Kropotkin's heirs can be found among those politicians and scientists who produced the 1950 and 1951 statements on the nature of race and racial difference for UNESCO. Poised as they were, Donna Haraway notes, on the boundary between fascism and colonization, on the one hand, and multinationalism, Cold War and decolonization on the other, they were aware that before World War II, versions of Darwinism, as well as other doctrines in evolutionary biology, had been deeply implicated in validating racist policies. (See Rachels and Beer in Chapter 4.) The constitution of UNESCO stated that the last war had been made possible by the doctrine of inequality of men and races, so new scientific 'facts' were needed to combat racial prejudice. Therefore the pivotal concepts of the 1950 document were those of a modern evolutionary synthesis in which natural selection and population biology was discussed in terms of complexity, biological efficiency and adaptive flexibility, with 'strong commitments to a version of the human place in nature that emphasized cooperation, human dignity, the control of aggression (war), and progress' (Haraway 1992: 197–9).

Although the American reaction to the document was on the whole quite favourable, English and French physical anthropologists expressed concern about the composition of the committee and certain aspects of its report, in particular, the inheritance of 'intelligence' and the question of '*a natural human predisposition to cooperation over competition*' (italics added). A second UNESCO committee was formed, and a second statement issued which did keep intact the possibility of social cooperation. However, in a Cold War climate, by 1975 a claim for a genetic predisposition to cooperation, unless it was figured in strict investment terms called inclusive fitness, would be the kiss of death for any research. And an affirmation that 'every man is his brother's keeper' would be revised, by the end of this century, to read as 'everyone is his/her sibling's banker' (Haraway 1992: 200f.).

If this seems an exaggeration, one need only remember Mrs Thatcher's exhortation that the Good Samaritan, if he hadn't earned the means to do so, would not have been able to help his neighbour. And presumably, he would have haggled with the innkeeper for a reduction in price and, when he returned, sold the victim travel insurance to cover future risks on the road. This kind of biblical commentary is routine in the sermons of the Christian Coalition in the States, so it is not altogether surprising that the Bank of Scotland considered setting up a joint direct banking operation in North America with the evangelical preacher and leader in the Coalition, Pat Robertson. In the first 'megachurch' in London, the Kingsway International Christian Centre, over 6,000 members attend its services every Sunday. In a potent rewriting of the game/competition model, it presents itself as 'the Church where champions are raised', and this year's convention was entitled 'Gathering of Champions', with its key motifs victory, power, success and achievement.

In the physical sciences, the possibility that cooperation might be a potent force in evolution is slowly gaining ground, especially through the work of Margulis and others on symbiosis. She has shown, through her research into cell biology, that we are composite individuals, made up of ancestral symbiotic associations that have become permanently interwoven. Cells as organisms exist in structural communities comprised of organisms with different abilities and potentialities, communities which appeared at the very beginning of life on earth and have persisted from then on. The sharing of the genome, as practised among bacteria, and the intrusion of one bacteria-type into another, made new composite organisms. We must, she says, dispense with extravagant anthropocentric labels to describe the driving forces behind evolution, and realize that 'our classification schemes blind us to the wildness of natural organization by supplying conceptual boxes to fit our preconceived ideas' (Margulis 1996: 167–84; 1998: 68).

In research on symbiotic associations, Tom Wakeford shows that the apparent conflict between this view of interactions between organisms and the Darwinian view has arisen because the latter evolutionary theory has mainly looked at animals, in particular vertebrates, and taken its conclusions largely from their patterns of behaviour. But more recently, observations of microbes have revealed examples of associations that are not satisfactorily explained simply as the product of gene mutation. In a comment which refers us back to the beginning of this book, he says that microbes have had a bad press at least since the time of Pasteur, being seen mainly as agents of disease. But, he says, they are also powerful agents of evolution, and are important in ecology for two reasons. Firstly, they are flexible and can change very quickly from one type of metabolism to another. Secondly, 'they invented every major sort of metabolism on Earth: photosynthesis, respiration, nitrogen fixing'. If, he says, we understand the importance of these liaisons as not just some trifling oddity but as something fundamental, 'we see that symbiogenesis, the creation of new organisms by means of microbes combining physiologies, is as important a perspective on evolution as the traditional gene-centred version' (Wakeford 1999: 7–8). Today we still rely on the indivisible benefits accruing from these metabolic exchanges.

In the next chapter I shall return to the composition of the conceptual boxes from which the 'rules', such as those of competition, are taken and used. In particular, I shall look at the effects on women and nature of a particular conceptual order which ranks human beings in relation to God. I return briefly now to the rabbi's exemplary tale, and to the question it poses of how we deal with indivisible benefits. The men's *EarthScape*, the desert, was not a neutral array of sand dunes, a mere unchanging backdrop to their encounter, but a physical dynamic reality with which their lives were actively and thoroughly implicated. They knew, we may presume, that it too is subject to perturbations from wind, storm or sun which trigger responses from it in accord with its own structural integrity.

When my husband first heard the story, he thought about the men's dilemma for a while and then said: 'In the desert the nights are cool. If the men decide to wait until then to make their journey, they can share the water, walk further, and both may live.'

11 Women and the ordering of Nature

The ancient identity of nature as nurturing mother, who provides for the needs of mankind in an ordered, planned universe, links women's history with the history of the environment and ecological change. ... But another opposing image of nature as female was also prevalent: wild and uncontrollable nature that could render violence, storms, droughts and general chaos. Both were identified with the female sex and were projections of human perceptions onto the external world. The metaphor of the earth as a nurturing mother gradually vanished as a dominant image as the Scientific Revolution proceeded to mechanize and to rationalize the world view. The second image, nature as disorder, called forth an important modern idea, that of power over nature.

(Carolyn Merchant 1996: 76f.)

In the previous chapter I outlined a certain competitive 'order of action' as the prevailing model of human interrelationships, and referred to a Platonic schema in which the representation of order is distanced twice over from its original reference. In this chapter, I want to consider this original reference, this prior order. It is the conceptual box marked 'Ontology', with 'order of Being' stamped on its lid. Curled up inside it is the presupposition that our actions result from, or depend on, or are in some way determined by the relationship between what we are in ourselves and what others (things or persons) are in themselves. Ontology as such, the conception of things being ordered on the basis of what they are, usually leaves unspecified the organizational principle on which the beings themselves are ranked in relation to each other. Classic Christianity, however, has formalized an extremely effective neo-Platonist principle of order known as hierarchy. Its mimetic effects on behaviour towards women and nature are the subject of this chapter, and by extension, its effects on the quality of inter-human and human–nature relationships. My particular concern is with binary codes based on hierarchical ordering and their validation of certain violent interactions between men and women and between them and their material environments.

Scientific organizational principles alluded to earlier, such as cellular formation or nutritional modes, take certain observable individual characteristics, marks or behavioural habits of organisms as criteria for deciding which beings will be included or studied in various taxonomies (Foucault 1974: 128–45; Ingold 1995: 57–9). General conceptions of how reality is ordered, however, cannot be so specific or so easily decided. They derive from ancient and often obscure ontological presuppositions, all the more powerful for being unstated or taken for granted. Foucault refers to them as 'the *site*, the mute ground upon which it is possible for entities to be juxtaposed' (Foucault 1974: xvii). One such foundational concept, which though largely muted in western culture is no less powerful for that, is hierarchy: an organizational principle governing the ordering of being which is itself ordered on a notion of primary Being (routinely capitalized). With such a notion, we have moved, as mentioned in the previous chapter, from an Aristotelian schema to a Platonic one. If this primary Being is identified with God as revealed in Jesus Christ as the ultimate reference point to which we are bound, then we have moved to a Christian ordering of the universe. This principle of ranking beings in relation to God, the supreme Being has, to a large extent, determined western cultural perceptions of human identity as distinct from the identity of nature, as well as what it means for us to be male rather than female. Its characteristic feature is its implicit/explicit acknowledgement of the sacredness of central authority, and its acceptance of certain key male figures, characterized in certain ways, as symbolizing, embodying and exercising that authority.

Hierarchy as a principle of order

The binding together of ontology and theology, of what we say we are and what we say God is, is called ontotheology. Ontology, in this instance, explores the meaning of the verb 'to be' rather than taking it as exemplified in 'beings'. It understands 'Being' as a verb (Levinas 1985: 38). It becomes ontotheology when, after Heidegger, it takes the idea of God's being as 'the mute ground' of all being. Modern (or postmodern, depending on the context) discussion of the subject focusses to a large extent on Heidegger's formulations of the concept of ontotheology and Levinas' rejection of them. Ontotheology, or 'the Science of God', attempts 'to provide the grounds for all beings as such and within the wholeness of the whole' (Blond 1998: 11–12; 67–106; 177–194). The Christian ontotheological presupposition can be summed up in Paul's words, that 'in God we live, move and have our being' (Acts 17: 27–8). Such linking of our being with divine being grounds the organizational principle called hierarchy, literally, sacred government, in which our being, in relation to all other beings, is ordered by God. My concern here is to show the *effects* of that on western culture in its ordering of women and nature. These effects, as we shall see, owe much to the fact that from its formative stages onward, that culture was shaped by, and shaped a *SocialScape* and a *PoieticScape* that has been male dominated.

The late-fifth-century Christian mystic and neo-Platonist known as Denys (or Dionysius) the Areopagite is credited with first use of the term *hierarchia* (hierarchy), a coinage from two Greek words meaning 'sacred', and 'source or

principle'. He expounded the principle while writing about 'the two hierarchies', the celestial and the ecclesiastical. The first 'consists of three ranks, each
consisting of three types of angelic being'. The second hierarchy also consists of
'three ranks of three', of which the first rank consists 'not of beings but of rites –
sacramental rites'. The second rank in this hierarchy is that of sacred ministry:
bishops, priests and ministers. The third rank is that of the laity, and includes
monks (in the Eastern Church, there is a tradition of resistance on the part of
monks to being ordained), the baptized, and those excluded from the
celebration of the sacraments. 'The purpose of the hierarchies is assimilation to
God and union with him [*sic*]. This is accomplished by each being fulfilling its
proper role in the hierarchy' (Louth 1990: 162–78). The aspect of hierarchy
which I want to highlight here, and one too often ignored or forgotten, is that
it ranks or grades all beings, even the angelic ones. And as each rank is graded,
so is its role (or order of action). And each rank, grade or role is assumed to be
determined by divine decree. A pervasive image of this divine order is expressed
in the popular hymn, *All things bright and beautiful,* sung to a God who
determines the relative high and low estate of the king and of the poor man
lying at the castle gate.

This divine ordering is made explicit by Denys positing the two hierarchies
(celestial and ecclesiastical) as in fact part of a triad of being, with the Thearchy,
or Trinity, ranked above the other two. The concept of hierarchy was, then,
actually a cosmic, theocratic pattern of government which visibly evolved into
'Christendom'. In it the Trinity presides above the angels, who are above the
ecclesiastics who are above the laity. This ranking is more than order: it refers
also to what this sacred ordering makes possible; the knowledge and activity of
those so ordered (the order of action). Denys' overall understanding of
hierarchy sees it as the overflowing of God's love, of God's active search for
humankind and gentle persuasion of fallen human beings.

A very important principle for him is that we do not receive our *being* from
other creatures ranked higher than us, for we are created immediately by God,
and each of us has an immediate relation to God by virtue of God creating each
of us. However, those ranked above us have a mediating role between us and
God, conveying and ordering knowledge of God (revelation) and directing our
activity in accordance with God's will for all members of the hierarchy. They
are, for Denys, a community seeking to draw near to God and draw others near
to God. They are a community being saved and mediating salvation, and their
presence expresses the transcendent love of God made immanent (Primavesi
1991: 89–99).

This magnificent vision of order and harmony throughout the world shaped
Christian and western consciousness for centuries, most obviously in its religious
and political order. Its organizing principle of graded levels of being carried
through, for Denys, into the material order, manifested for him most clearly in
physical church structures, where the architecture gives primacy to the
sanctuary. A computer-generated model of a traditional church seen from
above, without its roof, reveals a hierarchically ordered space, where the

sanctuary and its ministers stand at the apex of the building and the congregation fan out below them. The hierarchical order of action for those who used the building followed from this, with the ministers in the sanctuary separated from the laity outside and below it, the latter dependent on the ministers for access to God through sacramental mediation. The physical and spiritual boundaries between the orders were thus established, impregnable because ratified by the highest authority, God.

The ordering was formalized internally and externally, and its systematic application became and remains normative in theological and church systems. The 1960s Second Vatican Council document on the Church, *Lumen Gentium*, contains a long chapter on 'The Hierarchical Structure of the Church' (Abbott 1966: 37–56). In a recent interesting and influential theological/scientific study, *On the Moral Nature of the Universe: Theology, Cosmology and Ethics*, Nancey Murphy and George F. R. Ellis argue that the hierarchical ordering of the natural and human sciences is marked by 'top-down causation' and 'emergent order', in which with each step 'upward' in the hierarchy of biological order (from cell to organism to community) novel properties emerge that were not present at the 'simpler' levels of organization. In the light of this they define 'top-down causation' as both *effects*, which determine the detailed evolution of the hierarchical system, and *action*, which occurs when human volition is involved. They propose a hierarchy of the natural sciences which for them is incomplete without a metaphysical, or preferably theological 'top layer'. This unifies the hierarchies by providing a single theory of divine *purpose* which answers 'the ultimate questions arising from each branch of the hierarchy'. For them, the purpose is that 'humankind (or at least ethically aware self-conscious beings) might exist', and the ultimate questions, in particular those raised by violence, are answered by a theology which sees God as refusing to do violence to creation, whatever the cost to God. This view, for them as Christian pacifists, holds direct implications for human morality in that it implies a self-renunciatory, nonviolent ethic, one modelled on 'God's own self-sacrificing love' (Murphy and Ellis 1996: 19–37, 202f.).

In secular monarchies, particularly where, as in the Holy Roman Empire and the British monarchy, the monarch's 'divine' right to rule was, and is, ratified by the established Church or religion, hierarchy endorsed the political and military authority of royal institutions. Clifford Geertz gives a fascinating historical account of the symbolics of spiritual power previously attached to monarchies as diverse as those of England, Morocco and Java. These symbolics might seem, at first sight, irrelevant as well as redundant in today's secular society. However, he points out that though both the structure and the expressions of social life change, the inner necessities that animate it do not. Thrones, he says, may be out of fashion, but political authority still requires a cultural frame in which to define itself and advance its claims, and so does opposition to it. It is no accident that Stuarts get Cromwells and Medicis Savonarolas. It is, he says, only a certain view of 'the affinity between the sort of power that moves men and the sort that moves mountains' which died in the French Revolution (to the degree that it did). The sense that there is such an affinity did not die (Geertz 1993b: 121–46). It is interesting here to see how Yeltsin and other Russian leaders have publicly allied themselves with the renascent Russian Orthodox Church. And vice versa. In the 1996 edition of the annual *Catholic Directory of England and Wales*, a list of Roman pontiffs is followed by that of members of the college of cardinals, who 'rank as princes of the blood royal'.

This assumed affinity between sacred and secular order, internalized and no less powerful for its religious origins becoming increasingly remote, has, however, been contested this century by political and liberation theologians for its conjunction of deity and domination (Nicholls 1994); or monotheism and monarchy (Moltmann 1981); or monotheism and violence (Schwartz 1997); or capitalist hegemonies supported by right-wing churches (Hinkelammert 1983, 1986, 1997; Assmann 1983). It is contested also by those theologians who find hierarchical authority structures exercising undue and oppressive influence on the lives of women (Ruether 1983; Morton 1985; Primavesi 1991). Standing back, as it were, from these hierarchical structures within which they are enmeshed, are those philosophers and theologians who see that in classical hierarchical organization, where women and children are assigned to the lowest grade or rank, even that is denied to what is called 'Nature'. The dividing line between human and animal is so absolute that non-human 'beings' in our environments, monera, protoctista, fungi, animals and plants, are below any grade. They are totally 'de/graded'. They are considered, if at all, to be outside of that community seeking to draw near to God and draw others near to God; outside that community whose presence expresses the transcendent love of God made immanent. The secular version of this has been evident in the struggle by animal rights activists within the European Union to have farm animals graded as 'sentient beings' and not as 'agricultural products'.

I am not saying that divine 'collusion' with grading, degrading and exclusion is routinely or publicly claimed, endorsed or enforced, or that Denys is required reading for constitutional historians. But as Geertz points out, political, religious and military power still requires a cultural framework, a *SocialScape* and a *PoieticScape* in which to define itself and advance its claims, and while the ecclesiastical institutions remain the most visible hierarchical framework, 'inner necessities' for an order of action and of being also remain potent within social and political structures. It is at that subliminal level that hierarchy, with its assumption of affinity between divine and human power, retains its power. Civil religious ceremonies, such as a presidential inauguration, the state opening of parliament or armistice commemorations in Europe, are its most public expression today.

It is no accident then, that some of the most contested contemporary issues in public life have been women's challenges to a political and ecclesiastical order of being which excludes and degrades them (challenges epitomized in their claim to the right to vote and to officiate in the sanctuary) and the challenging of political and economic order by environmental movements which see that, for practical purposes, 'Nature' and its role have been degraded in or excluded from the community of being. Both these movements challenge what Geertz calls 'the master fictions', that is, the hierarchies of being and the mimetic processes by which the prevailing social order condones certain acts of violence toward certain classes of being: in Nature's case, by making it a 'nonbeing'. The early chapters of this book described the exclusion of organisms other than the human from our frame of reference, and addressed the painful question of what it might mean if we accepted their vital role in the world and our dependence on them. For at the heart of hierarchical separation lies a claim to divine and human independence of and power over nature and any being identified with nature. An understanding of the nature and extent of this religious, political and ecological apartheid is necessary if we are to address the overarching question of a coevolutionary theology: 'Why have *we* made and why do we insist on certain "orders of merit" in God's relations with us and with all other creatures in our environments?' Part of the answer at least lies in hierarchy's validation of violence in the name of God. Part of the response to this will be an attempt to describe a non-hierarchical, coevolutionary organizing principle which does not allow us to perceive ourselves as 'above', or 'outside' nature, but as belonging to it and constituted by it.

Modes of hierarchical ordering

Theology from a coevolutionary perspective sees that hierarchical ordering will remain theologically effective as long as we subscribe to a system in which the *value* of 'being' (whether ours or that of any other living entity) is ranked in relation to a supposed order of nearness (among human beings) to the highest Being, God. Hierarchy assumes that the 'highest' value of all is ascribed to God's Being which, through a type of top-down causation, is taken as the source of all value. By implication, whatever is placed furthest away, in the 'lowest' states of being, is furthest from God, and so of 'lesser' value. God 'functions' as the definitive source of value and at the same time, sets limits to one level of value in relation to another. So even though Denys was at pains to insist on the principle of immediate causation, or creation of each being by God, there is at least an implicit claim in hierarchy that the value of each one's being is not the same. It derives from where one is ranked relative to others' ranking. This is most evident in the common perception of ordination, or 'Holy Orders', as giving the ordained a rank above that of the laity which marks them out from lay people and enables them to act (on God's behalf) in ways not open to others. In such ranking, it makes perfect sense to make the penultimate 'Holy Order' that of cardinal, synonymous with that of a royal prince.

In Gaia theory, however, and in a coevolutionary theology, the existence of each organism 'counts' in respect of the whole, and each can be valued for what it is in itself. Intrinsic value can be attributed to bacteria as to ourselves. This rests on the fact that taking the nature of an individual's structural coupling into account, each entity is considered a unique being and therefore, essentially ungradeable. At a practical level of course, one may 'count' more than another.

And it is an unfortunate fact that the unique value of each organism, as Rachel Carson found, often becomes apparent to us only after it has become extinct.

For those who, like Gutierrez, base the intrinsic value of each human being on the gratuity of God's love for each one, for the least one, for the most forgotten one, that love too is essentially ungradeable. The loveworthiness of each is not derived from class, wealth, education, religion, gender or race, nor is it based on relative moral worth. It is based on their uniqueness before God. For me, when he and de Las Casas see the poor as altogether fresh and vivid in the memory of God, this echoes Jesus' claim about God's direct interest in sparrows and in each lily in the field. It extends the notion of intrinsic value beyond that of human life. Yet usually, the most value given other creatures, and the most usual defence of their right to a habitat, is their contributing to 'quality of life': *our* life, not theirs.

In Christian church documents based on hierarchical ordering, there are explicit limits set and boundaries to be kept between one rank of being and another. There is presumed to be a defining and predetermined hierarchic 'blank space' between God and the other states of being which could only be bridged by *the* mediator between God and man [sic]: Jesus Christ. He brought knowledge of God to men, who then preached this knowledge to other men, women and children. This ontological limit to knowledge of God is so accepted as to be largely unrecognized. No trickle-down effect on nature is envisaged in orthodox theology, although popular understanding has St Francis preaching to the birds and to the wolf. Yet here too, the presumption is that *he* was telling *them* about God, since it was assumed that otherwise, they would not have this knowledge. The idea that he might have heard something about God from them would have been dismissed as, at best, ridiculous.

However, an intimation of the reverse order of mediation is given in the saying attributed by some to St Francis and by others to Rabindranath Tagore:

I asked the tree,
Speak to me about God
And it blossomed.

In classic Christianity, however (classic in the double sense of standard teaching and standard taxonomy), the only bridge between divine Being and those in the 'lower' states, that is, below the human, was the human person himself, with his metaphoric role described as steward, guardian/custodian or pastor/shepherd. (For practical purposes, we can discount angels.) Such male metaphors excluded, and continue to exclude, women from a mediating role at the same time as they stress male human similarity to God. Doing so, they inherently devalue women. For in hierarchical systems, there is an inbuilt tendency not only to value some more than others, but by doing so, to devalue those others; not only to grade, but to degrade. And in this degrading, there is an implicit capacity for and acceptance of violence. The more something is degraded, the more it can be exploited, discarded, destroyed. Validation of violent relationships is one of the primary reasons for the continuance, consciously or not, of a hierarchical ordering of being, and therefore for consistently critiquing it and ultimately, rejecting it.

The place of Nature and women in hierarchical ordering

The devaluing process within hierarchy has been recognized by feminist theologians and philosophers as a significant factor in the ordering of women and nature (Primavesi 1991: 195–222; Plumwood 1993: 165–90). In a hierarchical pyramid which ranks God at its apex, and men (for practical purposes) immediately below God, then women, children, animals, plants and the soil/dirt/earth form its base. Once this 'ranking' has been established, God-concepts function in relation to women, children, animals and the earth as validation of their exploitation and subordination. God is presented as the ultimate arbiter who distinguishes them from men in order to degrade them. When this distinction is publicly expressed in binary codes which rank 'male' characteristics above 'female' ones, the degrading is formalized. The binary codes in themselves, as we saw, can be taken as a linguistic device for implying a whole which cannot be adequately expressed. But as Luhmann pointed out, they are more often used as devices for declaring allegiance to one position or person against another, or for affirming the status of one against another. So Christian binary codes of sacred/secular; human/animal; spiritual/material always reflect, implicitly at least, a prior hierarchical ordering derived from neo-Platonism or ontotheology.

It is a moot point here whether hierarchy precedes patriarchy or merely sanctifies it. What matters is that when binary codes routinely attribute opposed male/female characteristics to men and women, such as rational/emotional; objective/subjective; logical/illogical; strong/weak; active/passive, the attribution is not neutral. What matters is not the position of one word relative to another, but their connotations within a hierarchical ranking (Curthoys 1997: 70). The effects of this are obvious in a culture where, for centuries, the relative status of men and women in society has reflected this ranking. It has affected the power relations between men and women, whether religious, political, economic or social. It has affected the relations between men and their environments. The effects of this last, and its allied effects on women, have been quantified in studies of the disproportionate impact of environmental degradation on women, children, indigenous peoples and the poor (Brubaker 1994; Robb 1995).

Degradation of the biophysical environment itself reflects hierarchical attitudes which reduce it to instrumental or commodity value alone. The degradation has been validated, consciously or not, by the identification of male/female with culture/nature, with overtones of mastery by the male. This conceptual relational field has been one of the most contested areas of feminist discourse, with the contest centred, for the most part, on whether or not women are to be identified with nature or with culture. Much of the analysis has been done by secular feminists, who are often blind to the fact, as Curthoys points out, that there is a prior devaluing inherent in the terms which the terms in themselves do not carry. The understanding of this 'prior devaluing' offered here is that it rests in large measure on prior Christian hierarchical descriptions of the order of being, where women and nature are presumed to belong on the level of the 'fallen', 'uncontrollable' and 'disordered', and their subjugation and the recovery of order validated publicly as 'divine rule', or civilization. (Primavesi 1991: 85–110; Merchant 1996: 27–47). And I do not find it convincing when theologians protest that this is not what Denys meant by hierarchy. This is what it has meant for women and nature up to now, as secular scholars like Merchant, Plumwood and Curthoys make clear.

Effects of hierarchical ordering

What has it meant for God, and for the function of God-concepts? My theological concern in critiquing hierarchy is that within its perspective, God functions as hierarch, as an idol who presides over an order of being in which the poor, women and nature are devalued and their oppression validated. For throughout history, as Hugo Assmann avers, the God of the rich and the God of the poor are not the same God. Perspective really matters here. God, he says, has been pulled from one side to the other. As hierarch, he has been the last of the Roman Emperors and the first and last of the medieval kings, until now he is a captive of capitalism, playing the role of the god of the mighty dollar: 'in God we trust'.

This, Assmann says, is 'true idolatry':

> Idols are
>   the gods of oppression.
> Idols are
>   the shining fetishes
>   with divine names
>   and broad smiles,
>   with creeds
>   with worship
>   with prayers
>   with laws
>   with sacred and divine power
>   power to oppress
>   power to exploit
>   power to kill.
>
> The dominators,
> the idolatrous,
>   will never make the mistake
>   of declaring themselves atheists.
>   (Assmann 1983: 204f.)

On the contrary, as Assmann knows, the dominators parade their Christianity. Pinochet, when under house arrest in Britain in 1998, had his personal chaplain flown over from Chile to celebrate Mass in the house. Pinochet is described, and describes himself, as 'a devout Catholic'. Within such idolatrous hierarchies, 'God' is assumed to sanction the effects of military, political, social and economic oppression, visible in the violence inflicted through militarism; in inequality of power and the incapacity to achieve well-being; in exploitation by industry, enslavement by debt and bioserfdom imposed by agrochemical corporations.

A particular element in the hierarchical devaluing of women, one already mentioned in the discussion of poetic imagination and binary codes, is the distinction made between reason and emotion. This has affected men and women alike, although in different ways, with men taught to consider themselves and their actions as the embodiment of reason; women and their actions as the embodiment of emotion. This distinction has worked entirely in men's favour, since in a Platonic, neo-Platonic or Christian hierarchical schema, normative male traits, such as reason, are considered superior to those of women. (This is, of course, a circular argument, since men arrived at this conclusion, supposedly, through the exercise of their reason.) However arrived at, it was, and is, assumed to be a valid distinction, and the denigration of emotion, passion or empathy as a constituent in action still holds. In Kant's teaching on morality, he argued that an action is moral only if it is based solely on reason. Actions done from duty, he said, must completely exclude the influence of desire or inclination. It is not that moral persons must be without feelings, but that they must be able to suspend them in order to act in obedience to the universal law of morality. By implication, women, who must cultivate their sensibilities for their roles as wives and mothers, are either less capable, or even incapable of being moral agents, not because of a biological deficiency of the kind Aristotle would have argued for, but because their social roles 'preclude full development of their rational faculties' (Tuana 1992: 58–70).

It is clear, I think, how uneasily this sits with a poetic, empathetic self-perception, one emotionally empowered to respond imaginatively to stimuli from one's environment. It is clear too, I hope, that the distinction between reason and emotion is not in itself degrading: it degrades only because it belongs within a prior devaluing, within an ontotheological hierarchy which, by attaching 'emotion' to women, degrades that particular human faculty. So if, in a moment of reversal, reason were attributed to women in this determinative sense, then emotion would be ranked above it. In regard to animals, the 'rationality thesis' mentioned in Chapter 4 equated reason with 'the divine element' in men which distinguished them definitively from all other beings. The degrading effects of dualistic oppositions on perceptions of women and nature are the result of a hierarchical way of thinking, rather than determining the way we think about ourselves. If this is not made clear, we confuse the form (binary code) with the content (hierarchy) and concentrate on dismantling or reversing those forms rather than examining their content (Curthoys 1997: 71f.).

Women and Nature

One of the strongest and most enduring hierarchical distinctions made by men has been that between them and women/nature. This has been paralleled by an identification of women with Nature, which has led historically to a personification of 'nature' as female, and to images of it as maternal, nurturing, fruitful, passive and virginal, images bolstered by metaphorical clusters around seed, womb, fertility and barrenness which imply an active partner, man (Merchant 1980; 1996). The enduring relationship between him and woman, 'husbandry', is used to describe his closest working relationship with the earth, with its connotations of 'penetrating' virgin forest or soil, sowing seed on the analogy of marital sowing, and ploughing for the procreation of children. I have discussed the history and analysis of this type of identification and personification in some detail elsewhere (Primavesi 1991: 33–6, 46–54, 61–4). When made on the basis of a hierarchical order of being, it has led to femaleness, either in women or Nature, being defined, in every sense, solely from the dominant male perspective. Indeed within this order, the male form itself has been taken to define complete or perfect humanness, and the use of the male form, whether in body or in language, taken as generic. An *Atlas of Physiology and Anatomy of the Human Body* on my shelf, first published in 1906 and reprinted in 1984, illustrates the male body alone.

This physical apartheid has been linked, as I said, to another important element in women's struggle for identity, the dichotomy between nature and culture, in which men are identified with culture. One of its supporting pillars has been the distinction in Hellenic culture between the supremacy of order (*cosmos*) over meaningless desolation (*chaos*). The achieving of this supremacy formed part of the worldview of the Greeks and of every European and Northern ruling class which followed them. Carolyn Merchant traces its influence through the American capitalist project, where the city epitomizes 'the transformation of female Nature into female Civilisation through the mutually reinforcing powers of male energy and interest-earning capital'. The city is the locus of power operating in the natural world, sweeping everything towards its centre: the bridge between civilized female form and the raw matter of the surrounding hinterlands, transforming natural resources into capitalist commodities (Merchant 1996: 47f.). (Civilization, as we know, wears very large shoes and leaves very heavy footprints when imposing order on her sister Nature.) Building cities became synonymous with building culture. Culture then became identified with the supremacy of male power over *chaos*, with adapting and imposing order on a very earthy substantiality which included slaves, foreigners, pagans or country-dwellers, women and potentially unruly freedmen, and which, prior to its ordering through cultural categories and projects, remained in a state of flux.

Christianity, from this perspective, can be seen to have overcome its chaotic origins in Galilee and, through the preaching of Paul in the cities around the Aegean, and then through its assimilation into the Roman Empire, to have become largely an urban religion (Meeks 1983). Its ceremonies became confined within hierarchical church structures, the largest being built in/or creating cities, with those outside city boundaries under the jurisdiction of urban episcopal centres. Any other form of worship was, and is, anathematized as 'pagan'.

A defining moment in the Christian *PoieticScape* of the city was the metaphorical cluster in the New Testament book *Revelation*, which opposed one city, Jerusalem, which comes down from God out of heaven, with another, Babylon, dwelling place of demons, haunt of foul spirits (Revelation 3: 12; 18: 2–3). Augustine's magnum opus, *The City of God*, built on these metaphors, presents the spiritual history of the City of God as invisibly intertwined with the secular history of the City of Man. The first represents the collectivity of the saved, the second the 'lump of perdition'. In the latter, 'the lust for domination lords it over its princes as over the nations it subjugates; in the other, both those put in authority and those subject to them serve one another in love, the rulers by their counsel, the subjects by obedience'. At the Last Judgment, these cities will separate from each other finally and visibly. Then the City of God will appear as the New Jerusalem.

Catherine Keller, making this analysis, remarks that Augustine's allegorical dualism reinforces a foundational (indeed uncritical) loyalty to the imperial and civil order. His secondary metaphors of the *civitas pellegrina*, the pilgrim city, passing through the degraded *civitas terrena*, the earthly city, obeying its rules but not becoming attached enough to challenge the unjust ones, led, she says, to a sublime aloofness. 'The Augustinian reduction of all things creaturely to means to the timeless End secures the Western disconnection of spirit from the time rhythms of the earth.' The 'timelessness' of eternity, Augustine argues, means that 'in eternity there is no change'. In other words, says Keller, 'changelessness is the very essence of the immovable God, whose omnipotence is steering us unwaveringly through time towards the final confrontation. Then life will be frozen eternally into one of the two possible conditions'. Once free of time (and the earth), the self will again reflect the image of God, in which it was created. Or rather, Keller notes, in which men were created. For Augustine, women, while redeemable as such, only possess the image of God inasmuch as they are coupled with men, as body to head (Keller 1996: 97–103).

Exploiting Augustine's 'complex insinuations', she sees an ecclesial triumphalism gradually taking over which fostered a militant we/they attitude; an uncompromising hostility toward all sorts of unbelievers which formed the basis of expectations of a literal victory over the enemies of Christ. By the eleventh century, the construct of Muslim as 'infidel' emerges, and in the Crusades, the glittering vision of the City of God (Jerusalem) gets literalized with a vengeance: the hope for the 'spiritual' triumph of Europe fastened itself upon the acquisition of the fabulous material wealth of the *old* Jerusalem. After all,

Revelation, with its metaphor of a bejewelled Jerusalem, had promised Christians her riches (Keller 1996: 104).

Defining Nature

These historic processes have built on and built up a perception of nature/earth, women/body as material, irrational, passive, dependent and immanent, needing to be subordinated to and dominated by culture, man, reason and spirit which are rational, active, independent and transcendent. This perception has been publicly and religiously expressed in Christian teaching about women which described them, after Eve, as temptresses, fallen, lacking a soul and incapable, by nature, of redeeming themselves or mediating the knowledge of God to others. Hierarchical principles, such as male control of the household, of the city and of public order, were given the seal of sacred authority, with God envisaged for and experienced by women as fathers, husbands, patriarchs, kings, lords, stewards, custodians, popes and bishops (Primavesi 1991: 46–8; 198–202).

All of these principles of control have been applied in a most thoroughgoing fashion to western man's relationship with nature. And it seems to me that in the west, for men and for women, it is our concept of nature, prior to its identification or personification with either sex, which must change and is changing. Some of the changes are charted in *Remaking Reality: Nature at the Millennium*, in which the editors point out that political-economic transformations, technological changes of astonishing power and unfathomable extent and apocalyptic pronouncements of ecological catastrophe have put 'nature' on the agenda as never before. They and the contributors argue for a concept of 'social nature', that is, a nature ordered up, manipulated and constructed, as well as animate, unpredictable and consequential. They do this while describing three different, and co-existing concepts of nature: 'first' nature: a Marxist term for a bourgeois concept and representation of nature as external to society (and implicitly, the city); 'second' nature, described by Donna Haraway as 'not preexisting its construction, but something made by us, materially and semiotically (and implicitly, encompassing whatever is within as well as beyond the city boundary); and 'third' nature, a term used by Wark for the simulated natures of visual media, or the extraordinary optics of the geographical information system (GIS), all of which provide powerful means of manipulating nature as 'information'. These approaches, the editors conclude, show that it is 'increasingly impossible to separate nature off into its own ontological space. Thus, the remaking of nature(s) has wider implications – it becomes, quite simply, a focal point for a nexus of political–economic relations, social identities, cultural orderings, and political aspirations of all kinds' (Braun and Castree 1998: 3–42).

I cannot do justice here to the range and depth of the contemporary discussion, but the bibliographies in the above volume will help those who want to pursue it. (An allied topic is that of 'wilderness', and again, Max Oelschlaeger provides a good guide to that discussion.) It is, however, clear that there are important connections between a hierarchical ordering of nature and the Marxist perception of 'bourgeois' 'first' nature, and between hierarchical power relations and their implications for the role and perception of women, nature and culture in the concept of 'second' nature as a place and product of human construction. Also important is the acknowledgement that it is now impossible to separate nature off into its own ontological space, or to consider it as outside a nexus of political–economic relations and social identities. Included in this latter perception are the complexity of human–environment relations and the preconceptions we bring to their description (Milton 1998: 86–99). For me, this has meant using autopoietic theory to reimagine 'nature', with the focal point that theory's stress on the paradoxical nature of our structural coupling with our environments. It has also meant taking some dimensions of human–environment relations – *SelfScape*, *SocialScape*, *EarthScape* and *PoieticScape* – and using them to reveal the complex, interactive and transformative character of that tight coupling.

R. G. Collingwood, in *The Idea of Nature*, finds no less than seven definitions given by Aristotle for the Greek term *physis*, usually translated as 'nature', one of which, *the essence of things which have a source of movement in themselves*, Aristotle regarded as the true and fundamental meaning. This definition is, according to Collingwood, to be understood as 'what things are when left to themselves', before 'culture' or society adapts them to our needs and desires, or, as he puts it, before they are interfered with by us (Collingwood 1960: 80f.). (This corresponds to 'first' nature.) But, as Haraway and others point out, and as Gaia theory and its study of the interactions between life and its environment demonstrates, once we have arrived, as it were, on the scene, the things are no longer left to themselves. Once life, in the form of living organisms, emerged from earth's environment, 'nature' was no longer 'alone'. It was subsumed in a relationship between things as they are in themselves and what they are when they are relating to other things: a relationship of identity-in-difference. It was subsumed in the order of being called organism-with-environment/environment-with-organism. What kind of anthropology, what ordering of our being emerges from this coevolutionary, relational premise of interdependence and interactivity?

Belonging to the Gaian order

The premise of a hierarchical paradigm is a Platonic, neo-Platonic, Christian anthropology, based on assumed ontological spaces between the human and the animal which precede and establish dichotomies between culture and nature, between reason and instinct, between morality and physicality. Social anthropologist Tim Ingold enumerates and then vigorously challenges these 'stale dichotomies', as he calls them. His work brings together some of the important anthropological issues raised by a coevolutionary world view. Specifically, his descriptions of what it means for us to belong to, and to dwell within the order of organism-in-environment parallels an autopoietic order, in which being and activity are so related as to assume fundamental similarities between humans and animals while exploring differences between them.

This paradoxical similarity/dissimilarity, according to Ingold, resides in the fact that 'the difference between (say) a goose and a man is not between an organism and a person, but between one kind of organism-person and another. … [P]ersonhood is not the manifest form of humanity; rather the human is one of the many outward forms of personhood' (Ingold 1996: 132f.). Within this one world, he says, humans figure not as composites of body and mind but as undivided beings, 'organism-persons', relating as such both to other humans and to non-human agencies and entities in their environment. 'Between these spheres of involvement there is no *absolute* separation, they are but contextually delimited segments of a single field.' It is, therefore, as entire persons, not as disembodied minds, that humans engage with one another and, moreover, with non-human beings as well. And vice versa. 'They do so as beings *in* a world, not as minds which, excluded from a given reality, find themselves in the predicament of having to make sense of it.' He coins the term '*interagentivity*' to describe the constitutive quality of their world (Ingold 1996: 128–9).

Ingold's descriptions of personhood as a relational event, a process, an activity, remind me of Gerard Manley Hopkins' lines:

> Each mortal thing does one thing and the same;
> Deals out that being indoors each one dwells;
> Selves – goes itself; *myself* it speaks and spells
> Crying *What I do is me: for that I came.*
> (Hopkins 1930: 53)

The relationship between being, activity and environment is such that, in regard to the assumed dichotomy between nature and culture, Ingold concludes: 'The world can exist as "nature" only for a being who does not belong there, and who can look upon it, in the manner of the detached scientist [*sic*], from such a safe distance that it is easy to connive in the illusion that it is unaffected by his presence.' This accords with the autopoietic premise, and with Ingold's own, that there can be no organism without an environment, and no environment without an organism. For environments are forged through the activities of living beings, and as long as life goes on, both are continually under construction (Ingold 1998: 170; this, for me, is another way of describing coevolutionary process). Therefore he takes the human condition to be 'that of a being immersed from the start, like other creatures, in an active, practical and perceptual engagement with constituents of the dwelt-in world'. This ontology of dwelling, he contends, provides us with a better way of coming to grips with the nature of human existence than the alternative western ontology. Its point of departure (reminiscent of the 'rationality thesis') is that of a mind detached from the world, one which has literally to formulate that world prior to any attempt at engagement. For Ingold, however, and for an organism structurally coupled with its environment: '[A]pprehending the world is not a matter of construction but of engagement, not of building but of dwelling, not of making a view *of* the world but of taking up a view *in* it' (Ingold 1996: 120f.).

What view of God does this kind of understanding offer? How does it accord with the view of God offered by a hierarchical order of being? This will be considered in the next chapter.

12 The ordering of God

> To be, even for God, is to respond to all others and to have an effect upon all others. Thus God experiences the world's effect. Granted, to say this is to take the relational understanding of the world and to push it to its implications for the way God relates to the world, and as such, these statements, are necessarily provisional, like all generalizations. Yet what they indicate is consistent with a relational world, and therefore can be taken as legitimate speculative implications for our understanding of God.
>
> (Marjorie Suchocki 1994: 62)

Marjorie Suchocki's theological observation takes for granted a relational understanding not only of the world but of God, an understanding which presupposes that there is a relation between God and world, world and God. In Chapter 6, in the discussion of contingency, it was suggested that this could be seen as a relationship of love, with the world as subject of God's love and, therefore, God as the ultimate subject of the world's love. The nature of this love (other than that it is conditional on freedom) is not at issue here. It merely serves to highlight the fact that when God is defined as 'love', this presupposes that the relation between God and world belongs to the definitions or basic constitutions of God and world, and that without the experience of the effects of their love for each other, God and world would not be the same (Naess 1989: 28). In our own self-making, we are constituted by physical, emotional, social, cultural, expressive and religious recursive relations between us and our environments which affect both us and them, making us and them what we and they are. An autopoietic concept of God perceives God in this way also, as in some way constituted by God's relation with the world environment and its relation with God.

This means that as beings in the world, we express in the word 'God' a particular understanding of that world dependent on where we are in time and space, and that that situation shapes the words we use to describe our understanding of God. We have no others. To use Ingold's logic of language about nature, when we describe God's relationship with the world we inhabit, it is not a matter of taking up a view *of* that relation, but of taking up a view *within* it. There is no other place from which we can express such a view. The world has been, and is, integral to human expressions, verbal and active, conscious and unconscious, of perceived relationships between us and our environments, between them and us, and between us and God.

So descriptions of God as hierarch, as king, as father and ruler arise naturally in patriarchal societies. Descriptions of God as totally transcendent, inhabiting a changeless, unearthly realm, arise naturally in a culture dominated by neo-Platonism. It generates (as in Augustine) descriptions of the City of God as one of eternal happiness, in which necessity has no place, in which no lassitude slackens activity nor any want stimulates labour, and in which, 'along with other great and marvellous discoveries which shall kindle rational minds, there shall be enjoyment of a beauty which appeals to reason'. In this philosophical milieu, these descriptions conflict directly with descriptions of the earthly city. Its citizens do not know 'the Founder of the holy city', preferring their own false gods who are 'deprived of His unchangeable and freely communicated light' (Augustine, Book xxii, 30; Book xi, 1). This version of the binary code heavenly/earthly had a particular resonance for Augustine in 413. Just three years earlier the barbarians had sacked Rome, the city that some had thought would stand forever.

This conjunction of cultural, philosophical and political environments makes an important point about our descriptions of God and the world. They have a self-validating effect, that is, we tend to see or hear or express, from within our environments, whatever resonates with those descriptions. Furthermore, the descriptions themselves are validated because they shape our actions in ways which bring about what we believe, hope or fear may be the case (Bateson and Bateson 1988: 138). The fall of Rome validated Augustine's Platonic perception of God as one who transcends all worldly order, and at the same time, governs it. His description of the two cities validated his view of himself as one corrupted by original sin and therefore divided in himself between the two loves exemplified by the two cities: the earthly city as the love of self and the contempt of God; the heavenly city as the love of God and contempt of self (Book xiv, 28). For our descriptions of *how* God is perceived to relate to the world (and vice versa) can be seen, ultimately, as a matter of vital personal concern, one which shapes, and at the same time validates, certain interactions with our environments, and by doing so, validates our perception of ourselves. And in shaping our actions to correspond with that perception, they can also be of vital concern to those with whom we interact.

Moving on from Augustine and his episcopal response to imperial disaster, political reactions to natural disasters often display the same pattern of self-validation, both of one's view of God and of one's role *vis-à-vis* the disaster. The Great Irish Famine of 1845–52, for example, was seen by Sir Charles Trevelyan, British Chief Secretary to the Treasury and in charge of famine relief, as God's punishment on the Catholic Irish for their stubborn attachment to all the superstitions of popery. Ireland, for him, was a 'prodigal son', and God's relationship with the Catholic Irish was that of a father ready to starve his children into returning to 'authentic', 'true' Christianity (Primavesi 1997: 142).

In Trevelyan's case, such relational God-concepts validated certain relief policies which merely exacerbated people's suffering. These effects correspond to what I have called the 'function' of the word 'God', which, depending on the way in which God's relationship with the world is described, can be positive or negative depending on who is making the description and how it affects their actions.

Staying within the context of British nineteenth-century patriarchal society, to call God 'Father' validated, both for women and men, a whole raft of relationships based on an assumption of male social, economic, political, educational and religious superiority, which itself assumed, on the part of men and most women, the inferiority and consequent subordination of women and of nature. John Stuart Mill described women as existing in 'the primitive state of slavery lasting on through successive mitigations without losing the taint of its brutal origin, that is, the law of the strongest' (Mill 1869: 130f.). It made no difference, he said, that all men, except the most brutish, desire to have the woman most nearly connected with them not a forced slave, but a willing one.

I am concerned here to set hierarchy and hierarchical thinking within its historical contexts and to show it effective in different historic processes, rather than to show it as 'wrong'. I say this even though theologically it can never be right to abuse God, as it were, to validate abuses of power. But the impulse to do so will persist unless we realize some at least of the interactions between a theological *PoieticScape* and the power relationships within the *SocialScape* where that theology is situated. There are always assumed affinities between the 'power that moves men and the power that moves mountains'. If, like Mill, we realize some of the implications of these assumptions for those who suffer most from the abuses of power, then we may react positively against this kind of theological abuse.

Today, even given the rise of environmental and feminist consciousness, patriarchal theological descriptions still dominate the public Christian *PoieticScape*, east and west. God continues to be modelled on 'the great patriarch in heaven who rewards and punishes according to his mysterious and arbitrary will'; the one who demands 'dependent obedience' (Christ and Plaskow 1979; Holloway 1991). The theological task then becomes 'the liberation of God'. Is God free to be God: 'mysterious, awesome, and yet attractive and beckoning', the *mysterium tremendum et fascinans* of Rudolf Otto? (Otto 1958). Does this paradoxical God inspire us to interact with all living beings lovingly, justly and freely? Or violently, coercively, degradingly? Does this God leave the world, and us, free to evolve in our own way? For later examples in this chapter will show the sad truth of Lévinas' dictum, that an ontotheology which subordinates relationships with others to a relation with 'Being' leads inevitably to imperialist domination, to tyranny (Lévinas 1969: 46f.).

Hierarchical relations between God and world

In hierarchical ordering, God's constitutive relations with the world are described in terms of absolute power, of domination over the earth and all it contains. Therefore this God is the sole, the only one, since, being omnipotent, 'he' cannot have an equal. Monotheism and hierarchy imply each other. This divine monarchical power is unaccountable, unlimited, atemporal, unchangeable, and therefore, totally other than any power experienced or wielded by any person, or by any natural power such as that of wind, wave or fire. God as sacred ruler (hierarch) is 'outside', 'above' all those who claim power in his name. He reigns alone, and is therefore omnipotent, omnipresent, omniscient (and male). In classic Christian terms, formulated by Anselm, 'all necessity and impossibility is under his [*sic*] control' (quoted in Blond 1998: 208). There is no question of this God being affected in any meaningful way by any other being. There is no way in which the ontological gulf between them can be bridged or a reciprocal relationship with this God described .

Where did this understanding of God come from, and how has it functioned within the western world? Regina Schwartz traces it back beyond the neo-Platonist, theocratic formulations of Denys and Augustine, back beyond Paul's exhortation: 'Let every person be subject to the governing authorities, for there is no authority except from God, and those authorities that exist have been instituted by God' (Romans 13: 1), to the formation of identity in prebiblical societies. In those social orders, religious myths could be seen to mirror the social order or the sacral order design the state. 'Then too, figuring identity under a sovereign deity and figuring identity under a sovereign state could have a common source: some predilection for subjection, for imagining identity "under" ... ' (Schwartz 1997: 16). Schwartz here expresses succinctly 'top-down' interrelationships between God and world, and within the world, based on a predilection for ranking ontological and social order in a relationship of subordination to God's absolute sovereign power, seen as the 'top layer' of power experienced in that world. She also summarizes the validating effect of God's perceived sovereignty, validating the power of those with subjects 'under' them.

How does this affect those living in such a society, one determined by God's perceived relationship to them? Firstly, there is a transferral of ultimate responsibility for what happens in the social order to an omnipotent God seen as dwelling outside it. In this respect, God's omnipotence, or absolute sovereign power, poses particular problems for human freedom, not only by legitimating an abdication of responsibility for one's actions, but also by endorsing whatever authority is in power regardless of its behaviour. If God is supposed to decide everything which happens in the world, and someone enslaves or murders me, then it follows that God has decided that also (Hartshorne 1984). Our role is to be obedient to those in authority. This, we saw, is part of Keller's criticism of Augustine's attitude to Roman rule and its coercive power. This century, the same logic held in western fascism as it took hold in predominantly Christian patriarchal societies: in Germany, Italy and Spain. Its anti-Semitic aspect was ruthlessly endorsed in Catholic Poland where, even after the 'liberation' of the concentration camps and the disclosure of their horrors, the few Polish Jews left alive who returned to their homes found themselves subjected to such abuse and hatred that they were forced to return to displaced persons' camps in Germany (Belton 1998: 71–114). It is not accidental that it was a Jew, Levinas, who clearly discerned the implicitly tyrannical effects of Heideggerian ontotheology with its subordination of interpersonal relations to a relation with a 'Being' identified by Christians as 'their' God. The tragic irony here, of course, is that this 'God' was supposed to be the 'One' proclaimed by Jews and Christians alike (Lapide and Moltmann 1979).

The concept of divine omnipotence also affects our perception of the freedom of society, and of the world, to evolve in unpredictable ways. Yet, as we have seen in the discussion of contingency, a world without risks/chance is not now scientifically or philosophically conceivable (Hartshorne 1984: 12). Some of the reasons for this were mentioned at the conclusion of Chapter 6, where I defined contingency as predictable unpredictability consequent on the complexity of interactions in our world. Contingency offers us a world already constituted, but never completely constituted: in other words, one in which we see ourselves and other organisms not as predetermined (by God), but as free (within the limits of our structural couplings) to affect the evolution of that world, for better or for worse.

In Chapter 7, I claimed this limited freedom in respect of the responsibility we bear for the effects of present actions on future generations. This responsibility is knotted into our present and future relationship with others. It is not simply a matter of proximity in space, or in kinship (Lévinas 1985: 96f.). It is mixed into the composition of the earth, water and air we inherit and pass on to others. Jeremiah warns us that if fathers eat sour grapes, their children's teeth are set on edge. If we hand over responsibility for the effects of our actions to God, then we hand over accountability for the quality of our present relationships and their future effects, on the (sometimes voiced) assumption that God will intervene (or not, as in the case of the Irish famine) to prevent future generations suffering from them. Our freedom disappears in direct proportion to the totalizing of divine omnipotence. We are left with what Hartshorne, echoing Lévinas, calls a 'tyrant idea of God'. In contrast to this, he says, modern science shows us a paradoxical world which can be explained neither by pure chance (contingency) nor the absence of pure chance (Hartshorne 1984: 69).

Another feature of divine omnipotence is the assumption that an omnipotent God, who wields all power over the life and death of bodies, whether that of the earth itself, or of any other identifiable body on it composed of earthly material, has no body. The Christian appeal to the body of Jesus does not help, since the gospel accounts and ecclesiastical tradition teach that his body, life and death were also subject to the command or will of his Father's voice. This God is, and remains, only a voice: a disembodied voice recorded in stone (later shattered by men) or in texts (written by men); yet invoked by them as supreme judge in the court of final appeal. It grants, or withholds, life, fertility, and knowledge to our bodies, and can impose, or not, pain, exile, slavery and death on them. The voice of command is literally that – and nothing more. There can be no appeal, to compassion or to experience of suffering, against the edicts of that voice. It is the voice of reason, speaking from a realm beyond emotion, imagination or weakness.

> Let no one doubt
> that the god of the rich
> is unsullied transcendence.
> It has its residence
>   in the kingdom of 'other values'
>   totally spiritual
>
> It is the *divinum commercium*
> that can exist only
>   among entities
>   that are totally spiritual.
>
> (Assmann 1983: 210)

Finally here, this unearthly God, Ruler of the spiritual Jerusalem, is changeless. For time and consequent change is, as Keller pointed out, of the earth. God's relationship with the world, however, takes place outside time, in a 'changeless' zone. Therefore, since evolution is 'change through time', God does not evolve in any way which relates to our own evolution: to our own experience of life and death and the emergence of new life forms.

This problematic view, says Prigogine, was discussed by Aristotle, who opposed the principles of heavenly motion, such as immutability and determinism, to those involving a basic contingency which rule the sublunar, natural world (Prigogine 1989: 90). What Prigogine is questioning here, he says, is Einstein's God, the ideal of classical rationality, one who 'does not play dice'. The model Prigogine offers elsewhere, of a Talmudic image of God who has to, as it were, cope with the basic contingency of the natural world, and learns to do so after twenty-six failed attempts to exclude it, is in direct contrast to that of Einstein. This 'reparadoxized' God experiences the world's effect (Suchocki) and learns from it, if you like, that continuing existence (whether of God, world or ourselves) depends on contingency *and* immutability, on freedom *and* determinism. And as God learns from the natural world, implies Prigogine, we learn more about God's paradoxical nature.

Therefore, describing a relationship with God which does not allow for change, either in God, in us or in our theological descriptions, will not be taken as an authentic description in the world disclosed to us by modern science. Yet the presumption in traditional theology is that we are still bound by modes of address and theological descriptions which have lost their paradoxical nature. Behind this lies the further presumption that ideas and knowledge about God exist in a heavenly realm governed by classic rationality and unaffected by the evolution of ideas and knowledge about the natural world. The 'deposit of faith' is presumed sealed against time and its effects. And our own evolving *SelfScape* is discounted every time we are asked to step back into a theological *PoieticScape* dominated by an immutable, omnipotent God.

Similarly, our communal relationship with God is presumed to remain unchanged from schooldays to grave, as are the metaphors or prayers one uses. School hymns, dutifully sung by adult choirs, portray God as a father and us as his children, or as a king with complete control over everything ruling a universe which he has made by a word of command: 'the ultimate monarch at the top of the cosmic pyramid'. This 'kingafap' system (King-Almighty-Father-Protector), as theologian/hymn writer Brian Wren calls it, gives, he says, a distorted vision of God, one which supports male dominance through the hegemony of male God-language (Wren 1989). The refusal by many church institutions even to consider change in this patriarchal imagery can be seen, ultimately, as a refusal by them to accept evolution in God description: as a refusal to consider Christians as members of an evolving society affected by the evolution of knowledge. One of the most popular appeals addressed to God, *Abide with me*, runs as follows:

> Change and decay in all around I see
> Oh thou who changest not
> Abide with me.

From a coevolutionary perspective, we should at least be able to add:

> Change and new life in all around I see
> O thou who changes too
> Abide with me.

Hierarchy, however, is underwritten by what Schwartz calls 'inviolable transcendence'. Such a God cannot evolve, since evolution is essentially a vast, immanent, in part observable and in part disintegrative operation of interlocking changes. Every particular change, it is true, can be seen as an effort to make change unnecessary, to keep something constant in the face of change (Bateson 1991: 276). As Margulis remarks: 'we change in order to stay the same'. Which is one reason why the 'kingafap' system continues to entice the Christian imagination. It offers a God who cannot, or rather does not have to adapt to, take risks with and, ultimately, relate reciprocally to emergent forms within a changing world. Instead he [*sic*] can, and presumably did, inscribe an unchanging algorithm in the world whose divine purpose is our existence (Murphy and Ellis 1996: 202f.). The world and its life forms, it is assumed, could not have evolved in any other way, or to any other end. Such absolutizing of God's power, however, demystifies, desacralizes the evolving world. It remains the Augustinian *City of Man*, the earthly, decaying city through which we make our pilgrimage to the heavenly, unchanging Jerusalem where God walks on sapphire pavements (Exodus 24: 10).

Omnipotence and identity

What role does God play when Augustine's cities, epitomizing sacred and secular power, are related to each other? It is easy to imagine, as Geertz notes, that the secular 'city' has broken any ties with the heavenly one. Schwartz, however, shows that monotheism, and its correlate, divine omnipotence, is related to, and continues to foster and validate earthly notions of collective identity. Its central tenet, one people established under one God, binds the sphere of the sacred to that of nationalism, and hence to other collective identities. It is tragically the case that these identities have been, and are, largely fostered through violence, violence validated through descriptions of a God who, supposedly, perpetrates it on one people in favour of another.

She concentrates on various ways in which this identity was forged in prebiblical and biblical times, one of which was the violent cutting of covenants between absolute ruler and people. The Hebrew phrase, *karat berit*, literally, 'he cut a covenant', describes the institution of identity through violence. Animals are cut in two and fire passes between them; human flesh is cut at circumcision. The fact that severing an animal typically attended covenant ceremonies in the ancient Near East hardly helps, Schwartz remarks, to familiarize the bizarre passage in Genesis where God first makes his covenant with the father of the Hebrew people. A heifer, a goat and a ram are cut in two by Abram and the halves arranged opposite each other. When the sun sets and darkness falls, a blazing torch appears and passes between the pieces. Then God makes the covenant giving Abram 'the land of the Kenites, Kenizzites, Kadmonites, Hittites, Perizzites, Rephaim, Amorites, Canaanites, Girgashites and Jebusites' (Genesis 15: 5–21).

Ancient Israel, she says, is formed as a people and as a nation in this scene. It is instituted through servitude (to God) and subsequent freedom; through immense land acquisition (from other peoples); and in a narrative framed by the account of severed pieces of animals (violence commanded by God). 'Why? In ancient Near East rituals, the cut made to the animal is symbolically made to the inferior who enters into the covenant with a superior. ... Does "cutting a covenant" create Israel's identity or destroy it? Must identity be forged in violence?' She cites the biblical scene described in making the covenant at Sinai, where the covenant is cut in stone rather than flesh, as one where, as Rene Girard suggests, we might expect substitutive violence to be in full play. Instead, she says, 'the violence is not symbolized, it is literalized. And it is not deflected away from those who are part of this covenanting community, it is suffered by them'. After Yahweh's commands are written, Moses builds an altar at the foot of the mountain, and directs certain young Israelites to offer holocausts and immolate bullocks to Yahweh. He takes half of the blood and puts it into basins; the other half he casts on the altar. After reading the Covenant to the listening people, and their responding that they will observe it, he takes the blood and casts it towards them saying: 'This is the blood of the Covenant that Yahweh has made with you.' Not, Schwartz notes, this is the 'book' or 'words', but 'the blood'. And, she says, the blood that subsequently flows is not that of bulls. For when Moses comes down from the mountain he discovers the people worshipping another deity, in spite of the stipulation on the tablets in his hand that they must obey one exclusively. So he rallies the Levites to him: 'Whoever is for the Lord, come to me. ... This is what the Lord says: "Gird on your sword, every one of you, and quarter the camp from gate to gate killing one his brother, another his friend, another his neighbour" ' (Exodus 32: 26–8). About three thousand perished that day.

Schwartz points out that far from being a dead metaphor, 'he cut a covenant' is a loaded phrase, carrying all the resonances not only of making a covenant but also of severing it and being severed by it. 'Yes, Israel's identity is instituted by transcendent omnipotence, but that omnipotence threatens to destroy the very identity it is called upon to establish. God is both the guarantor and the threat to Israel. What was once the fragility of identity has become outright violence, a violence made explicable, perhaps even bearable, as the will of an omnipotent sovereign whose wrath could be managed through obedience' (Schwartz 1997: 16–34).

Schwartz is careful to point out that the Bible conceives of Israel's relation with God in diverse ways which broadly fall into two modes: that of negation, in which the Other (god or people) is rejected/obliterated, with identity negatively asserted and tied to rejection (Plaskow 1990: 96–107); and that of what she calls multiplicity, a logic which sustains contraries without obliterating them, which multiplies difference and keeps to the fore the provisional character of identity. In this mode, she says, Israel in opposition against not-Israel ends up being elaborated into a different understanding, of Israel not *against*, but *among* many nations. This she calls an antidote to the poison of 'identity-in-opposition'. It is the 'identity-in-difference' argued for in a coevolutionary theology; the acceptance of the truth of multiple perspectives based on the multiplicity, the plenitude of the mystery we call 'God'. If accepted, it would at the very least reduce violence perpetrated in the name of God.

Christianity and identity

I shall examine such a potentially positive relationship with God in some detail in the next chapter. The biblical record, however, as Schwartz points out, not only details vast numbers of peoples and animals obliterated in Yahweh's name, but also immense land acquisition. Both of these negative modes have marked Christian/western expansionism worldwide. Vast numbers have been obliterated/colonized/enslaved, and their lands acquired, in the name of the 'New Covenant' of Jesus' blood. This is the reality of 'identity-in-opposition' throughout western history, in which identities are seen to compete so radically that one must be exterminated in order to validate the other. Its 'mute ground' has been given a Christian male voice whenever power 'over' is inscribed as a theological notion, and so the deadly competition is surrounded by an aura of piety. Schwartz reminds us that the belief that collective identity is forged by a monotheistic 'covenant' *against* the claims of others to an alternative identity is loudly and eloquently proclaimed in the Scottish Covenants of 1638 and 1643, in the Covenantal Oath of the Afrikaners, and even, according to some interpreters, in the US Constitution. These are among the most explicit political heirs of this notion. Nor is it confined to Protestants. The proclamation of the Catholic Spanish Emancipation of the New World put the covenant to work in the demand that the Indians convert; that they recognize the Church as Mistress and Superior of the world and Universe, and the Supreme Pontiff as Superior and lord. *Or else*: 'I shall make war on you on all sides and in every way I can, and subject you to the yoke and obedience of the Church and his Majesty; and I shall take your wives and children and make them slaves' (Schwartz 1997: 25f.). Which they did.

Schwartz's in-depth discussion of violence perpetrated in the name of transcendent, omnipotent deity is careful, as I said, to offer glimpses of another vision of monotheism, one of multiplicity or plenitude; of a God of endless and inexhaustible giving. It is and always has been possible, as Willard Swartley shows, to validate the cases for and against war, slavery, Sabbath observance and a hierarchical interpretation of women and men's roles by using different biblical sources or interpreting the same ones differently (Swartley 1983). But as history shows, and Schwartz admits, the alternative vision of monotheism is difficult to sustain, caught up as it is in that dark universalism that turns other gods into idols (Schwartz 1997: 36f.). It becomes almost impossible to sustain when in colonization an identity negatively asserted is bound up with competing claims to possession of land.

In 1492, all non-Christians, that is, Jews and Muslims, were expelled from Spain and their land and property confiscated (unless they converted to Christianity). In the same year, Christopher Columbus set out, with the authority of the Christian King and Queen, the blessing of another Pope, and in the name of the cross, to conquer the lands and destroy the lives of other 'enemies'. Columbus wrote in his diary on the first voyage in 1492: 'Your Highnesses, as Catholics, Christians and Princes who love the holy Christian faith and wish to see it increase, and as *enemies* of the sect of Mahomet and all idolatries and heresies, have seen fit to send me, Christopher Columbus, to the said parts of the Indies to see … what way there may be to convert them to our holy faith' (italics added; Dussel 1990: 39).

While it is certainly true that the real motives for the conquest, as Enrique Dussel points out, may be traced to the economic and political expansionist projects of the trading powers in Christendom, this cannot cloak the fact that it was validated by Christian militarist categories of designated *enemies* – Muslims, heretics, idolaters. The genocide and abuse of indigenous peoples' bodies and lands which began in 1492 would not have been possible without an appropriate militarist theology, in which the physical military violence was accompanied by theologically violent language about the native peoples who, 'thanks to terror combined with preaching, received the Christian religion' (Dussel 1990: 61).

In an essay entitled *1492: The Violence of God and the Future of Christianity*, Pablo Richard cites examples of this militarist theology with its hierarchical ordering and its degrading and violent effects. It ranks 'barbarians', that is, the native peoples, as being 'as much inferior to the Spaniards as children to adults and women to men'. War against the indigenous peoples was just because they refused to accept the domination of those who are 'more prudent, powerful and perfect than themselves' and because 'matter should obey form, the body the soul, appetite reason, brute beasts human beings, the wife her husband, children their father, the imperfect the perfect, the worse the better, for the universal good of all things'. Western colonial Christendom survived, he says, not because of its credibility, but because it had the power to impose itself (Richard 1990: 59–67). That this violent power was bolstered by such hierarchical ordering is, as I said in the previous chapter, a major argument for consistent critique and replacement of that ordering.

Identity and land ownership

For theology from a coevolutionary perspective, one of the most important aspects of Schwartz's study of violence, monotheism and identity is her highlighting the fact that it delineates people as those who belong to a land, and that this is its deepest, most lasting and undoubtedly most troubling political legacy. She cites Bosnia as a place where people who conceive of themselves as having distinct identities lay claim to the same territory. This scenario was replayed in all its horror in Kosovo and East Timor. In Israel, political claims to the same piece of land are reinforced, for many, by the belief that their right to it is historical, ancient and divine. 'So achingly familiar, so ubiquitous, is the notion of possessing land, that it is difficult to call attention to how odd it is.' Imagine, she says, trying to explain to a civilization from another planet, who live on it without any urge to carve its surface into pieces and label and assign ownership to them, why we obsessively delineate territory, build walls and plant flags, no matter how small or large, fertile or barren the piece in question may be. Horrific acts of human violence have been and continue to be committed in the service of what is, after all, an idea: 'the notion that a "group" (an imagined community) must "possess" (how can land be owned?) a "piece" (note how the earth is imagined in pieces) of land' (Schwartz 1997: 40). And, of course, turn its indivisible benefits into those divisible among themselves.

This objectifying and commodification, expressed in the language of pieces, of possessors and possessed, reveals much about our relationships with land and its non-human inhabitants. Is this border-obsession, asks Schwartz, some extension of the borders of our personal identity? Is our skin not adequate enough border? With this, she takes us back to the concept of an autopoietic identity in which we cannot rightly view what lies beyond the permeable boundary of our skin as being something which belongs to us, but rather view ourselves as belonging within it. And from this perspective, can we claim to 'own' it? Does it not rather 'own' us? Do I not depend on it for the energy exchanges which fuel my metabolism? What, and who sustains my dwelling in a particular place?

Schwartz's own questions about land lead her to consider the role of what she calls the myth of scarcity in land disputes (as we saw in the case of water, one of the 'engines' of capitalist economies which drives its competitiveness). It rests on the belief that resources are scarce, that there is not enough land to produce the goods we need and so what land there is must be ruthlessly acquired, perpetually defended. 'But people do not possess land. Such a notion of land possesses them, for the land becomes soaked in the blood of the peoples who claim it. We cannot really own anything, despite (or because, since desire is propelled by lack of) the overwhelming desire to do so' (Schwartz 1997: 41).

And yet, she says, with more and less subtlety, biblical narratives fully elaborate the notion that a defining feature of a people is its divinely ordained right to land. With the dangerous consequence that an obvious threat to its identity is loss of that land. Precisely that fear drives the plot of the biblical narrative. But something else drives it as well and complicates the plot: a theology which says that an omnipotent God owns the land, and that it belongs to him to do with as he chooses. God has given but, as the story develops into one of exile from the land, it is obvious that God has also taken away.

How do the writers cope with this? They do so by keeping God's omnipotence intact, and investing everything in their faithful response to the divine will. And that will is that they should be a radically monotheistic people. Therefore as long as they cling to the one God, the land is theirs. Any betrayal of that God through pluralism, and the land is taken away. God's gift, and the generosity which inspires it, appears to be conditional: conditional on their obedience. 'Everything about the land – who lives on it, who tills it, whether it is watered, whether it yields its fruits – is divinely ordained' (Schwartz 1997: 44–47). On certain divine terms and conditions.

Despite this biblical obsession, Schwartz points out that the ancient Israelites did not invent the idea of defining a people by land, for it was part of the empire building – by the Akkadians, Amorites, Assyrians, Egyptians, Persians and Romans – which filled the theatre of the ancient Near East. It is also the case that the biblical writers included a critique of attaching land to identity, in an alternative vision of nomadism, a suspicion of settled agriculture, and even an idealization of wilderness. However, through the accidents of religious history, the aspiration of a people in exile to have a home has left a troubling legacy of belief in land entitlement as synonymous with the very will of God. His omnipotence offered some longed-for stability amid political and economic chaos, conditional, of course, on obedience to his will rather than that of an emperor. 'Fidelity to the one God persistently frames the discourse of land.' In the Hebrew narrative of Adam and Eve, instead of the later Christian stress on the sexuality of the original sin, the emphasis is on land, from the opening pun on man's name to the conclusion of the curse: 'from dust you were taken and to dust you will return'. (I have explored some of the pertinent implications of this narrative elsewhere. Primavesi 1991: 204–43.)

Here, with Schwartz, I want to concentrate on the perception that in this myth of human 'origins', we are seen as condemned to a general exile from a perfect land (Schwartz 1997: 48–54). This earth we now inhabit is, because of a primal act of disobedience, only second best. It is not where 'God' intended us to be. Its 'being' has no intrinsic worth, for, unlike Eden, God does not walk and talk with us here. 'Trailing clouds of glory do we come, from God above in heaven which is our home.' Wordsworth's *Ode on the Intimations of Immortality* expresses just one of the many subtle ways in which the exile motif reinforces an Augustinian perception of the city of man at an infinite distance from our 'home' in the city of God. And therefore, earth's continuing existence, and that of its non-human inhabitants, is not seen as a matter of ultimate concern to us. They 'belong' here. But we do not.

Schwartz brings us back to the effects this perception has had on some of the basic presuppositions of Christian colonization and its attendant violence, and consequently, to some of the most intractable political problems facing us today, when she says that defining identity in terms of land implies that either a people take land from another people (conquest), or the land is taken from them (exile). 'The logic runs something like this: because we were (or will be) made homeless, we can seize another's home; because we were (or will be) conquered, we can conquer.' Tragically, the peoples in question who inflict and therefore 'deserve' pain are rarely the same, but historical memory is so long and so dim that it is quite willing to confuse the identity of oppressors in order to allow the retributive process to proceed. Examples, alas, abound, from Northern Ireland to Africa to Australia. She cites a Lebanese guerrilla fighter who said in a recent interview that the Israelites had been his enemy for two thousand years, and a Serbian funeral oration which praised the deceased for dying for Serbia just as his ancestors had died in the battle of Kosovo Polje against the Turks in the fourteenth century. The real problem here, as I said earlier in this chapter, is that when the design and execution of this history is vested in a divine principle, when it is presented as the will of an omnipotent God who determines who shall live or die in the land, then responsibility passes, ultimately, from the Israelis, or the Serbians, or the Nazi guards, or Afrikaners, or the IRA, or the Hezbollah, or the KLA, to God (Schwartz 1997: 55–60).

The convoluted historical afterlife of the biblical narratives, both in their use by religious groups and their interpretation by scholars and preachers, is such that they have been appropriated for widely divergent purposes: to celebrate conquest *and* liberation from conquest. The consequences of overlapping and confusing the exodus and conquest paradigms are, says Schwartz, deeply troubling. She cites a Native American: 'As long as people believe in the Yahweh of deliverance, the world will not be safe from Yahweh the conqueror.' This disturbing fact makes some liberation theologians uneasy with the tendency to make the Exodus paradigmatic for liberation theology, for while liberation from slavery is a powerful model for peoples enslaved by economic colonization, it can also be made to justify retributive conquest and enslavement. The Voortrekkers of South Africa called their trek out of British-held territory, the proximate cause of apartheid rule, 'the Great Exodus'. Liberation and violence can, then, potentially at least, become inextricably linked, an important point in the Vatican critique of certain liberation theologies, although there, as I pointed out in Chapter 8, the violence is attributed to Marxist, not Christian, ideology.

Validation of suffering

Whatever the example of violence, and whatever its proximate cause, the 'disembodiedness' of God has the effect of distancing him from the actual suffering inflicted on bodies in his name; from the effects on them of human actions validated, ultimately, by invoking his power to inflict suffering for his own inscrutable purposes. (Although, as in Trevelyan's case, they have often been unhesitatingly interpreted to suit sectarian purposes, such as the return of the papist Irish to 'true', that is, evangelical Anglican Christianity.) His patriarchal image functions, or is made to function, in ways which distance him (and those who speak for him) from present earthly, bodily suffering, which is described by them as punishment for sin, for disobedience. His power to liberate us from slavery, from suffering, is made conditional on our behaviour rather than proceeding from divine integrity. In such subtle ways, God's image is reduced to one commensurate with human imposition of power over those subordinate to or weaker than their masters.

Does this image leave God 'free' to be God? I have been using patriarchal/male metaphors here, without qualification, since, as far as I am aware, this God is described in no other way. Usually, this image allows for no possibility, among the majority of those imposing the suffering, or among those observing it, of discerning God's presence among the sufferers. Which, in a liberation theology, is precisely where God is to be sought. But a God of unsullied transcendence, a disembodied God complicit with those inflicting suffering for some divine end, is 'above' all suffering, compassion, grief or any other emotion. This classically 'impassible' God closely resembles the God of global capitalism, wielding the 'invisible hand' of competition over 'free' markets and inflicting economic slavery on the majority of the world's population, apparently unaffected by the fact that the poorest 60 per cent of the world's population share just 4.5 per cent of the world's income, while 20 per cent of the richest share 83 per cent.

An alternative feminist vision

I shall conclude this chapter with Melissa Raphael's Jewish feminist theology of the Holocaust, one which has emerged from her desire to put aside what she calls childish but also very dangerous notions of divine omnipotence while holding on to a God who has point or purpose in the face of her people's suffering, slave labour and ultimately, mass death. She expresses, and sums up, better than any argument, what it means to believe God to be omnipotent, 'disembodied', distanced from bodies which are utterly degraded and so can be worked to death for human profit. These Jewish bodies, soiled, irredeemably material, were transported geographically and ontologically into the realm of the profane, processed into corpses – the primary product of the Final Solution – and then, secondarily, into soap and fertilizer. Her account is all the more valuable because she is not immediately concerned with the belief itself, or with its grounds, but with the possibility of theological responses from those who suffer its effects. What, or who can be God for them?

I cannot do justice to the complexity or specificity of Raphael's argument here, but will try not to oversimplify it either when I highlight some aspects of it pertinent to the discussion of a relational model of God and its effects. Focussing on the sufferer wrestling with the question of how, as a Jew, one could think about God at all within this most violent system of human relationships embodied in Auschwitz, she suggests that 'it was a particular patriarchal model of God, not God-in-God's self, that failed Israel during the Holocaust'. (She is talking here about a Jewish patriarchal model.) She wants to offer instead a model of relationship based on the recorded experience of some women's groups within the camps, a *PoieticScape* which conceives of God's redemptive presence in Auschwitz without divine or theological complicity with evil. She suggests that by means of their mutual care for one another, and for children, these women summoned Shekhinah (the traditional female image of the holy presence of God) into the very abyss of profanity. 'Because women are made in the image of God, Shekhinah suffered in the suffering of women.' So that what has been called the 'gender wounding' of Jewish women in the death and concentration camps was also a wounding of God. But conversely, that mutual care by which women restored the divine image to each other also restored God to God. 'For the erasure of the femaleness of God has divided God from God-self over millennia of patriarchal and religious domination.'

The historiography of Jewish women's experience during the Holocaust, a significantly smaller record than that of Jewish men, does not claim that the men's suffering did not, or does not matter to women, but that 'women suffered different horrors in the same hell'. Androcentric studies are oblivious to this shattering of something innate and important to women's sense of their own womanhood, shattered most cruelly in the forced gynaecological experiments and in the particular terror and grief of abortion, pregnancy and childbirth in camps and ghettos whose purpose and product was death. Against this background, Raphael makes use of Judith Tydor Baumel's study of the relationships between one particular group of ten women who, at great risk, sustained their relationship for two years and in three camps, Plaszow, Auschwitz and Bergen-Belsen. They did not limit their assistance to religiously observant women, or to those in their own group, but endangered their own lives to help women and children outside their circle. Such groups were not unknown among men in the camps, but the practical, domestic nature of women's reactions to extreme physical and emotional deprivation allowed their groups to develop more quickly and to be more stable than men's. They were permeated by 'the characteristically Jewish sense that the whole people of Israel bears responsibility for one another'.

Their mutual assistance, for Raphael, suggests a particular relational theology. As they were traditionally excluded from any role in public communal worship or in the study of Torah, they may, she thinks, have perceived themselves as in no need of a now doubly prohibited legal apparatus in order to remain close to God. Their quasi-maternal care for one another could remain a service not only to human beings, but through them, to God. They were willing, in the words of one of the group, to 'sanctify' God by 'adhering to our faith, by assisting as many Jews as possible and by remaining decent human beings'. This practice would have been grounded in a *kiddush hahayim*, the sanctification of God's name in life in community, or in this case, in the 'anti-community' of the camp. There, radical loss, physical debility and sadistic terrorization and cruelty rendered even the most ordinary act of human decency an extraordinary moral and physical feat, or quite simply impossible (Raphael 1999: 60f.).

For Raphael, their theology of mutual care and their preservation of their own freedom to act morally enacted a theology of Shekhinah, of a God who sets up her tent in our midst, wherever we may be; who, when the Nazis had destroyed the synagogues and homes of European Jewry, went with her children into the hiding places, ghettos and camps as a mothering presence. Raphael contrasts this with existing patriarchal Jewish models which, variously, offer Hitler, like Nebuchadnezzar, as the servant of God's will, that is, a new and vitalized form of Jewish existence. (Only a Jew, Ignaz Maybaum, could dare make such an analogy.) Or the God who 'countenances and executes unlimited suffering on his people in order to ensure the future of his own glorification through a resurgence of learning and observance of Torah' (Bernard Maza.) Or the one who, in the name of freedom, hides his face and turns away from the suffering ones (Eliezer Berkovits.)

Raphael does not intend to devalue all post-Holocaust patriarchal theology. Nevertheless, she says that it would make little sense for a feminist to attempt to reconcile God's supposed moral perfection with the facts of the Holocaust, or to ask God to stretch out his hand and do the sort of interventionist jobs that the patriarchal model of God failed to do in the Holocaust. It failed, she says 'because it *was* a patriarchal model, and therefore defined in such a way as to be incapable of surrendering certain divine rights, privileges and instrumentalist habits'. Such theology shares with all patriarchal ideologies the view that those devoted to supposed creative ends (whether those of the biblical God or of the Nazis), may deploy absolutely destructive means. Moreover, it shares with all oppressors the assumption that some human beings (whether women or indigenous peoples or Jews) are not entitled to the dignity of full subjecthood and free religious agency (Raphael 1999: 66f.).

In her theological exploration, Raphael discusses the objections that could be raised to her post-Holocaust theology of relation. The extracts I have given form part of an ongoing discussion. Their importance here is that they illustrate, as no argument could, the proposition of this chapter: that a God-concept which does not allow for reciprocal evolving relationships between God and the world is not only seriously, but dangerously, flawed. And following on from this, that the way in which we describe that relationship, and use that description to validate our lives and actions, will affect our self-making and our relationships with all other beings, either negatively or positively. And finally, that any God-concept which we use to exclude, degrade or deny value to the earthy substantiality of certain classes of being validates violence against them, and by extension, against the whole earth community.

13 Life as gift event

> I am the supreme and fiery force who kindled every living spark, and I breathed
> forth no deadly thing – yet I permit them to be. ... And I am the fiery life of the
> essence of God: I flame above the beauty of the fields; I shine in the waters; I
> burn in the sun, the moon, and the stars. And with the airy wind, I quicken all
> things vitally by an unseen, all-sustaining life. For the air is alive in the verdure
> and the flowers; the waters flow as if they lived; the sun too lives in its light; and
> when the moon wanes it is rekindled by the light of the sun, as if it lived anew.
>
> (Barbara Newman 1987: 69–70)

The twelfth-century abbess, writer and musician Hildegard of Bingen wrote this
hymn as part of a treatise entitled *On the Activity of God*. For her, this activity
encompasses the entire body of the universe and gives all things life, and she
personifies the activity here as Caritas, or divine Love: Caritas is 'God's love for
the world as well as the world's for God. She is the love that beckons us to
wonder but also the love that summons us to work' (Newman 1987: 79).

This lyrical theological description of the earth's life as wholly the work of
love seems remote (not only in time) from the description in the previous
chapter of 'the land given to us by God'. That view of the land came from those
to whom God gave it. For them, it confirmed that God was their deliverer. But
for those from whom it was taken, God was their oppressor. To some the gift
was a blessing, to others a curse. To some it brought life, and to others, death.

The ambiguity of the gift of land is tied to this paradoxical relationship
between life and death. The patterns of reciprocal relations between life, death
and land link them inextricably together. Our life, ultimately, depends on the
land. As does our death. Without land and its gifts of earth, air, water and
sunlight, there was (and is) no life, whether for the Israelites, their opponents,
or any other land creature. Hildegard's poetic theology makes the same point.
Life and land together can be seen as God's primary gift to us. But with it also
come 'deadly things'. I suggest in this chapter that human autonomy, no matter
how limited, plays an increasingly major role in deciding how and to whom
these deadly things come: how and with whom the indivisible benefits of
healthy soil, clean air and access to fresh water will be shared.

The nature of 'gift'

The primary ambiguity life/death is still linked to the idea of bestowal of gifts, although what God gives us has been narrowed down (through teaching that death came into the world through Adam) until 'God's gift' has become almost entirely identified with bestowing, or giving, life. The ambiguity was preserved in different Germanic languages where the German word '*Gift*' once meant both 'present' and 'poison'. Its reference to 'present', or life-bestowing, persisted in *Gift und Gabe* (presents) but has now become obsolete, so *Gift* is usually translated into English solely as 'poison' or 'malice', with a teasing reminder to English speakers of its obsolete usage because of its homophonic form. Marcel Mauss traces the double reference 'present' and 'poison' back to ancient German and Scandinavian 'drink-presents' where, in principle at least, the drink could be poison. There was always an uncertainty about the good or bad nature of the present because of uncertainty about the donor's intent (Mauss 1997: 30). In the last act of *Hamlet* a cup containing a poisoned jewel is offered by Claudius to Hamlet, and drunk in good faith, though to mortal effect, by Gertrude. Further south in Europe the Borgias too are credited (if that's the right word) with the possession of exquisitely crafted jewelled rings which could, with the flick of a finger nail, poison a guest's drink.

For a gift did not, and does not, stand alone in some relation-free zone. It always signifies some element in the relationship between giver and receiver. In the 'drink-present', every cup offered or taken was, potentially at least, a metaphoric 'poison chalice', with a high risk factor for the recipient (whether in accepting or rejecting it). This metaphor is routinely used today to describe political appointments, most often here that of British appointees to the post of Secretary of State for Northern Ireland. The recipient's vulnerability to the dangers of the appointment, together with his dependence on the goodwill of the donor, are all too evident. And in a relationship of dependence, that goodwill, or its absence, leaves open the question of whether or not the gift is intended as lethal (to the appointee's career) or life-giving.

Even outside the political arena the risk borne by the recipient is in direct proportion to his dependence on the donor's goodwill. This determines whether or not he will be harmed through the gift, or more precisely (since its appearance must, one might assume, be unthreatening for it to be accepted) through its unpredictable effects. Pierre Bourdieu has formalized these complex interactions between donor, gift and receiver in a model which reduces the event to a series of successive choices performed on the basis of a small number of principles which, with the aid of a combinatory formula, gives an account of an infinity of possible gift events. Phenomenally, they are as different as exchanges of words, objects or challenges. These proceed through a series of irreversible choices made by each participant, sometimes under pressure and often involving heavy stakes, even life itself, in response to other choices obeying the same logic (Bourdieu 1997: 193).

It is not surprising then, that from such an infinity of events the word 'gift' carries different nuances in different environments. It is clear, for instance, that in most Indo-European languages, the original sense of 'to give' is expressed in words which, depending on the context, may mean 'to take'. The gift may give life, or take it. The double possibility survives in English usage in the two opposed meanings of 'to take something to someone' and 'to take something from someone'. So 'to give' and 'to take' proclaim themselves as notions that are organically linked by their polarity (Benveniste 1997: 34).

These interactive relationships between giver and receiver, between giver and gift and between gift and receiver link them openly, materially, sensually, with the link made tangible (usually) in some object passed by one to the other, chosen by one for the other and received by one from the other. They are also (usually) linked privately and/or publicly in and across individual boundaries, through bodily, familial, political, emotional, sexual or economic relationships or contractual bonds. Strangers spontaneously giving gifts arouse suspicion rather than gratitude. An instinctive response would be on the lines of 'What's the catch?'

While real 'drink-present-poison' exchanges are no longer part of our cultural/political scene, the bond between giver and receiver is still marked by an asymmetry in power. The donor is assumed to have power to bestow something (or not) which the other lacks. When the gift is received, the perceived deficiency is remedied. If the gift could be given and is withheld, the asymmetry is intensified and the deficiency felt more deeply. If given, the receiver in some sense feels a need met by the other's generosity. The asymmetry between them creates and is experienced as a relationship of independence/dependence. With the receiver free to assert his limited independence only by refusing the gift.

This description of gift-giving provides an insight into the primary human experience of dependence: our own birth. We depend on another person to give us life, and once born, to sustain it. The gift presupposes a prior relationship: a physical coupling between a man and a woman. Even with the technologies of reproduction available today, the coupling of egg and sperm is (up to now) still needed, and both (unless human cloning is legalized) have to be donated. The mutual giving is embodied in the conception of a living being, culminating in its emergence as the mother 'gives' birth. And if we reverse the order and ask from whom *she* received the gift given her at birth, then a matrix of dependent/independent/dependent relationships appears which regresses almost to infinity. Or, on the basis of Gaia theory, to the moment when the first living organism emerged from its earth environment. It was that which 'gave' birth to the organism, and then, through inputs of energy, sustained its life.

Coming back to the present, or if you like, to the present moment in which the gift of life becomes present in every sense, we see that our life is still ultimately characterized by dependence. It is continually constituted by prior and present gifts which make our self-making possible: by gifts which presuppose and involve us in relationships with other people and with other organisms; with the air we breathe and the land we walk; with the food we eat and the love, joy and understanding we receive from others. Some of these gifts we hand on in modified energy exchanges. Some remain with us, becoming constitutive of bone and blood, of health or disease, of education and religion, of confidence or happiness. Every metabolic exchange contributes to these reciprocal processes. As does every autopoietic entity. Compounded of independence/dependence in relation to the earth, we act as givers/receivers in relation to it and to other living entities. Ultimately, however, unless we choose to assert our limited independence by refusing the earth's gifts, our dependence on them determines our life and death.

As I write this I remember a member of the Samaritans saying that suicide is often the only way in which some people feel they can assert their independence. And indeed feeling dependent is not generally felt to be desirable or healthy. Rightly so, since absolutized dependence is a pathological state. To a greater or lesser degree, this affects our perception of gifts, making it difficult (if not impossible) for some people to receive them graciously. They realize, consciously or not, that the asymmetry in power integral to the gift relationship does not allow them equality with the giver. Rather, it presupposes the opposite. Such an uncomfortable self-perception is customarily dealt with by countering the gift with another one, entering, as it were, into competition with the donor; the winner being the one whose gift outclasses the other.

This rejection of any appearance of dependence changes the character of the gift-giving. It turns it into a gift exchange, consciously or unconsciously excluding any acknowledgement of dependence. When gift exchanges become the norm, as they have done in affluent western culture, they signal a denial of dependence. Absolutized dependence in a relationship can, as I said, be pathological. But absolutizing independence as a defining feature of our interrelationships can be just as pathological. And today the pathology feeds into, and feeds on, a political, economic and social environment where 'dependence' on the state is synonymous with social stigma. In such a cultural climate, it becomes difficult if not impossible to recognize our dependence on the material environment, the land. This is seen by those living in the economic North not as a fact, but as a problem: not as a problem for them, but for subsistence cultures in the South. Those who live in the North assume they can simply exchange money for what they need.

For them, gift exchanges between 'equals' are the norm, with their 'equality' assured because it is assessed in terms of spending power related to the market value of the commodities exchanged. Gift exchange then becomes, in practice, another form of commodity exchange. Attention is focussed on the objects exchanged and their relative monetary or equivalent value, with the monetary value all important. The resources used to make the objects, whether labour or raw materials, are discounted. Advertising strategies present commodity exchanges as important cultural rituals at peak times in the calendar, such as Christmas. In this *SocialScape*, the relationship or bond underlying the gift is discounted, as is the real cost in resources. The price is what matters.

This form of gift exchange reveals its very concrete origins in those parts of the Indo-European world where slavery was the norm and 'value' was that possessed by a human body handed over for a certain price (Benveniste 1997: 42). The commodification of the human body endures today in the economic slavery of people whose self-respect, as Weil noted, is destroyed to the extent that they no longer count as persons, in their own or others' eyes. In her essay entitled *Women on the Market*, Irigaray sees our culture as one still based on the commodity exchange of women's bodies: one in which women's bodies are 'value-invested forms'; in which they derive their 'price' from their relation to the male sex; in which they relate to each other in terms of what they represent in male desire (Irigaray 1997: 174–89). Looking at multimedia images of women as 'value-invested forms', used to sell every type of consumerist commodity from cars to coffee, who can disagree with her? And whatever protests are made or heard about the commodification of women, those made about the rhetoric of commodification in respect to land and non-human species are met with indifference or disregard.

In this cultural climate, any feeling of dependence on the land and its gifts is excluded from our self-perception. Instead, the assumption of independence from the land leads to ever more agribusiness, ever more consumption, ever-increasing commodity exchanges, until we are told that the health of our society depends not on the land, but on 'consumers' who will, year on year, consume more and more of the land/ocean resource base. This attitude reverses the power relationship between us so that we assume that the land and its gift of life 'belongs' to us, a possession to be exploited, patented for human profit. And as we regard it as our possession, we feel free to exchange it and its resources for monetary equivalents.

The nature of gift event

These negative aspects of our relationships with the land reiterate a point made in many different ways throughout this book. Our descriptions matter. How we express our relationships reveals more than we can say, and the effectiveness of those expressions correlates in some way with our impact on the material environment. A *PoieticScape* in which the earth is described primarily as a resource bank for the human economy facilitates our treating those resources as commodities to be exchanged for our sole use and profit. Clearly, we need other ways of expressing our complex structural coupling with the *EarthScape*. In Chapter 11, I suggested symbiosis as a scientific model, one which allows for unitive, generative and generous qualities in the transformative interactions which constitute our *SelfScape*. The biological dynamics between microbes and plants from which symbionts emerge visibly embody their mutual dependence while preserving their individual character. The dynamics of this process can be seen as a series of continuous events in which organisms from distinct evolutionary pathways share their metabolic strategies, giving to and taking from each other what they need to sustain life.

Our lives too depend on such events, on such knotworks of actual giving and receiving in which what we give and receive from one another effects and promotes further life events. We too share and pool resources, and engage in mutually beneficial interactions. Hence Margulis' observation that from this perspective, as well as from that of our bacterial origins, 'we are all symbionts'. However, rather than simply adopting scientific symbiotic models for human relations, I want to build on the metaphorical cluster around 'gift' and giving, and describe human symbiotic interactions as 'gift events'. This allows me to stress qualities seen as specifically human, such as gratitude, generosity, imagination and the need to ritualize, which in some degree differentiate our structural coupling from that of other organisms.

In contrast to gift exchanges, a gift event is one in which if an actual object is given, its equivalent value in monetary terms is incidental to the value of relationship affirmed or established (Schrift 1997: 2). 'Gift event' focusses, above all, on the character of relational patterns in human liaisons and their positive and negative effects on our mutual self-making. Words like responsibility, commitment and dependence assume a new importance in this context. A gift event presupposes, for example, a conscious acceptance of and commitment to the fact that our lives depend on indivisible benefits, on our being given what we need to sustain life whether or not we can or do pay for it. And as those who give to us may or may not be the ones who receive from us, gratitude for what we receive becomes an appropriate and fruitful response.

A conventional model for a gift event is the practice of exchanging rings at wedding ceremonies. No one enquires about their price, for it is generally accepted that their value lies in the relationships they symbolize. Their circular shape is a symbol of a loving all-encompassing relationship without beginning or end. They signify too a continuing commitment by both parties to give each other every kind of 'good'. Both these characteristics are found in gift events. There is a cycle of cause–effect relationships (mini-events) of which the last, potentially at any rate, 'feeds back' its effect into the first; and the cycle is sustained through the mutual dependence and continuous generosity of those involved. Or sadly, it is destroyed by meanness or greed or pathological dependence on the part of any one of them.

There is an essential phenomenological aspect to gift events which reveals important interactions between *SocialScape* and *SelfScape* dimensions of our structural coupling. 'Gift' is an abstract noun or concept which need not refer to any particular thing. Concepts are essentially lifeless; tools of thought which allow us, implicitly at least, to separate the object designated as 'gift' from the 'event'. But it is the 'event', the *giving* by donor and recipient which constitutes the gift. It is not a gift until it is given. This phenomenological component, what happens between the donor and receiver, constitutes the gift as event. And the event cannot be abstracted from the relationships which it expresses, whether formalized or not. They determine its function: as 'present' or 'poison'; as life or death.

The same is true of 'life'. It too is an abstraction, a unifying concept imposed by us on the multiplicity of our lives. We only glimpse what it is, or might be, as we live it; particularly through our relationships with whatever it is which is keeping us alive. Or not. This vital distinction has been forcibly and memorably expressed by Arne Naess: *Life is wonderful, delightful, and fantastic; but to be alive is a completely different thing* (Rothenburg 1993: 38; original italicized).

I see a similar distinction to that between gift and giving, life and being alive, in Lévinas' critique of 'totalization' of 'Being' in ontotheology. He argues that the comprehension of Being in general (in the sense of defining it as a totality and exploring the logical/linguistic/expressive possibilities offered by the concept) can allow us to evade or to subdue the demand of the individual being confronting us. Ethics *'occurs'*, says Lévinas (Lévinas 1969: 45, 245; 1985: 12, 90). It is a qualitative component in an event, and does not occur outside events. Similarly to totalize or to try to comprehend 'gift' or 'life' in general, or to talk about them in the abstract, can be a way of evading or subduing the demands of giving to and receiving from individuals who are alive.

I am suggesting therefore that to talk about life as a gift *event*, with its effects lasting through time and space, does not allow me to evade or ignore the fact that other beings live well, or not, in part at least because of how I live and relate to them. They live healthily and happily, or not, because I try, or not, to live justly here and now. My weight bears down lightly or heavily on them through my ecological footprint. As I take less or more of my share of the environmental space available to me, I know that this means more or less for others. My living affects others and I am, in part at least, responsible for how it affects them.

To see life as a gift event is to see that I am alive because I am continuously gifted with what I need to live. I am gifted because other organisms and species have not evaded or ignored the demands I make on them. Ultimately, this fact does not allow me to evade or ignore my dependence on the earth. Or to ignore my responsibility to return it, at the very least, the gift of gratitude. This impulse to give thanks for the fruits and gifts of the earth has been the basis for religious rituals throughout the ages.

In an Orphic hymn to Nature used in ritual and sacred practice from at least 300 BCE to 500 CE, she is addressed as

> Goddess of earth, air and sea
> bitter to the worthless, sweet to those who honour you,
> all wise, all giving guardian queen of all,
> Bringing food, freely endowing us with ripening plenty.
> (Long 1992: 67f.)

A contemporary poetic example is Gary Snyder's *Prayer for the Great Family*. In a series of invocations and responses, he proclaims his gratitude to Mother Earth and to her Plants, Air, Wild Beings, Water, Sun and 'the Great Sky', acclaiming each for its particular gifts (Snyder 1974: 24–5).

In Judaism, the custom of blessing food before eating and drinking is a conscious affirmation of the bountiful blessings of the earth. Michael Lerner, writing on the need to update the Passover Seder to address the problems of the present moment, situates the blessing of the earth's vegetation within present ecological crisis. Seeing the earth not only as our sustainer, vital to our survival, but also as a sacred place, worthy of our respect and awe, he commits himself to saving the earth from ecological damage while thanking God for its beauty (Lerner 1992 : 508).

The Christian Eucharist (which literally means 'thanksgiving') again focusses on God's gifts symbolized in bread and wine. I shall comment on some aspects of the traditional Eucharistic celebration in the next chapter, but here quote a simple yet profound poem written in New Zealand and offered as a resource for worship in the World Council of Churches' Justice, Peace and Integrity of Creation programme:

> From air and soil
> From bees and sun,
> From others' toil
> My bread is won.
>
> And when I bite
> The soil, the air,
> The bees and light,
> Are still all there.
>
> So I must think
> Each day afresh
> How food and drink
> Became my flesh.
>
> And then I'll see
> The air, the sun,
> The earth, the bee
> And me, all one.
> (Orteza 1998: 21; penultimate line slightly adapted)

Scapegoats today

These religious expressions of what it means for us to be continually gifted with life and to respond to that gift stress the positive side of our receiving and giving, although their negative impact, as we see in Lerner, is never wholly absent from view. Indeed one particular religious use of the gift motif, rather than evading the painful ambiguities attached to life as gift event, makes it impossible for us to ignore them. It does this by personifying them in an individual, a scapegoat. The one chosen expresses for the community both its communal awareness of having been 'poison' for others, whether within or outside that community, and its desire to purge itself of that poison. It also expresses the fact that there are individuals or groups within the community to whom nothing but poison is given while every kind of sustenance is taken from them – hope, strength, happiness, family, even life itself.

In classical Greek *pharmakon* (gift) stood for both 'remedy' and 'poison'. Rene Girard focusses on a link between *pharmakon* and *pharmakos* (scapegoat/sacrifice), made possible (although Girard does not make the connection) by the commodification process of slavery in ancient Greek societies (Benveniste 1997: 37f.). There the distinction between person and object was annihilated, so that the designated *pharmakos* (scapegoat/gift) offered to the gods was an unfortunate individual. Sometimes a foreigner, sometimes a native maintained at public expense, this tragic individual was executed ritually, either at appointed times or in certain catastrophic emergencies. Girard describes these individuals as 'polluted objects, whose living presence contaminates everything that comes in contact with it and whose death purges the community of its ills'. He reads the Oedipus myth in this light, with Oedipus as an exemplary *pharmakos*: 'used as a kind of sponge to sop up impurities, and afterwards expelled from the community or killed in a ceremony that involved the entire populace' (Girard 1977: 94–6).

There are obvious links here (although again, Girard does not make them) with the story of Aaron, at God's behest, choosing a live goat (Azazel), and, laying his hands on its head, confessing over it all the sins of the people of Israel. Then the goat was led away into the wilderness 'bearing all their iniquities upon him' (Leviathan 16: 6–22). This passage is read each year in Jewish communities on Yom Kippur, the Day of Atonement.

In a passage read by Christians every Good Friday, the death of Jesus is configured according to the mysterious figure of God's suffering servant. He is a man of sorrows who has borne our griefs, been despised and rejected by men and smitten by God, who 'laid on him the iniquity of us all'. He is led like a lamb to the slaughter, cut off out of the land of the living and buried with the wicked 'although he had done no violence and there was no deceit in his mouth … yet he bore the sin of many, and made intercession for the transgressors' (Isaiah 53: 1–12). Paul applies this imagery directly to Jesus Christ, saying that 'for our sake, he (God) *made him to be sin* who knew no sin, so that in him (Jesus) we might become the righteousness of God (2 Corinthians 5: 21, italics added). These iconographies underlie Christian invocations to Jesus as 'Lamb of God, who takes away the sins of world'. And there is an enduring Roman Catholic link with the Roman *hostia* (a designated victim intended to compensate for the anger of the gods) in the Latin hymn *O Salutaris Hostia* addressed to Jesus in the Eucharist. It translates as: 'O Saving Victim'.

Girard makes an important and relevant point in respect to the Greek *pharmakos*. It had, he says, a dual connotation. On the one hand it was a woebegone figure, an object of scorn who was also weighed down by the guilt and sin of others; a butt for all sorts of gibes, insults and of course, violence. On the other hand, we find it surrounded by 'a quasi-religious aura of veneration'. This is very evident in the passage from Isaiah, in which the dreadful fate of the blameless victim will, in accordance with God's will, make many to be accounted righteous. He himself will see the fruits of his suffering and be satisfied, and God will confer on him a place among the powerful. This duality, this simultaneous presence of sin and goodness, violence and healing, punishment and reward, death and life, reflects, for Girard, the metamorphosis which the ritual victim is designed to effect. It draws to itself all the violence, sin and pollution infecting the community, and through its death transforms this baneful burden into harmony and abundance. It is not surprising, Girard concludes, that 'the word *pharmakon* in classical Greek means both poison and antidote for poison; both sickness and cure – in short, any substance capable of perpetrating a very good or very bad action, according to the circumstance and the dosage' (Girard 1977: 95).

These rituals, and the worldview which informs them, whether civil or religious, may seem far from those obtaining at the beginning of this Millennium. Yet the link between communities and scapegoats with their burden of sin, pollution and violence is still evident, even though today it would be called projection or transference. Scapegoats are routinely sacrificed in the media, the most common nominees being politicians, sports-people and television/film celebrities. Their number and the rapidity of their turnover cloaks their communal function.

But there are other living scapegoats in the world community today not readily discerned or acknowledged as such. They are the ones from whom everything is taken, everything needed to sustain life, and who receive nothing but poison in the form of poverty, pollution, commodification and death. Their presence reminds us of the painful ambiguities and knock-on effects attached to gift events, in which we may, or may not give others what they need to live; in which our greed makes lethal their dependence on us. Tragically, the magnitude of their numbers blinds us to their role and presence. They are the scapegoats for wars, for the arms trade, for the deforestation and despoliation of land which supports the capitalist economy and by extension, our consumerist lifestyles. They visibly bear the scars of pollution, violence and sin. Their identity is decided by a community who pushes them 'outside' its boundaries.

We see them in the countless refugees fleeing violence in Rwanda and Kosovo; in the tribal peoples expelled from their forest homelands; in the poor in the North and in the South living in environmental ghettos. And there are scapegoats beyond reckoning in the species crushed beneath the weight of our ecological footprint: decimated by forest fires in Borneo; by commercial overfishing in Antarctica; by pesticide saturation of farmland.

All of these bear not only the weight of violence and pollution, but also, as religious history indicates, they bear the marks of our sins. Unfortunately, they are not perceived in this way by many religious people. Once institutional slavery was abolished, in the form of buying and selling human bodies, the possibility of real scapegoating was assumed no longer to exist. But as previous chapters have shown, economic slavery, while its chains are not so visible, has been just as effective in reducing people to commodities. Now, in public at least, no one would dare call them an acceptable sacrifice to God. For now, as liberation theologians observe, they are sacrificed on the altars of Mammon.

The concept of religious sacrifice made to appease the gods, or at God's behest, was an intrinsic part of scapegoat rituals in antique religion. The story of Abraham's willingness to sacrifice his son Isaac, however interpreted, has close affinities with this tradition (Genesis 22). An allied theological factor has blinded Christians to the presence of contemporary scapegoats. As I said in the preface, theology has been constrained within the bounds of that history played out between 'Adam' and Jesus Christ. The historic sacrifice of the victims of extreme and sanctioned violence has been subsumed into the individual figure of Jesus, bearer of our sins and at the same time, of our righteousness. While this has been continually remembered and reenacted in Christian rituals, notably the Roman Catholic Mass, the tragic individuals in whose company he belongs have been lost sight of. On the scant historical evidence available to us, Jesus died as a victim of Roman militarism, a violent and cruel system of government which gave its citizenry the right to abuse, enslave and in certain circumstances execute its non-citizens – of whom Jesus was one. The account of his death has been taken as that of a once-for-all sacrifice, one in which Jesus, at some level, has atoned for all sin in a fashion which reconciles us with God once and for all. Liberation theologians have seen that by 'totalizing' Jesus the scapegoat, we are able to ignore and evade what his life tells us about the role of today's scapegoats in the systems of governance which we support and which support us. Lost too is their function in eliciting a sense of communal sin and repentance among members of the Christian community.

Sin is a theological concept familiar in western culture, assumed to be a matter between God and an individual (our *SelfScape*), or between one individual and another (our *SocialScape*). That personal concept of sin still holds true. What is less familiar is the concept of structural sin: sin which marks our structural coupling with all aspects of our environments and whose effects stretch beyond the individual into the very structure of our *EarthScape*. This extension of the concept, as we saw in Chapter 9, has come from theological reflection on findings from scientific socioeconomic and environmental analyses which focus on who is given enough of the earth's resources to live well. And if not, why not? Briefly, because the cycle of life-giving has been broken for the many by the greed and over-accumulation of the few. Out of these reflections have come such statements as: 'The poor person, the one who does not enjoy the fruit of his or her labour, is the manifestation of sin *in the system*. Sin, which is simply domination-of-the-other, is revealed when someone is poor. The poor are "the others" stripped of their dignity, of their rights, of their freedom, and transformed into instruments for the ends of the dominator, the Lord, the Idol, the Fetish' (Dussel 1984: 57).

As we saw in Chapters 7, 8, 9 and 10, one of the problems in dealing with structural sin is that we are all tight coupled with it through multiple interactions. There is no specific person (usually) to whom one can point and whose removal or repentance would remedy the situation. Nor need there be any specific intent to hurt anyone. Neither do the people within the system necessarily desire all its effects. 'It's nothing personal. It's strictly business.' Its impersonality means that violence and pollution are built into the system in which we find ourselves. 'I am entangled in it. ... We do not seek out for ourselves the society in which we live and the place we have in it, but are born into something which is already determined by the structures of sin, of separation from God' (Sölle 1990a: 55). And whether we are born in the South or in the North, the relationships between us are marked by the commodity exchange character of those structures.

This brings us back to the place played by 'land' in the gift event of life. It ties us, and our sins, into the whole structure of intricate relationships between people and the planetary *EarthScape*: into the globalization of trade agreements balanced in favour of the North and to the detriment of African, Asian and Latin American subsistence farmers. They, their families, their soil, their water, their plants, their livestock and their air are evidently our scapegoats. As are subsistence farmers in the North who struggle with the impact of agribusiness and its 'killing' of the countryside, its 'silencing' of spring. Rachel Carson saw that the logic of the gift is such that, by our lifestyles, we can and do turn the land to anti-gift, releasing its lethal potential not only against ourselves, but against all who share our life community.

How do we remedy this? The answer will depend on the environment in which we live, on the situation in which we find ourselves and how it affects our *SelfScape*, the personal, bodily dimension of our environment. Wherever we are, part of the answer will lie in a deepening sense of dependence on the gift events which sustain our lives. With this will go a deepening sense of the limited dependence of others on us for their life's sustenance. Who are the scapegoats sacrificed to my lifestyle? Who are those forced to give everything that makes life precious, even life itself, to feed my consumerist habits?

Such questions make us attentive to the complex interactions which sustain our energy exchanges, and to their potential for violence. As autopoietic beings we have freedom, limited it is true by the freedom of others, but freedom none the less to live as nonviolently as possible, to work for nonviolent movements and to participate in community and political initiatives which reduce consumption and pollution. Each of us, depending on our context, will have a particular focus: ethical consumerism and/or investment; restoring woodland or hedgerows; campaigning against the use of PVC in children's toys or against genetically modified crops. The list is as lengthy and varied as the issues are complex and interconnected, and the environmental sciences, together with environmental movements and justice and peace initiatives, offer models and opportunities for many kinds of 'work'.

In life as gift event, these practices cannot be separated in any real sense from one another. There is no absolute division between say, working for justice and peace within the human community and working for justice within the earth community. But there are certain specific areas, some of which have already been mentioned, in which theologians can work positively to reduce violence.

The first positive input would be a commitment to the truth of multiple perspectives about the subject of theology, God. This would mean that our understanding of God would be expressed descriptively, not prescriptively; in other words, that the models and metaphors we use to speak about God would be intended to demonstrate in as many ways as possible the truth of God's relationships with the world. They would not be intended to prove the absolute truth of one kind of relationship rather than another. This would also mean, ultimately, that the absolutist religious claims which in some respect underlie so many military conflicts today, whether it is Orthodox Christians against Muslims in Kosovo or Christian against Christian in Northern Ireland, would gradually lose their power to validate violence. This evolutionary development away from absolutist claims would gradually change the character of the functions we ascribe to God, as we become increasingly sensitive to the ways in which they validate violent action.

Positively too we can help cultivate Hildegard's insight that not only does God love and give life to the world, but the world loves and therefore responds to God. The profound relationship between them is experienced and expressed by every living being in its own fashion. The Gospel of Thomas has Jesus teaching this lesson:

> If your leaders tell you,
> *Look! This presence is in the skies!*
> remember,
> the birds who fly the skies have known this all along.
> If they say,
> *It is in the seas!*
> Remember,
> the dolphins and fish have always known it.
> It is not apart from you.
> It wells up within each and surrounds all.
>
> (Gospel of Thomas 3)

This insight into the relationship between God and the world increases our respect for the whole earth community, and by doing so, makes it easier for us to acknowledge our dependence on it. We can no longer pretend that the land belongs to us, and degrade it to a commodity. Rather, we come to see that we belong to the land. Neither can we treat 'life' as a patented possession. Rather it comes to be seen as the continuous, complex and mysterious interchange of gift events which constitute our being alive.

Setting God's relationship with the world within the largest possible context helps ground the notion of structural sin as violence against the earth community. Theologically, sin always implies a relationship with God. Therefore it makes sense of the notion of structural sin if we presume that there is, and always has been a relationship between God and the world. Then even if sin is still considered, as it has been throughout most of Christian/western history, as rebellion against God: 'Now it can be seen as unnecessary violence against any aspect of existence, whether through act or intent, whether consciously chosen or not' (Suchocki 1994: 17).

The historic figure of the scapegoat, laden with sin, violence and pollution, and condemned to die at the hands of the community, represents the ambiguity of life as gift event. The living scapegoats bearing that burden today do not allow us to exempt ourselves from responsibility for their deaths: for their living or dying depends on, and occurs within, the gift events in which we all give to and receive from each other. When we open our eyes to their presence, we see that these haunting figures have another ambiguous aspect. They also wear the aura of the holy, of the sacred, and so elicit, however inchoately, a quasi-religious awe and respect. That is the aspect of our response to them which I shall consider in the concluding chapter.

14 Sacred gift

> During the course of many conversations on 'the sacred' I came to a startling realization. The reason why a number of people so glibly label certain things 'sacred' or 'spiritual' or 'occult' is that in labelling that brief experience of such a feeling with those terms, they safely cut it off from daily life.
>
> (Dolores La Chapelle 1988: 128)

The adjective 'sacred' occurred in Chapters 11 and 12 in the discussion of hierarchy or sacred government, a system of order described by two Greek terms, the first, *hieros*, meaning 'sacred'. The system is based on a concept of power emanating from God the Trinity, a divine power seen to give life to each individual being. Hierarchical ordering of power has been institutionalized most effectively and comprehensively in Christian ecclesiastical structures and, as we have seen, has remained a potent force in western cultural perception of the roles and status of women and the earth. Sacredness, it is assumed, emanates from God and is primarily attached to power wielded in God's name. Those who wield it (and the places where it is wielded) become, as it were, sacred by association, surrounded by an aura of respect and awe most clearly seen today in that accorded to the Pope, patriarchs and bishops, and to church buildings. In a residual form, it still attaches to royalty.

What, we might ask, has such an image of the sacred to do with the desolate figure of the scapegoat? That is the question explored in this chapter.

The concept of the sacred

In spite of my reservations about the dangers of abstraction, it is necessary to speak here about 'the sacred' as a totality. For the most important aspect of the sacred, and the one I want to stress above all, is that it cannot be separated out from whatever we understand as the whole of existence. If it is separated out in any absolute sense, then it is no longer 'the sacred'. Adapting one of Hinkelammert's paradoxical formulations which will appear later in this chapter, we might describe the sacred as the internal transcendence of every living being. But as that cannot be divorced from the environments and events in which each being is interconnected with all others, then we cannot reduce the sacred to any one manifestation of being, but must extend the concept to the whole dynamic system of relationships between God and the world.

Within that system it is not possible either, in any real sense, to divide the powerless scapegoat from God's divine power. Both belong to the whole within which we exist, and to a sense of that whole which can only be perceived with awe. Having said that, Dolores la Chapelle's experience, which is by no means unique, raises a fundamental question: Why do we separate the sacred from daily life in any real sense? Which brings us back to another already posed: Why do we make distinctions between one person and another, one being and another, one place and another which, through binary codes based on a hierarchical system of ordering, devalues one in relation to the other? The answer which emerged was that having devalued one, we feel free to exploit it or destroy it.

A major task then for theology as an earth science is to resist any process or tendency towards such devaluation by stressing the connectedness, diversity and sacredness of all beings. Gift events between organism and environment connect us personally, interpersonally, communally, individually and systemically. At the same time, natural drift differentiates us one from the other. Each being does whatever it needs to selve, to be itself. This unity of life in diversity of beings is usually called 'biodiversity'. It holds life on earth in dynamic equilibrium, enhancing the potential for survival of new modes and forms of life through the generosity of gift events. Biodiversity is normally distinguished from numerical abundance as such, that is, the multiplication of similar entities, and is discerned at three levels now standard in environmental discourse: at the species level, at the genetic level and at that of the ecosystem. All are essential for the functioning of the dynamic system we call Gaia, which supports differentiation in life forms arising from natural drift *and* symbiotic fusions. Together with their environments they form the matrix which sustains the capacity for life within the world we inhabit (Primavesi 1998b: 47–59).

Dwelling as we do within this matrix, earth sciences help us perceive what to us is its paradoxical nature: its inclusion of the capacity for death as well as life. Theology as an earth science helps us sense this paradox as a whole: as a sacred whole. It opens us up directly to its mystery and to its reality. This moves us beyond satisfaction with intellectual coherence to the realization that the sacred gift event in our lives is not a once for all occurrence in a building or institution marked 'sacred'. It is revealed within the continuously evolving life-death-life relationships which sustain each *SelfScape*. And so it becomes as untenable theologically as it is scientifically to distinguish one person-in-environment from another in order to devalue or destroy its life. Releasing our *PoieticScapes* from such taxonomic restraints allows them to expand towards ever wider horizons. Eventually, this liberates the sacred from constraints placed on it by human logic until it encompasses the whole *EarthScape*. In theological terms, we give God room to be God: to be transcendent to and at the same time present within a world no smaller than the whole within which we exist; a whole which can only be glimpsed with awe.

In his dialogues with his daughter Gregory Bateson links that description of the sacred as 'the whole within which we exist' with another: 'that with which thou shalt not tinker' (Bateson and Bateson 1988: 148). He would not want to be more precise in his description, he says, because that would mean dissecting the whole in some fashion. Nor would I. For any question about the nature of the sacred which is asked, or answered, on the presupposition that 'the sacred' could be in any way 'tinkered with', that is, set apart from, or dissected out of the universe, would be, for him, and for me, a 'bad' question which would carry a bad answer. I say this in spite of the danger of 'totalizing' the sacred, since in our culture, as I said already, the opposite is the case. And if, as was proposed in Chapter 1, the horizons between the world described by theologians and the one disclosed to us by Gaia theory are to fuse, then theologians no less than poets (or theologians as poets?) must place a counter-reality in the scales of environmental discussion. Such would be an affirmation of the sacredness of the whole within which we have partial knowledge of God: as in a glass, darkly.

This is an important theological task today, not least because theological 'tinkering' has resulted in systemic theological apartheid. The range and influence of this system include the numerous codes by which we have segregated the human species from all others as uniquely capable of relating to God. I would also include hierarchical norms which have segregated some members of that species from all the rest and named them alone as mediators of the sacred. Within the Christian *SocialScape* one church community has segregated itself, or been segregated from another in the name of the God whose presence among them, it is claimed by each, makes their worship sacred.

This last point deserves special attention. Theological apartheid is both powerful and pernicious because it is validated and enforced in the name of God. God, it is assumed or claimed, has willed this segregation, and it is the 'mighty hand and outstretched arm of God' which wields the sword of separation. Once this function is ascribed to 'God', God can no longer be seen as related consistently and continuously to that whole which can only be glimpsed with awe, that is, *as sacred*. Ultimately, this segregates God from the One who 'laid the foundation of the earth; shut in the sea with doors and caused the dawn to know its place'. That God knows when goats bring forth young and has let the wild ass free to range the mountains. That God gives the horse his might and the hawk his wings. That God rebukes Job for 'darkening counsel' by using words which show no knowledge of what makes God, God (Job 38f.). That God is gift event within Gaia.

Theological apartheid blinds us to what human beings have always intuited as being essential to God: God must be God of the whole of time and space and all it contains; the One beside whom there is no other. Instead, theological apartheid constricts our vision so that we effectively narrow down God's function to validation of violence: violence inflicted by us on whatever it is we segregate out from the whole as 'non-sacred', as profane, because *we* regard it as distinct from all else. Or in a mirror image of this process, claim that whatever *we* have so distinguished alone deserves to be treated as 'sacred'.

The premise of apartheid, which is the superiority of one kind of being over another, makes the theological version as fallacious as any other propounded by men. It is falsified theologically because of the suffering it imposes in the name of God on those separated out on the basis of 'inferiority'. It is falsified further when it validates violence against God's gift to the world: the dynamic interactions and symbiotic relations between organisms and environments which sustain all life on earth. It is falsified scientifically when we realize that we are not in any actual sense superior to, but rather dependent on, other beings, including those not even visible to us: the micro-organisms whose ceaseless activity in the soil, the sediments, animals and plants is essential for the continued existence of life on earth (Lovelock 1991: 99).

There has always been human differentiation between parts and wholes, between one organism and another, one dimension of environment and another. It is part of our perception and expression of our own nature and of our interactions with other forms of life, as well as being the basis of modern scientific method. But it can only be differentiation within the whole. This is one of the aspects of Gaia theory which encourages scientists to engage in interdisciplinary research which itself recognizes that the whole is more than the sum of its parts. Similarly, discerning the sacredness, the wholeness of differentiated parts can be a unifying theological principle. All is sacred, or nothing is sacred. So when I put 'sacred' in front of 'gift', I am not choosing one type of gift – a certain book, a particular loaf of bread or plot of earth – to set it apart from all the others, or indeed from all our experience (and analysis) of an infinite number of gifts within the earth community. On the contrary, I am saying with Bateson, and with the Jewish women who, in the Holocaust, did not divide off the Shekhinah from the horrors of their life, that the sacred, as I understand it, is always related to, unifies and dwells in mysterious fashion within whatever event, experience or knowledge relates us to the whole.

This takes us back to the figure of the scapegoat and its ambiguous (to us) aspect. It is a contaminated presence, sopping up all impurities. But at the same time it is, quite rightly, surrounded by a quasi-religious aura of veneration. It is a polluted object, and at the same time a remedy for the community's ills. Poison and remedy cannot be separated out from it. And it is precisely this duality sensed by the community which makes them see the scapegoat as sacred *and* profane. Synonymous with the holy, it cannot be separated from its antonym without losing its paradoxical character.

Such a perception of the sacred is echoed in Dussel's impassioned claim that those I have named as the scapegoats of today, the poor, are the 'internal transcendence' (Hinkelammert) in the system which oppresses them. '*In* the system the only possible *locus* of God's epiphany is those who are non-system, what is other than the system, the poor. Jesus' identification with the poor (Matthew 25) is not a metaphor; *it is a logic*' (Dussel 1984: 57). But it is a paradoxical logic which forces those who claim Jesus as God to recognize the mysterious nature of that identification.

Because our knowledge of the whole is always partial, our expressions and descriptions of the sacred tend to partiality also. Therefore our sense of the sacred will always outstrip any logical descriptions of it we may give at any one time and in differing contexts. They attempt to hold in tension the ambiguity, the is/*is not* of divine presence. (I understand but do not agree with Dussel's dismissal of metaphor in this matter, but then I am working with a particular understanding of this language form.) Unless the tension is held and the ambiguity preserved, then God is portioned off, compartmentalized in some fashion – here, but not there, there but not here. 'The kingdom of God does not come because you look for it carefully nor does it come because they shout: "It's here!" Or: "There it is!" The fact is, God's kingdom is among you all' (Luke 17: 20–2).

One of the most effective tools for cutting the sacred off from daily life has been Christian binary codes. Overall, their separation of earthly, daily life from the heavenly existence which is to follow it has desacralized the gift events which support that daily life. Theologically, as I said, this separation corresponds to that made by Augustine between the earthly city and the heavenly city; between the love of self and the contempt of God; between the love of God and the contempt of self; or between 'natural' knowledge of God through the world and 'revealed' knowledge through Jesus Christ alone.

Such dissection has had disastrous effects on the Christian psyche (if one may so generalize), by definitively separating our mortal bodies, subject to death, from our immortal souls. It has also separated death from life, making death only a means to an end, which is life eternal. The sacred character of our present life, inextricably bound up with death, is lost. And as we are not given any reason to believe that any other species will enjoy eternal life, the sacredness of their present lives, and of their deaths, is all too easily denied.

Discerning the gift

Some of the effects of these defining codes appear in an instructive example given by Bateson himself of what happens when the sacred is 'tinkered with'; instructive in that it expands on what has been said about *pharmakos* and community. He looks at the fact that in the fifteenth century in Europe, many Catholics and Protestants were ready to burn each other at the stake, or were willing to be burnt, rather than compromise about the nature of the bread and wine used at the Mass. (There is a sad if twisted lineage connecting those burnings with the Catholic children burnt to death in their home in Northern Ireland by Protestants in 1998.) The traditional position (at the time the Roman Catholic position) was that the bread is the body of Christ and the wine is the blood. The Protestants, Bateson remarks, said that the bread is not the body of Christ – it *stands for* the body – and the wine is not the blood – it *stands for* the blood. The contested proposition, in terms of what was said about metaphor earlier, is that the bread is/*is not* the body, and the wine is/*is not* the blood. Just as the gift is/*is not* poison; is/*is not* remedy.

Bateson does not want to suggest (nor do I) that either the Catholic or the Protestant formulation is better than or more accurate than the other. I see both in terms of what I said about metaphor holding together paradoxical insights into the nature of reality. Therefore the dissecting of the paradox, its literalization by one side rejected in favour of a corresponding literalization by the other, has the effect (on both sides) of validating the consequent violence in the name of a 'dissected' God. It is a tragic example of what happens when, in Bateson's terms, we 'dissect' the sacred, or in Pauline terms, 'do not discern the (whole) body of the Lord'. It is a tragic and continuing example of theological apartheid made visible in churches built side-by-side to keep one set of believers segregated from the other. Inside them, a particular piece of bread or cup of wine is separated not only from that used next door, but from all other bread and wine (or other food and drink), while at the same time the claim is made that it alone is, or stands for the sacred body and blood of Christ.

Bateson views the problem as one mirrored in various pathologies of the mind which he studied over many years. There are in our minds, he says, various layers of operation. There is ordinary 'prose' consciousness, where what you perceive to be true is true in the sense in which you perceive it. The cat is on the mat if you see it there. That's the normal waking state for most of us, in which we also see that what we perceive can be a symbol, distinguishing between the actual cat's hunger and the symbolic cat on a petfood tin. This kind of consciousness, he says, resides in the left hemisphere of the brain, and there it makes perfect sense to say that the bread 'stands for' or is a symbol for the body.

But in the right hemisphere, in the part of our mind which dreams (or daydreams) you cannot draw those distinctions. There, the bread *is* the body, or it's irrelevant. In that place in the brain, there are no 'as ifs', and metaphors are not labelled as such. This, he said, is a major problem with schizophrenic people he treated over the years. They are, so to speak, more Catholic than the Catholics. In my terms, they absolutize the 'is' and erase the *is not*.

For him, the richest use of the word 'sacred' is that which will say that what matters is the *combination* of these insights. In other words, *at the same time* the bread *is*/is not the body of Christ. This keeps the paradox of God's presence intact. Any fracturing of the two is, shall we say, anti-sacred. It shatters our ability to sense the combination encompassed by the one word, sacred. The body of the *pharmakos*, bearing profanity, pollution and guilt, was sacred. The Jewish women in Auschwitz preserved Shekhinah by sanctifying life in death.

Bateson makes the apposite comment that the word sacred itself (like the word gift) is always 'two-sided'. The original Latin word *sacer* means 'both so holy and pure as to be sacred, and 'so unholy and impure' as to be sacred. Girard makes the same point about the relationship between violence and the sacred, an ambivalence which underlies most theological metaphors. So God is at once *fascinans/tremendum*, bewitching and enchanting/terrible and threatening (Trias 1998: 95–111). It is, Bateson says, as if there's a scale – on the extreme pure end we have sacredness, then it swings down in the middle to the secular, the everyday, and at the other end we again find the word *sacer* applied to the most impure, the most horrible. (This can be seen as analogous to the scale between life and death.) There is, he remarks, a notion of magical power implied at either end of the scale, and if the pure end is violated, disaster follows, so that the pure end confers not a blessing, but a curse (Bateson 1991: 265–9). This sense of power, of power over life and death or in life and death, whether or not it is dubbed magical is, as we saw in hierarchy, always attached to the sacred, and is evoked by (though not necessarily described as) that sense of 'internal transcendence' noted by Dussel.

In a fine example of paradoxical description, Bateson warns against invoking the disaster consequent on dissecting the sacred by advising us to keep the is/*is not* levels of the sacred '*not* separate, and *not* confused' (a piece of advice which echoes, for me, the fifth century paradoxical formula worked out at the Council of Chalcedon to describe the mystery of Jesus' incarnation as God/man). In regard to the fifteenth-century controversy between Protestants and Catholics about the bread and wine, Bateson implicitly rebuts the Platonic ontotheological presupposition of a hierarchical order of being when he remarks that the bread and wine *are* sacred objects, not because they represent the body and blood of Christ, but because they are the sustainers of life. So we can, if we wish, *secondarily* relate them to Christ (Bateson 1991: 270).

On this premise, I would suggest that when we reflect on the image of Jesus inviting us to remember him by taking bread and wine, blessing and sharing it, saying: 'This is my body; this is my blood', we look at that image in present time and understand the bread and wine as his body and blood because they sustained his life: just as food and drink now sustain ours. Without them, he would have had no body. Without them, we would not be here to remember his body in the present. The continuity between his life and mine lies ultimately in our shared dependence on the gifts given us by the land. I, like him, depend on earth and its photosynthesizing labours; on water and its cleansing power; on air and the chemicals it transpires; and above all, on the heat of the sun fuelling Gaian biogeochemical cycles. His incarnation, like mine, depended on all of these.

The Buddhist monk Thich Nhat Hanh catches this awareness of dependence perfectly when he says that looking at a plate of food, we see within it the whole universe sustaining our existence (Nhat Hanh 1996: 449). Similarly in the poem in the previous chapter the poet realizes that each day afresh, for each of us, food and drink becomes our flesh. The records we have of his meals teach us that in Jesus' eyes, there was no 'ordinary' food as opposed to that designated 'sacred'. All food and drink was blessed by him, as it is blessed today by every devout Jew. And when he shared it, he did not distinguish between those he gave it to on the grounds of their being sinners or righteous. Indeed, his table companionship was condemned by the religious authorities of his day precisely because he ate and drank with tax-collectors and sinners, an association which would have made the food, by association, unclean, unholy (Primavesi 1989: 25–58).

The sacredness of food and drink *as they are in themselves* gives them their life/death potential. The earth sciences deepen our understanding of them as sacred when they reveal the complex and diverse relationships between our food and drink and 'all that there is'. The sense of awe this properly deserves is, it must be admitted, a difficult sense to cultivate in today's fast food culture where the rituals of consumerism reduce food to something bought and consumed or sold and discarded, valued solely in monetary equivalents. The sense of awe is equally difficult to sustain when Christians use food and drink designated as 'sacred' as a means of segregating themselves from others, including other Christians who would, one might suppose, be eligible to share food and drink dispensed in Jesus' name. Sacred food and drink then functions as a way of distinguishing in order to degrade: or to grade one Christian 'worthy' as opposed to an 'unworthy' one. This can only happen when communities cannot accept the indivisibility of the sacred and the profane, of sinner and righteous, both in themselves and in the bread and wine before them. In short, when they cannot accept these as or with grace.

Gift as grace

The word 'grace', and its cognate 'gratuitousness', emphasizes an essential quality in gift events. When Regina Schwartz writes about the 'oddness' attached to possessing the land 'given' to us by God, the oddness is not attached to the notion of possession alone. A theology of 'land' as God's gift, but conditional on the Israelites' obedience, destroys the particular quality which makes it a gift: that it is unconditional, undeserved, and not necessarily reciprocated in any way, a quality summed up in the term 'gratuitous'. Anything else is not a true gift event. For no matter what asymmetry there may be between giver and receiver, one assumes that if it is truly a gift, both are free to handle it as they please. One does not 'earn' a gift.

Gratuitousness is the essential quality which lifts a gift definitively out of the realm of commercial or commodity exchange. There are certain qualities required of gift and giver to make it gratuitous. Firstly, the gift needs to be in some way precious to the donor, even irreplaceable. There must be no equivalent sought, or expected. Jesus observed and commended this type of gift event when the widow threw her farthing into the box of offerings. He was saddened when the rich young man proved incapable of it.

The giver must bring an even more extraordinary quality to the event. If there is to be a real gift, there must be no reciprocity, return, exchange, countergift, debt or feeling of debt. 'If the other *gives* me *back* or *owes* me or has to give me back what I give him or her, there will not have been a gift, whether this restitution is immediate or whether it is programmed by a calculation of a long-term deferral' (Derrida 1997: 128). It does not matter, says Derrida, whether the gift is good or bad. If something similar is returned, the gift is annulled. 'It is annulled each time there is restitution or countergift. Each time, according to the same circular ring that leads to "giving back", there is payment and discharge of a debt.' Derrida holds to this even though, he says, 'all the anthropologies, and indeed the metaphysics of the gift have, *quite rightly and justifiably*, treated *together*, as a system, the gift and the debt, the gift and the cycle of restitution, the gift and the loan, the gift and credit, the gift and the countergift'. Nevertheless he departs from this tradition and takes as his point of departure the axiom: 'There is gift, if there is any, only in what interrupts the system. ... For there to be gift, *it is necessary* that the recipient not give back, amortize, reimburse, acquit himself, enter into a contract, and that he never have contracted a debt' (Derrida 1997: 129).

And, says Derrida, it is necessary that the donor not recognize the gift as gift, lest even that symbolic equivalent to himself, of perceiving the intentional nature or meaning of the gift, annul it as gift. There is, he says, no more gift as soon as the other receives it, for if she keeps it as gift, if it signifies gift for her, there is no more gift (Derrida 1997: 130).

This almost inexorable extension of the notion of gratuitousness in gift event may well give us pause, even make us blench at its total demand. But I see that as its paradigmatic power, in that it makes us perceive and continually readjust the norm of what we may be capable of. It is a decisive counter-reality to that of commodity exchange, giving us room to go beyond the limits of the norm, in particular, the norm of monetary equivalence. Instead, it opens up the mystery of our continuous structural couplings with the material environment, most of which, for us, remain below the level of consciousness where they might signify as gifts. When have we heard the wind, sea, earth or water ask for a return from us? Or for a contract? But then when, for our part, have we 'gifted' them?

Looking for an image to illuminate Derrida's relentless logic, I find it in the example Bateson gives of what he calls 'religion/sacred/prayer'. He takes Coleridge's *The Rime of the Ancient Mariner*, and homes in on what for him is the fulcrum, the turning point of the whole poem. The mariner with the dead albatross around his neck, surrounded by the corpses of those who have died of thirst, watches the water snakes moving in tracks of shining white:

> Within the shadow of the ship
> I watched their rich attire:
> Blue, glossy green, and velvet black,
> They coiled and swam; and every track
> Was a flash of golden fire.
>
> O happy living things! No tongue
> Their beauty might declare:
> A spring of love gushed from my heart,
> And I blessed them unaware:
> Sure my kind saint took pity on me,
> And I blessed them unaware.
>
> The selfsame moment I could pray;
> And from my neck so free

The Albatross fell off, and sank
like lead into the sea.

(Coleridge 1970: lines 272–91)

Bateson is not suggesting that blessing the water snakes caused the rain that then came. That, he says, would be precisely secular logic (in our case, that of gift 'exchange'). What he suggests is that the nature of prayer, religion and, I would add, gift event, is that he blessed them *unaware*. If he had worked out how to get rid of his guilt by blessing the sea snakes, the albatross, remarks Bateson, would be hanging round his neck to this day (Bateson and Bateson 1988: 73f.).

Bateson calls this story a parable: a parable which is a sudden realization or discovery of the mystery of *life*. I take paradox to be the formal principle of parable, and Derrida formulates the paradox of the gift event as follows: 'For there to be gift, it is necessary that the gift not even appear, that it not be perceived or received as gift' (Derrida 1997: 131). One of the problems for those who analyze the 'logic' of this kind of giving is precisely this aspect of it: that it is, in fact, an antilogic. It is profoundly and radically antithetical to the prevailing capitalist logic which assumes investment for return and its accompanying structure of competitive accumulation. A true gift event, however, which actually constitutes our biological structural couplings, reveals relationships which neither call for, nor calculate, nor expect any return. Indeed, that is their very essence. Therefore they are viewed with incomprehension, suspicion and often, implicitly at least, downright rejection in a capitalist economy oriented toward ever-increasing return (for the donor/investor/trader) on any transaction. Commodity exchanges are based on the presupposition that at worst, you get an equivalent return in the exchange, and what you really expect is to get more than you give. The notion that something could be given without any return at all is, for most economists/policymakers/administrators, literally unthinkable.

This mindset has created a major policy logjam in the welfare systems of late capitalist economies. How do you deal with those in society who cannot offer any visible return in quantifiable, that is, productive labour with a monetary equivalent? For it is almost universally accepted that it is unacceptable to get no visible return for whatever 'benefit' is given them. Which is why the notion of indivisible benefits has all but vanished from public infrastructure policies and planning. Ultimately, a welfare payment is only seen as acceptable if it benefits, through those who receive it, the growth of the economy. Therefore we have 'workfare', 'jobseekers allowance' and other macroeconomic schemes which presuppose a return in the form of labour or tax. Otherwise, it is assumed, you do not deserve to be given anything in the first place, an attitude endorsed with the rhetoric of 'preventing the growth of a dependency culture'. This is, as I have acknowledged, a danger in gift events. But is there not a worse danger in creating an exchange monoculture dominated by one system only? Is there not, on the basis of our autopoietic interactions, the possibility of a diversity of exchanges?

The 'first' donor?

It is hardly surprising that secular theorists of the logic of gifts find it puzzling to account for gift events, above all to describe a primary event which gratuitously set the life cycle in motion. 'Why are there gifts at all?' Religions throughout the ages have discerned the sun as the primary giver in the life cycle, and expressed their awe and gratitude for the gift, and their dependence on it, in various rituals, some of which, such as human sacrifice, now appal us. But their discernment of the sun's leading role in the energy cycle of planet and organism was correct. There are, however, few religious sun worshippers in contemporary western culture, and the question of the primary giver or First Cause has, to a large extent, been subsumed into theology.

Theology would seem to have an advantage here, since it can simply answer that the donor is God. But what kind of God? How does God function within gift relationships? Schwartz's analysis, as well as the prevailing notion that God grants any gift – whether life, prosperity, children or health – only on condition that we abide by certain rules, shows that theological descriptions, and the prescriptions abstracted from them to validate certain kinds of violence, vitiates the grace, the gratuitousness which constitutes sacred gift. It loses the antilogic of the event.

Going back, however, to Derrida's formulation of the paradox of gift event, and Bateson's parable illustrating it, there are parables throughout Judaism and Christianity which express God's relationship with the world in antilogical terms. They shock us out of any complacency about our partial perspectives by setting them, and their validatory role, against a theological *PoieticScape* which foregrounds the gratuitous, unconditional nature of divine relationships with the world (Primavesi 1989: 44–58).

One such is a rabbinic parable in which God shows Moses the great treasure troves in which are stored up the various rewards for the pious and the just: in this place the rewards for those who give alms; in that place, for those who look after orphans, and so on. At length they come to a treasure of gigantic size. 'Who's this for?' Moses asks. God answers: 'The other treasures are rewards for those who deserve them because of their deeds; but this I give to those who are not deserving, for I am gracious to those also who have no claim to my graciousness, and generous to those who do not deserve my generosity.'

Elie Wiesel recounts an Hasidic parable whose antilogic runs contrary to every form of theological apartheid. A young Hasid, a follower of the great Maggid of Mezeritch, married the daughter of a fierce Mitnagged who forced him to choose between his family and his Rebbe. But after a few years he could not resist the impulse to visit the Maggid. When he returned his angry father-in-law marched him to the local rabbi for judgment. The rabbi consulted the *Shulkhan Arukh* and decreed that since he had broken his promise he had to divorce his wife immediately. The young man found himself on the street without any support. Inconsolable, he sickened and died. When the Messiah comes, the young man files a complaint against his father-in-law and against the rabbi. The former says: 'I obeyed the rabbi.' The rabbi says: 'I obeyed the *Shulkhan Arukh*.' And the Messiah says: 'The father-in-law is right, the rabbi is right and the Law is right.' Then he kisses the young man and says: 'But I, what have I to do with them? I have come for those who are not right' (Wiesel 1984: 125f.).

One of Jesus' parables mentioned already is that of the Last Judgment in Matthew 25, where the blessed are summoned to be with God and the damned sent to hell. The blessed are named as those who have fed the naked, clothed the starving, given drink to the thirsty and so on. They are amazed, and ask: 'But when, Lord, did we do this?' Like Coleridge's Ancient Mariner, they did it unaware.

Such parables are too uncomfortable for us to spend much time in them. But they transform our perspective on the sacred by using language to subvert the notion that any chosen description, distinction or translation, whether theological or scientific, can fully express the reality of 'all there is'. With this realization of limit comes the awareness that a God who eludes verbal categories has broken other bounds as well. The usual confines within which we place and then describe God are seen to be all on our side of the horizon. Paradox shows them up for what they are, and dismantles them sufficiently to give God room: room to be God of the whole earth system: enchanting and terrible, giver of life and death, not separate from and not confused with the world and its sacred gift events.

Bibliography

Abbott, W. M. (ed.) (1966) *The Documents of Vatican II*, London and Dublin: Geoffrey Chapman.

Agius, E. (1998) 'Obligations of Justice towards Future Generations', in E. Agius and S. Busittil (eds), *Future Generations and International Law*, London: Earthscan.

Allardt, E. (1993) 'Having, Loving, Being', in M. Nussbaum and A. Sen (eds), *The Quality of Life*, Oxford: Oxford University Press.

Assmann, H. (1983) 'The Faith of the Poor in Their Struggle with Idols', in *The Idols of Death*, New York: Orbis.

Augustine (1950) *The City of God*, trans. M. Dods, New York: Random House.

Balasuriya, T. (1984) *Planetary Theology*, London: SCM Press.

Barbour, I. (1992) *Ethics in an Age of Technology*, London: SCM Press.

Barr, J. (1992) *The Garden of Eden and the Hope of Immortality*, London: SCM Press.

Bateson, G. (1991) *A Sacred Unity*, San Francisco: HarperCollins.

Bateson, G. and Bateson, M. C. (1988) *Angels Fear*, London: Rider.

Batstone, D. *et al.* (eds) (1997) *Liberation Theologies, Postmodernity, and the Americas*, London: Routledge.

Beer, G. (1983) *Darwin's Plots*, London, Boston, Melbourne: Routledge & Kegan Paul.

—— (1986) 'The Face of Nature: Anthropomorphic Elements in the Language of The Origin of Species', in L. Jordanova (ed.), *Languages of Nature*, London: Free Association Books.

Behe, M. J. (1998) *Darwin's Black Box*, New York: Simon & Schuster.

Belton, N. (1998) *The Good Listener: Helen Bamber*, London: Weidenfeld and Nicholson.

Benjamin, W. (1997) *One-Way Street*, trans. E. Jephcott and K. Shorter, London and New York: Verso.

Benveniste, E. (1997) 'Gift and Exchange in the Indo-European Vocabulary', in A. D. Schrift (ed.), *The Logic of the Gift*, London: Routledge.

Bettenson, H. (ed.) (1963) *Documents of the Christian Church*, Oxford: Oxford University Press.

—— (1975) [1943] *Documents of the Christian Church*, London, Oxford, New York: Oxford University Press.

Blenkinsopp, J. (1995) 'Global Stewardship: Toward an Ethic of Limitation', in M. Ryan and T. Whitmore (eds), *The Challenge of Global Stewardship*, Indiana: Notre Dame Press.

Bloch, E. (1995) [1959] *The Principle of Hope*, Vol. 1, 3 vols, trans. N. Plaice, S. Plaice and P. Knight, Massachusetts: The MIT Press.

Blond, P. (ed.) (1998) *Post-Secular Philosophy*, London: Routledge.

Bourdeau, P., Fasella, P. M. and Teller A (eds) (1990) *Environmental Ethics*, Luxembourg: Commission of the European Communities.

Bourdieu, P. (1997) 'Selections From the Logic of Practice', in A. D. Schrift (ed.), *The Logic of the Gift*, London: Routledge.

Bramah, E. (1936) *The Wallet of Kai Lung*, Middlesex: Penguin Books.

Brandt Commission (1980) *North–South: A Programme for Survival*, A. Sampson (ed.), London and Sydney: Pan Books.

Braun, B. and Castree, N. (eds) (1998) *Remaking Reality*, London: Routledge.

Brubaker, P. K. (1994) *Women Don't Count*, Atlanta: Scholars Press.

Bunyard, P. (ed.) (1996) *Gaia in Action*, Edinburgh: Floris.

Capra, F. (1997) *The Web of Life*, London: Flamingo.

Capra, F. and Spretnak, C. (1985) *Green Politics*, London: Paladin Grafton Books.

Carley, M. and Spapens, P. (1998) *Sharing the World*, London: Earthscan.

Carson, R. (1955) *The Edge of the Sea*, New York: New American Library.

—— (1965) [1962] *Silent Spring*, London: Penguin.

Chapelle, D. La (1988) *Sacred Land, Sacred Sex, Rapture of the Deep*, Colorado: Finn Hill Arts.

Christ, C. and Plaskow, J. (1979) *Womanspirit Rising*, San Francisco: Harper and Row.

Chardin, T. De (1965) [1955] *The Phenomenon of Man*, London: Fontana.

Cohen, G. A. (1993) 'Equality of What?', in M. Nussbaum and A. Sen (eds), *The Quality of Life*, Oxford: Oxford University Press.

Coleridge, S. T. (1970) [1834] *The Rime of the Ancient Mariner*, New York: Dover Publications

Collingwood, R. G. (1960) *The Idea of Nature*, Oxford: Oxford University Press.

Curthoys, J. (1997) *Feminist Amnesia*, London: Routledge.

Darwin, C. (1985) [1859] *The Origin of Species by Means of Natural Selection*, J. W. Burrow (ed.), London: Penguin.

—— (1996) *On Evolution*, eds T. F. Glick and D. Kohn, Indianapolis: Hackett Publishing Co.

Dear, J. (1944) *The God of Peace*, Maryknoll: Orbis Books.

Derrida, J. (1997) 'The Time of the King', in A. D. Schrift (ed.), *The Logic of the Gift*, London: Routledge.

Devall, B. (ed.) (1993) *Clearcut*, San Francisco: Sierra Club Books.

Dowie, M. (1995) *Losing Ground*, Cambridge, Mass.: MIT Press.

Dussel, E. (1984) 'An Ethics of Liberation: Fundamental Hypotheses', *Concilium* 172, 2.

—— (1990) 'The Real Motives for the Conquest', *Concilium* 6, 30–46.

Dyson, F. (1992) *From Eros to Gaia*, New York: Pantheon Books.

Dyson, G. (1997) *Darwin Among the Machines*, London: Allan Lane, The Penguin Press.

Eliot, T. S. (1968) *Four Quartets*, London: Folio Society.

Elliot, R. (1995) *Environmental Ethics*, Oxford: Oxford University Press.

Ellman, R. (1987) *Oscar Wilde*, London: Hamish Hamilton.

Fisher, P. (1998) *Wonder, the Rainbow and the Aesthetics of Rare Experiences*, Cambridge, Mass.: Harvard University Press.

Fiumara, G. (1995) *The Metaphoric Process*, London: Routledge.

Fortey, R. (1997) *Life. An Unauthorised Biography*, London: HarperCollins.

Foucault, M. (1974) *The Order of Things*, London: Routledge.

Fox-Keller, E. (1983) *A Feeling for the Organism*, New York: Freeman and Co.

—— (1992a) 'Nature, Nurture and the Human Genome Project', in D. J. Kevles and L. Hood (eds), *The Code of Codes*, Cambridge, Mass.: Harvard University Press.

—— (1992b) *Secrets of Life, Secrets of Death*, New York and London: Routledge.

—— (1995) *Refiguring Life*, New York: Columbia University Press.

Franklin, U. (1990) *The Real World of Technology*, Toronto: CBC Enterprises.

Friel, B. (1981) *Translations*, London: Faber.

Frostin, P. (1988) *Liberation Theology in Tanzania and South Africa*, Lund: Lund University Press.

Galbraith, J. K. (1991) [1958] *The Affluent Society*, London: Penguin Books.

Galtung, J. (1982) *Environment, Development and Military Activity*, Oslo, Bergen and Trondheim: Universitetsforlaget.

Geertz, C. (1993a) [1973] *The Interpretation of Cultures*, London: Fontana Press.

—— (1993b) [1983] *Local Knowledge*, London: Fontana Press.

Gibellini, R. (1987) *The Liberation Theology Debate*, trans. J. Bowden, London: SCM Press.

Girard, R. (1977) *Violence and the Sacred*, Baltimore: Johns Hopkins.

Glick, T. and Kohn, D. (eds) (1996) *Darwin on Evolution*, Indianapolis: Hackett Publishing Co.

Grant, R. M. (1990) *Jesus After the Gospels*, London: SCM Press.

Gustafson, J. A. (1994) *A Sense of the Divine*, Cleveland: The Pilgrim Press.

Gutierrez, G. (1991) *The God of Life*, trans. M. J. O'Connell, London: SCM Press.

—— (1996) 'Option for the Poor', in J. Sobrino and I. Ellacuria (eds), *Systematic Theology*, London: SCM Press.

Hallman, D. G. (ed.) (1994) *Ecotheology*, Maryknoll, New York: Orbis Books.

Haraway, D. (1991) *Simians, Cyborgs, and Women*, New York: Routledge.

—— (1992) *Primate Visions*, London New York: Verso.

—— (1997) *Modest Witness @ Second Millennium*, London: Routledge.

Harnack, A. (1981) *Militia Christi*, Philadelphia: Fortress.

Hartshorne, C. (1984) *Omnipotence and Other Theological Mistakes*, Albany: SUNY.

Harvey, G. (1997) *The Killing of the Countryside*, London: Jonathan Cape.

Harvey, V. A. (1995) *Feuerbach and the Interpretation of Religion*, Cambridge: Cambridge University Press.

Heaney, S. (1995) *The Redress of Poetry*, London: Faber and Faber.

Helgeland, J., Daly, R. J. and Patout Burns, J. (1985) *Christians and the Military*, London: SCM Press.

Hessel, D. T. (ed.) (1996) *Theology for the Earth Community*, Maryknoll, New York: Orbis Books.

Hinkelammert, F. (1983) 'The Economic Roots of Idolatry', in *The Idols of Death and the God of Life*, New York: Orbis.

—— (1986) [1977] *The Ideological Weapons of Death*, trans. P. Berryman, Maryknoll, New York: Orbis.

—— (1997) 'Liberation Theology in the Economic and Social Context of Latin America: Economy and Theology, or the Irrationality of the Rationalized', in D. Batstone *et al.* (eds), *Liberation Theologies, Postmodernity, and the Americas*, London: Routledge.

Holloway, R. (1991) *Who Needs Feminism?*, London: SPCK.

Hopkins, G. M. (1930) *The Poems of Gerald Manley Hopkins*, London: Humphrey Milford.

Hynes, P. (1989) *The Recurring Silent Spring*, New York, Oxford: Pergamon Press.

Ingold, T. (1992) 'Culture and the Perception of Environment', in E. Croll, and D. Parkin (eds) *Bush Base: Forest Farm*, London: Routledge.

—— (ed.) (1994) *What is an Animal?*, London: Routledge.

—— (1995) 'Building, Dwelling, Living', in M. Strathern (ed.), *Shifting Contexts*, London: Routledge.

—— (1996) 'Hunting and Gathering as Ways of Perceiving the Environment', in R. Ellen and K. Fukui (eds), *Redefining Nature*, Oxford: Berg.

—— (1998) 'Culture, Nature, Environment', in B. Cartledge (ed.), *Mind, Brain and the Environment*, Oxford: Oxford University Press.

Irigaray, L. (1997) 'Women on the Market', in A. D. Schrift (ed.), *The Logic of the Gift*, London: Routledge.

Jordanova, L. (ed.) (1986) *Languages of Nature*, London: Free Association Books.

Katz, C. (1998) 'Whose Nature, Whose Culture?, in B. Braun and N. Castree (eds), *Remaking Reality*, London: Routledge.

Kee, A. (1990) *Marx and the Failure of Liberation Theology*, London: SCM Press.

Kellenbach, K. von (1994) *Anti-Judaism in Feminist Religious Writings*, Atlanta: Scholars Press.

Keller, C. (1996) *Apocalypse Now and Then*, Boston: Beacon Press.

Kevles, D. J. and Hood, L. (eds) (1992) *The Code of Codes*, Cambridge, Mass.: Harvard University Press.

Kumar-D'Souza, C. (1996) *The Universality of Human Rights Discourse*, A. Gnanadason *et al.* (eds), Geneva: WCC Publications.

Lapide, P. and Moltmann, J. (1979) *Jüdischer Monotheismus*, Munich: Kaiser Verlag.

Leakey, R. and Lewin, R. (1992) *Origins Reconsidered*, New York: Doubleday.

Lear, L. (1997) *Rachel Carson*, London: Allen Lane, The Penguin Press.

Lenton, T. (1998) 'Gaia and Natural Selection', in *Nature* 394, 439–47.

Leopold, Aldo (1970) [1949] *A Sand County Almanac*, New York: Ballantine Books.

Lerner, M. (1992) 'Critical Support for Earth Day', in M. Lerner (ed.), *Tikkun Anthology*, Oakland: Tikkun Books.

Lévinas, E. (1969) *Totality and Infinity*, Pittsburgh: Duquesne University Press.

—— (1985) *Ethics and Infinity*, Pittsburgh: Duquesne University Press.

—— (1996) *Autrement quiêtre ou au-dela de líEssence*, Paris: Kluwer Academic.

Lewontin, R. C. (1993) *The Doctrine of DNA*, London: Penguin Books.

Llewelyn, J. (1991) *The Middle Voice of Ecological Conscience*, London: Macmillan.

Long, A. (1992) *In a Chariot Drawn by Lions*, London: The Women's Press.

Louth, A. (1990) [1981] *The Origins of the Christian Mystical Tradition*, Oxford: Oxford University Press.

Lovelock, J. (1990) 'Gaia and the Balance of Nature', in A. D. Schrift (ed.), *The Logic of the Gift*, London: Routledge.

—— (1991) *Gaia, The Practical Science of Planetary Medicine*, London: Gaia Books.

—— (1995) [1988] *The Ages of Gaia*, Oxford: Oxford University Press.

Luhmann, N. (1986) *Love as Passion*, trans. J. Gaines and D. L. Jones, Cambridge: Polity Press.

—— (1989) [1986] *Ecological Communication*, trans. J. Bednarz Jr, Chicago: University of Chicago Press.

—— (1990) *Essays on Self-Reference*, New York: Columbia University Press.

—— (1994) [1982] *Liebe als Passion*, Frankfurt: Suhrkamp.

Madeley, J., Sullivan, D. and Woodroffe, J. (1994) *Who Runs the World?*, London: Christian Aid.

Margulis, L. (1996) 'We are All Symbionts', in P. Bunyard (ed.), *Gaia in Action*, Edinburgh: Floris.

—— (1997) *Slanted Truths*, New York: Springer-Verlag.

—— (1998) *The Symbiotic Planet*, London: Weidenfeld & Nicolson.

Margulis, L. and Sagan, D. (1995) *What Is Life?*, London: Weidenfeld & Nicholson.

Marx, K. *et al.* (1994) *Alienation and Social Criticism*, R. Schmitt and T. E. Moody (eds), New Jersey: Humanities Press.

Maturana H. R. (1987) 'Everything Is Said by an Observer', in W. Thompson (ed.) *Gaia; A Way of Knowing*, Great Barrington, Mass.: Lindisfarne Press.

Maturana, H. R. and Varela, F. J. (1998) *The Tree of Knowledge*, Boston and London: Shambhala.

Mauss, M. (1997) 'Gift', in A. D. Schrift (ed.), *The Logic of the Gift*, London: Routledge.

Mayhew, P. (1989) *A Theology of Force and Violence*, London: SCM Press.

McClellan, D. (1990) *Utopian Pessimist*, New York and London: Poseidon Press.

McKelway, A. J. (1990) *The Freedom of God and Human Liberation*, London: SCM Press.

Meeks, W. (1983) *The First Urban Christians*, New Haven: Yale University Press.

Merchant, C. (1980) *The Death of Nature*, New York: Harper and Row.

—— (1996) *Earthcare*, New York: Routledge.

Merleau-Ponty, M. (1996) [1962] *Phenomenology of Perception*, trans. C. Smith, London: Routledge.

Metzger, B. M. (1977) *The Early Versions of the New Testament*, Oxford: Clarendon Press.

Midgley, M. (1996) *Utopias, Dolphins and Computers*, London: Routledge.

Mill, J. S. (1970) 'The Subjection of Women', in J. S. Mill and H. T. Mill, *Essays on Sex Equality* (edited by A. S. Rossi), Chicago: University of Chicago.

Mill, J. S. *et al.* (1993) *Justice*, M. Fisk (ed.), New Jersey: Humanities Press.

Milton, K. (1998) 'Nature and Environment in Indigenous and Traditional Cultures', in D. Cooper and J. Palmer (eds), *Spirit of the Environment*, London: Routledge.

Moltmann, J. (1981) [1980] *The Trinity and the Kingdom of God*, London: SCM Press.

—— (1992) [1991] *The Spirit of Life*, trans. M. Kohl, Minneapolis: Fortress Press.

Moltmann-Wendel, E. and Moltmann, J. (1991) *God*, trans. J. Bowden, London: SCM Press.

Morton, N. (1985) *The Journey Is Home*, Boston: Beacon Press.

Murphy, N. and Ellis, G. F. R. (1996) *On the Moral Nature of the Universe*, Minneapolis: Fortress Press.

Myerson, G. and Rydin, Y. (1996) *The Language of Environment*, London: UCL Press.

Naess, A. (1974) *Gandhi and Group Conflict*, Oslo: Universitetsforlaget.

—— (1989) *Ecology, Community and Lifestyle*, Cambridge: Cambridge University Press.

Nash, R. F. (1989) *The Rights of Nature*, Madison: University of Wisconsin Press.

Newman, B. (1987) *Sister of Wisdom*, Aldershot: Scolar Press.

Nhat Hanh, Thich (1996) 'Earth Gathas', in R. Gottlieb (ed.), *Sacred Earth*, London: Routledge.

Nicholls, D. (1994) [1989] *Deity and Domination*, London: Routledge.

Nussbaum, M. C. (1995) *Poetic Justice*, Boston: Beacon Press.

—— (1999) *Sex and Social Justice*, Oxford and New York: Oxford University Press.

Nussbaum, M. C. and Sen, A. (eds) (1993) *The Quality of Life*, Oxford: Clarendon Press.

O'Connor, J. (1994) 'Socialism and Ecology', in C. Merchant (ed.), *Ecology: Key Concepts in Critical Theory*, New Jersey: Humanities Press.

Oelschlaeger, M. (1991) *The Idea of Wilderness*, New Haven and London: Yale University Press.

Oosterhuis, H. (1968) *Your Word is Near*, trans. N. D. Smith, New York: Newman Press.

Orteza, E. (ed.) (1998) *Five Loaves and Two Fishes*, Geneva: WCC Publications.

Otto, R. (1958) [1917] *The Idea of the Holy*, London: Oxford University Press.

Pannenberg, W. (1993) *Towards a Theology of Nature*, T. Peters (ed.) Louisville Kentucky: Westminster/John Knox Press.

Parsons, H. *et al.* (1994) *Ecology*, C. Merchant (ed.), New Jersey: Humanities Press.

Peet, R. and Watts, M. (eds) (1996) *Liberation Ecologies*, London: Routledge.

Plaskow, J. (1990) *Standing Again At Sinai*, San Francisco: HarperCollins.

Plumwood, V. (1993) *Feminism and the Mastery of Nature*, London and New York: Routledge.

Prigogine, I. (1990) 'Environmental Ethics in a Time of Bounded Rationality', in Ph. Bourdeau, P. M. Fasella, and A. Teller (eds), *Environmental Ethics*, Luxembourg: Commission of European Communities.

Prigogine, I. and Stengers, I. (1985) *Order Out of Chaos*, London: Flamingo.

Primavesi, A. (1991) *From Apocalypse to Genesis*, Tunbridge Wells: Burns & Oates.

—— (1995a) 'The Spirit of Genesis: Liberation and Environmental Theology', in S. Bergmann and G. Eidevall (eds), *Upptäckter i Kontexten*, Lund: Institutet for Kontextuell Teologi.

—— (1995b) 'Faith in Creation', in A. Race and R. Williamson (eds.), *True To This Earth*, Oxford: Oneworld Publications.

—— (1996) 'A Just and Fruitful Creation', in J. Rogerson (ed.), *Industrial Mission in a Changing World*, Sheffield: Sheffield Academic Press.

—— (1997) 'Earth the Original Ark', in H. Browne and G. Griffith-Dickson (eds), *Passion for Critique*, Prague: The Ecumenical Publishing House.

—— (1998a) 'The Recovery of Wisdom: Gaia Theory and Environmental Policy', in D. Cooper and J. Palmer (eds), *Spirit of the Environment*, London and New York: Routledge.

—— (1998b) 'Biodiversity and Responsibility: a Basis for a Nonviolent Environmental Ethic', in U. King (ed.), *Faith and Praxis in a Postmodern Age*, London and New York: Cassell.

—— (2000) 'Ecology's Appeal to Theology', in *The Way*, Vol. 40.

Primavesi A. and Henderson, J. (1989) *Our God Has No Favourites*, Tunbridge Wells: Burns and Oates.

Prins, G. (1995) 'The Challenge of Ecology', in A. Race and R. Williamson (eds), *True to this Earth*, Oxford: Oneworld.

Quarrie, J. (ed.) (1992) *Earth Summit*, London: Regency Press.

Rachels, J. (1990) *Created From Animals*, Oxford: Oxford University Press.

Rahner, K. (1978) *Foundations of Christian Faith*, trans. W. Dych, New York: Seabury Press.

Raphael, M. (1999) 'When God Beheld God: Notes Towards a Jewish Feminist Theology of the Holocaust', in *Feminist Theology* 21, 53–78.

Rich, A. (1980) *On Lies, Secrets and Silence*, London: Virago.

Richard, P. (ed.) (1983) *The Idols of Death and the God of Life*, New York: Orbis.

—— (1990) '1492: The Violence of God and the Future of Christianity', *Concilium* 6, 59–67.

Ricoeur, P. (1975) 'Biblical Hermeneutics', *Semeia*, 4.

—— (1984) *Time and Narrative*, Vol. 1, trans. K. McLaughlin and D. Pellauer, Chicago: University of Chicago Press.

—— (1986) *The Rule of Metaphor*, trans. R. Czerney, K. McLaughlin and J. Costello, London: Routledge.

Robb, C. S. (1995) *Equal Value*, Boston: Beacon Press.

Rogers, P. (1994) *Firekeeper*, Minneapolis: Milkweed Editions.

—— (1997) *Eating Bread and Honey*, Minneapolis: Milkweed Editions.

Rolwing, R. J. (1994) *Israel's Original Sin*, San Francisco: Catholic Scholars Press.

Rothenburg, D. (1993) *Is It Painful to Think?*, Minneapolis: University of Minnesota Press.

Ruether, R. (1983) *Sexism and God-Talk*, Boston: Beacon Press.

Ryan, M. A. and Whitmore, T. D. (eds) (1997) *The Challenge of Global Stewardship*, Indiana: Notre Dame Press.

Sampson, A. (ed.) (1980) *North–South: A Programme for Survival*, London: Pan.

Samuelson, N. M. (1994) *Judaism and the Doctrine of Creation*, Cambridge: Cambridge University Press.

Sapp, J, (1996) 'Symbiosis in Evolution: Cooperation in Conflict', in P. Bunyard (ed.), *Gaia in Action*, Edinburgh: Floris.

Schmitz-Moormann, K. (1997) *Theology of Creation in an Evolutionary World*, Cleveland Ohio: The Pilgrim Press.

Schrift, A. D. (ed.) (1997) *The Logic of the Gift*, London and New York: Routledge.

—— (1997) 'Introduction: Why Gift?', in A. D. Schrift (ed.), *The Logic of the Gift*, London: Routledge.

Schüssler-Fiorenza, E. (1994) *Discipleship of Equals*, New York: Crossroad.

Schwartz, R. (1997) *The Curse of Cain*, Chicago: Chicago University Press.

Segundo, J. L. (1985) *Theology and the Church*, trans. J. W. Diercksmeier, Minneapolis: Winston Press.

—— (1988) *An Evolutionary Approach to Jesus of Nazareth*, trans. J. Drury, London: Sheed and Ward.

Sen, A. (1993) 'Capability and Well-Being', in M. Nussbaum and A. Sen (eds), *The Quality of Life*, Oxford: Oxford University Press.

Snyder, G. (1974) *Turtle Island*, New York: New Directions Books.

Sobrino, J. (1985) *The True Church and the Poor*, trans. M. J. O'Connell, London: SCM Press.

Sobrino, J. and Ellacuria, I. (eds) (1996) *Systematic Theology*, London: SCM Press.

Sölle, D. (1984) [1973] *Suffering*, trans. E. R. Kalin, Philadelphia: Fortress Press.

—— (1990a) *Thinking About God*, London: SCM Press.

—— (1990b) *The Window of Vulnerability*, Minneapolis: Fortress.

Solomon, J. (1992) *Getting to Know About Energy*, London: The Falmer Press.

Song, C. (1988) *Theology From the Womb of Asia*, London: SCM Press.

Stone, C. D. (1987) *Earth and Other Ethics*, New York: Harper and Row.

Suchocki, M. (1994) *The Fall to Violence*, New York: Continuum.

Suzuki, D. and McConnell, A. (1997) *The Sacred Balance*, Vancouver: Greystone Books.

Swartley, W. (1983) *Slavery, Sabbath, War and Women*, Scottdale, Penn.: Herald Press.

Swidler, L. *et al.* (1990) *Death of Dialogue*, London: SCM Press.

Tannen, D. (1998) *The Argument Culture*, London: Virago.

Taylor, M. C. (1984) *Erring*, Chicago: The University of Chicago Press.

Thomas, L. (1974) *The Lives of a Cell*, London New York: Bantam Books.

Thompson, W. I. (ed.) (1987) *Gaia, a Way of Knowing*, Massachusetts: Lindisfarne Press.

Trias, E. (1998) 'Thinking Religion', in J. Derrida and G. Vattimo (eds), *Religion*, Oxford: Polity Press.

Trible, P. (1984) *Texts of Terror*, London: SCM Press.

Tuana, N. (1992) *Woman and the History of Philosophy*, New York: Paragon House.

Varela, J. F. (1993) 'Cognitive Science and Human Experience', in J. F. Varela, E. Thompson and E. Rosch, *The Embodied Mind*, Cambridge, Mass.: MIT Press.

Volk, T. (1995) *Metapatterns Across Space, Time, and Mind*, New York: Columbia University Press.

—— (1998) *Gaia's Body*, New York: Copernicus.

Wackernagel, M. and Rees, W. (1996) *Our Ecological Footprint*, Gabriola Island, BC: New Society Publishers.

Wakeford, T. (1999) 'Liaisons in Life', in *Gaia Circular* 2, 1, 7–8.

Walker, I. R. (1994) *Faith and Belief*, S. Thistlethwaite (ed.), Atlanta: American Academy of Religion.

Watts, M. (1998) 'Nature as Artifice and Artifact', in B. Braun and N. Castree (eds), *Remaking Reality*, London: Routledge.

Webster, R. (1995) *Why Freud Was Wrong*, Basic Books, New York.

Weil, S. (1957) 'La Personne et Le Sacré' in *Écrits de Londres*, Paris: Gallimard.

—— (1987) *Formative Writings 1929–1941*, D. Tuck, D. McFarland, and W. Van Ness (eds), trans. D. McFarland and W. Van Ness, London: Routledge.

—— (1990) 'On Human Personality', in D. McClellan, *Utopian Pessimist*, New York: Poseidon Press.

Welch, S. (1997) 'Dancing with Chaos: Reflections on Power, Contingency and Social Change', in D. Batstone *et al.* (eds), *Liberation Theologies, Postmodernity and the Americas*, London: Routledge.

Welker, M. (1994) *God the Spirit*, Minneapolis: Fortress Press.

Wengst, K. (1987) [1986] *Pax Romana*, trans. J. Bowden, London: SCM Press.

Wertheim, M. (1997) *Pythagoras' Trousers*, New York: W. W. Norton.

White, L. (1967) 'The Historic Roots of our Ecologic Crisis', in R. Gottlieb (ed.), *This Sacred Earth*, London: Routledge.

Wiesel, E. (1984) [1972] *Souls on Fire and Somewhere a Master*, London: Penguin Books.

Winch, P. (1989) *Simone Weil*, New York: Cambridge University Press.

Wittgenstein, L. (1961) [1921] *Tractatus Logico-Philosophicus*, trans. D. F. Pears and B. F. McGuiness, London: Routledge & Kegan Paul.

Wren, B. (1989) *What Language Shall I Borrow?*, London: SCM Press.

Index

absolutism and violence 165–6
Adam 14–16, 18, 39; and Jesus 38–9; his sin reappraised 20–1
Adam and Eve and land 148–9
Agius, E. 73
Allardt, E. 84–5, 105
anthropocentrism: preserves respect for life? 58–9; projected onto the non-human 56–7
antilogic in gift event 178
Assmann, H. 129–30, 142
Augustine: against Julian of Eclanum on death 38–9; earthly and heavenly cities 132, 149, 172
autonomy and dependence 17–18
autopoiesis 2–4, 17–18; and God concepts 153; its paradoxical nature 31
autopoietic entities: and environment 3; cells as 2–3; described 28–9; interaction between 3
autopoietic entity: Gaia as 5
autopoietic identity 24–5, 28
autopoietic interaction: discounted in Darwinism 109–10
autopoietic properties 28

Balasuriya, T. 96
Bateson: on tinkering with the sacred 170, 172–3
Bateson, G. 1, 27, 31, 46–7, 70, 77, 99, 113, 138, 143, 170–4, 176–8
Batstone, D. 95
Beer, G. P. K. 22, 38, 50–5, 118
Behe, M. J. 46
Belton, N. 141
benefits divisible and indivisible 112–13
Benjamin, W. 114

Benveniste, E. 156, 158, 162
Bettenson, H. 96
biblical world view 25–6
binary codes: in Christianity 66–8; prior devaluing in 128–30
biodiversity 169
Bloch, E. 69
Blond, P. 122, 140
boundary 2
Bourdieu, P. 155
Bramah, E. 113
Brandt Report 82–3, 87
Braun, B. 133
Brubaker, P. K. 128
Buddhism and nonviolence 17

canon: Vincentian 96
capital as object of theological reflection 102
capitalism: and liberation theology 106–7; as civil religion 106; its implicit use of God concepts 95–6; justified by a literalist stance on Darwinism 54–5; values humans as commodities 105–6
Capra, F. 2, 4
Carley, M. 87–8
Carson, R. 1, 11, 13–14, 33, 39–40, 44–6, 78, 127, 165; *Silent Spring* 33
Castree, N. 133
cell as autopoietic entity 2–3
chaos/cosmos 131–2
charity: and nonviolence 59; as action 64–5; of the imagination 64–5, 68–9, 88
Chartres Cathedral 72
Christ 20, 35, 38, 41, 44, 72, 106, 122, 127, 132, 162, 164, 172–4
Christ, C. 139

Christian absolutism 35–6
Christian binary codes: derive from hierarchical ordering 128; sacred/secular 172–4
Christian fundamentalism 45–6
Christian theological presuppositions: and the exploitation of nature 48; God became man (Incarnation) 40–2; humans uniquely created 39–40; man alone made in God's image 42–4
Christian theology: and evolutionary theory 37–49; its usual focus 18
Christian violence 38–9
Christian world view: alien to modern 89–90
Christianity: and the city 132–3; and the preferential option for the poor 106; its contribution to oppression 90; its evolution 15–16; its text-based nature 15; its view of Marxism 89–90
classification: determines relationships between human and non-human 52–3; of life forms 51–2; by nutritional modes 51–2
coevolutionary perspective: and structural coupling with environment 109; its effect on theology and science 45; on judgment 72–3; on justice 79–80
coevolutionary process 134–6
coevolutionary theology 36; and the intrinsic value of every being 126–7; its critique of hierarchical ordering 125–33; multiple perspectives about God 165–6; non-human world's response to God 166–7; sacredness of all beings 169
Collingwood, R. G. 134
commodification of humans 157–8
commodity exchange and gift event 177–8
commodity production: and the situation of producers 102–6; as object of theological reflection 102
commodity relations and Darwinian evolutionary theory 108–9
competition: Darwin's metaphor literalized into a natural law 116; implies endemic violence 116–17; liberation from 116–20; rules of 109–10
competition and cooperation 56–7, 117

conformity and self-making 113–16
consumerism 52
contingency: and hope 68–71; and unpredictability 65–6, 69–71
contingency, logical: coped with by using binary codes 66–8; 'deparadoxizing' 66–7; negates impossibility and necessity 66; there is no 'why' 66
contractual obligation and justice 75–6
cooperation and competition: in the emergence of life 17–18
cooperation as force in evolution 117–18, 119
cosmos/chaos 131–2
coupling, structural or tight 3–4, 24–5, 27, 82, 109–10; and poiesis 60; in reimaging the idea of nature 133–5; specific human forms of 158–9
creationism: and human evolution 18
Curthoys, J. 128–31

Darwin, C. 13–14, 30, 37, 39–41, 43, 46–7, 50–1, 53, 55–6, 58–9, 67, 69, 108–10, 113, 115–16; and androcentrism 50–1; and Marx 55; and natural selection 46–8; his Platonic schema 67
Darwinism: and environment 108–9; consequences of taking it as law 116–17; implications of as seen by Asa Grey 41–2; limitations of 108–10, 116; 'struggle for existence' 53–4; validating racist policies 118
death 21; as boundary dissolution 2–3; origin of 51; traditional Christian view of 38–9
debt and gift 175–6
deep ecology 43
Denys the Areopagite 122–3
dependence and autonomy 17–18
Derrida, J. 175–8
Descartes and the role of the imagination 60
Devall, B. 82
devaluing: the process of 34
Dickens, C. imagining a different *SocialScape* 63
dignity of all life forms 58–9; and respect for freedoms 59
distinction and differentiation: in religious discourse 65–8

distinguishing: to respect or to degrade 22, 34–5, 68–9
division or distinction? 32–4
doctrine: development of 39–40, 45–6
Dowie, M. 78
drink as gift, as poison 155
Dussel, E. 146, 164, 171, 172, 174
Dyson, F. 33
Dyson, G. 47, 62

earth: as a single evolutionary process 17; as a system 17
EarthScape: as context to meet needs 85; as resource base 84; human structural coupling with 158–9; missing from evolutionary descriptions 55–8; provider of quality of life 87–8
EarthScapes, SocialScapes, SelfScapes, PoieticScapes tightly coupled 91–2
ecofeminism: philosophical agenda of 34
ecological footprint 85–7, 102; and sustainable use of resources planning 86–7; as indicator of resource consumption 86; contrasted with environmental space 88–9
ecology and liberation 91–2
economic slavery and commodification of humans 157–8
Economic Structural Adjustment Policy 64
economic structures bring freedom, bring slavery 93
Elliot, R. 43, 48
Ellis, G. F. R. 124, 143
emotions: and reason 130–1; in science and theology 33–4
energy 82; access to its sources 83–5
environet 62
environment: and evolution 47; as *EarthScape* 9–12; as multidimensional 6–12; as *PoieticScape* 9–12; as *SelfScape* 7–12; as *SocialScape* 8–12
environmental degradation: those most at risk from 75–6, 107
environmental ethics 43
environmental interaction: energy extraction and absorption 81–3
environmental justice 77–9
environmental space 87–9, 102; contrasted with ecological footprint 88–9
eternal life and present lives 172

ethic of nonviolence 16–17, 19, 22–3, 64–5; as remedy for structural sin 165
ethics founded on distinction between human and non-human 43
eucharistic doctrines: and the sanctioning of violence 172–4; used to grade/degrade 175
evolution: a single process 2–3; and Christian faith 20–1; and environment 47; and immutability in God 143–4; and the emergence of humans 44–5; cooperation or competition? 108; from a Gaian perspective 16–17, 20; has no goal 46–8; implications of as seen by Asa Grey 41–2; of religious truth 39–40; patterns of 17–18; unveiling and revealing God 12
evolution and molecular biology 47
evolutionary descriptions: competitive individualism in 54–5; determined by anthropocentrism 53; omits *EarthScape* 55–8; their nature and function 50–9

farming practice, modern: Harvey on consequences of 72–3, 78–9
feminism 16, 43–4
fetishism: in Marx's analysis of the spirit of Northern institutions 102, 104–6; Marx's concept of 110
Fisher, P. 15
Fiumara, G. 60–3
food as grace 174–5
Fortey, R. 45
Foucault, M. 122
Franklin, U. 112
free market mechanisms: bring death 93
freedom 69–71; and respect for all life forms 58–9; as space for hope 70; to do no harm 73
Frostin, P. 106–7
future: consequent on present choice 72–3

Gaia: belonging to 134–6; natural drift and symbiotic fusions 169; place of humans in 14–15
Gaia theory 14, 18–19; and the intrinsic value of every being 126–7; and the sacred 171
Galbraith, J. K. 54–5, 110
Galtung, J. 5

Gandhi and nonviolence 17, 59, 64–5

Geertz, C. 7, 124–6, 144

gift: and debt 175–6; as grace 175–8; as life-giving, as poison 155, 161–2; discernment of 172–5; essential qualities of 155–8, 175–7; implies dependence of receiver on donor 156–7; relationship between giver and receiver 155–6

gift events: and land 165; express relationships 159; give and take in 155–6; human response to 159; nature of 158–61

gift exchange: commodity exchange 157

gift of earth: and life and death 156–7, human dependence on 156–7

gift of land: blessing for some, curse for others 154

gift of life 156–7

gift relationship: asymmetry of power in 156–7

Girard, R. 144, 162, 173

God: and suffering 150–3; and the Jewish Holocaust 150–3; as 'kingafap' 143–4; as changeless 142; as gift event within Gaia 170; for theologians in North, in South contrasted 93–107; from a Gaian perspective 12–14; omnipotent, disembodied, beyond suffering 150–3; origin of the concept of omnipotence 140; 'reparadoxized' 142

God and world 17; in dialogue 16

God as idol in hierarchical ordering 129–30

God concepts 17, 19; and autopoiesis 153; and evolution 143–4; and human self-perception 14; as liberating 100; function of 13–14, 90, 99–100; how can be used to sanction violence 13–14, 19, 48–9, 138–9, 170–1; in capitalism 95–6, 101–6; in hierarchical ordering 128; in Irish famine 138–9; in liberation theology 99–101; justifying suffering 150; no function outside relational fields 99–100; their emergence in liberation theology 97–8

God of life: and the idols of death 106; as understood by the poor 105–6

God, as primary giver 178

God's function: in capitalist societies 105–6; in the lives of the rich 102

God's gift to the world 171

God's omnipotence: and collective identity 144–5; and human freedom 140–3; and human subjugation 140–1; and unpredictable evolution 141

God's relationship with world 137, 166–7, 178–9; Augustine's view of 138; our language about emerges from 137–8

grace 175–7

gratitude in response to gift event 158–61

Gutierrez, G. 97–9, 105, 127

Haraway, D. 54–7, 92, 115, 118, 133–4; situated knowledge 92

Hartshorne, C. 140–1

Harvey, G. 73, 78

Harvey, V. A. 13

hierarchical ordering: modes of 126–8

hierarchical relations between God and world 140–4

hierarchy 121–2; and the Fall 123; its effects 122; origins of the term 122–3; within Christianity, devalues women 127–8

hierarchy as principle of order 122–6; and affinity between sacred and secular 124–5; and degradation of environment 128–9; and militarist theologies 146–7; condones violence 125–8; degradation within 125; effects of 129–30; enforces apartheid 125–6; Ingold's challenge to 134–6; Murphy and Ellis' perception of 124; within Christianity 127–8

Hildegard of Bingen: on the activity of God 154

Hinkelammert, F. 94–6, 98, 100–2, 104–6, 108, 125, 168, 171

Holloway, R. 139

Holocaust, the Jewish: and the sacred 171; and the Shekhinah 171; and women's experience of God in 150–3

Hopkins, G. M. 135

human and prehuman: no radical discontinuity between 16–17

Human Development Index 16

human genome project 57–8

human identity: forged through violence 144–50
human origins 17–19, 39
human self-perception 1, 2, 18–23, 57–8
human species and other species 40–1
human uniqueness 33–4
humans: alone created in God's image? 42–4; as autopoietic entities 28–9; distinguished by language 61–2; distinguished from non-humans by rationality 43–4; evolution of 44–5; our bacterial ancestry 17; perception of where we belong 149; still evolving 44; their status before God 17
Huxley and Kropotkin 117–18
Hynes, P. 78

identity: and land ownership 147–50; in difference, in opposition 145–6
idolatry in hierarchical ordering 129–30
idols of death and the God of life 106
imagination: a force for change 63–4; and emotion 64–5; and non-existent possibilities 63–5, 69; and the *SocialScape* 63–4
IMF, SAP, World Bank 74–5
immanence and transcendence 67
imperialism of North over South 92
impulse towards change 16
incarnation: and Gaian cycles 174; Christian doctrine of 40–2
individuals' response to environment 2
inequality: measured by ecological footprint 86; measured by environmental space 87; resulting from unchecked economic forces 83
inequality and quality 84–5
Ingold, T. 9, 15, 26, 29, 43, 51–2, 115, 122, 134–5, 137
intrinsic value 65; each being essentially ungradable 126–7
Irigaray, L. 158

Jesus 41, 42; and Adam 38–9
Jesus' identification with the poor: Dussel's logic of 171–2
Job: God gives, God takes away 67
judgment: present choice, future consequences 72–3
judgment, justice, and continuing growth 76–7

Julian of Eclanum: against Augustine on death 38–9
justice: and contractual obligation 75–6; and judgment 72–80; and power 74–5; and the whole earth community 19; and trade 74–5; as fairness 73–4; as loving attention 81; as nonharming 72–3; as nonviolence 81; between generations 73–4; done where no violence is done 73; environmental 77–9; from a coevolutionary perspective 79–80; North and South 81–92; Rawls' theory of 73–7, 84–5; Rawlsian theory presumes a competitive model 116; rights model of 74–6

Keller, C. 15, 21, 37, 45, 57, 132–3, 140, 142
kingafap view of God 143
knowledge: situated versus universalist 92
Kropotkin's reaction to Huxley 117–18

La Chapelle, D.: sacred and profane 168–9
land: as gift 175; its gifts of life and death 154, 157; ownership and identity 147–50
language: Lacan's 'circuit of' 37; stability and change 61–2; what happens when linguistic codes mix 27–8
last judgment 72
Lear, L. 40
Lévinas, E. 14, 70, 122, 139, 141, 160
Lewontin, R. C. 58
liberation: and ecology 91–2; and violence 149–50
liberation theology: and capitalism 106–7; Frostin's paradigms of 106–7; its agenda 94–5; its context 108–9; its critique of capitalism 98–9; its option for the poor 97–9
life: its emergence 17–18; what it means to be alive 14, 16
lifestyle: and Gaia 14; and theology 17, 19
Llewelyn, J. 110
Long, A. 160
Louth, A. 123
love your neighbour as yourself 110–11
Lovelock, J. 2–5, 16, 22, 33, 45, 171

Luhmann N.: 2, 8, 31, 48, 63, 65–70, 72, 90, 128; and the effects of binary coding 67–8; and the necessity of contingency 65–7

Madeley, J. 75
Margulis, L. 2, 4–6, 17–20, 22, 28–31, 45, 51, 82, 108–9, 119, 143, 159; her five kingdoms of life 51, 59
market economy and overconsumption 82–3
Marx, K. 53, 55, 90, 92, 100–2, 104–5, 110; and Darwin 55
Maturana, H. R. 1, 2, 3, 4, 10, 17–18, 24, 27, 30, 33–4, 47, 51, 56, 61, 82
Mauss, M. 155
Meeks, W. 132
men and God: in concentration camps 152–3
Merchant, C. 13, 121, 129, 131
metabolism 2; and boundary 2–3
metaphor: and literalization 30, 113, 172–4; and the function of paradox in 29–32; in Aristotle 62; paradox and *PoieticScape* 61–63; Ricoeur 62
metaphoric process: and emergent perceptions 62–3; makes for stability and change 61–2
microbes as agents of evolution 119
microorganisms and the well-being of all life forms 18–19
Midgley, M. 43, 75
militarist language in evolutionary descriptions 58
Mill, J. S. 139
Milton, K. 134
mimesis and poiesis 113–16; Aristotle's 115; 'go and do likewise' 114–15; in Ingold 115–16; Plato's 115
molecular biology and evolution 47
Moltmann, J. 125, 141
money as commodity 105–6
money-making: as object of theological reflection 102
monotheism: and divine omnipotence 140, 144–6; and land ownership 148
Monsanto 57–8
Morton, N. 125
multiple perspectives as viewed by Northern theology 96
Murphy, N. 124, 143
Myerson, G. 62

Naess, A. 16–17, 59, 79, 137, 160
Nash, R. F. 43
natural drift 46–8; in theology 48–9
natural selection or natural drift? 46–9
Nature: as female 121; as not sacred 48–9; 'first', 'second', 'third' 133–4; her face and Darwin's wedges 13–14
Nature redefined 133–4
Nature reimagined: using autopoietic theory 133–5
Neoplatonism 122–3, 128, 130, 134–5, 138, 140
Newman, B. 154
Nicholls, D. 125
nonviolence 16–17, 19, 22–3, 64–5; as remedy for structural sin 165
North as industrialized market economy 83
Nussbaum, M. C. 16, 63–5, 69, 79, 84; imagination as force for social change 63–5

ontology 121–2
ontology and theology 122
ontotheology 122; and Christian binary codes 128
organism: and environment 3–4; as autopoietic system 28–29
organisms 15–21; human relationship to 16–19; plants and animals distinguishable? 15–16; relationship of each to God according to its kind 19–20; their multifaceted reality 15–16
original sin 20–1, 35
Otto, R. 139
overconsumption 82–3

Pannenberg, W. 13, 70
parable of the Great Treasure 178
parable of the Hasid and the Messiah 178–9
parable of the Last Judgment 179
paradox 29–32; as the power behind metaphor 30; in theology 31
partiality as unavoidable 31–2
Peet, R. 91–2
perception: as response to environment 2; how possible? 1, 2
pharmakos in classical Greek 162–3
Plaskow, J. 139, 145
Platonic schema 31, 50–3, 56–7, 67, 70–1, 115, 121–2, 130, 134–5, 174

Plumwood, V. 34, 128–9

poiesis: the imaginative element in structural coupling 60

poiesis and mimesis 113–16

PoieticScape: and metaphor 61–3; as aspect of environment 91; coupling organism to environment 60–1; Descartes 60; descriptions matter 158; Fiumara 60–1; its evolution 24–8; many dimensioned 91–2; Maturana and Varela 61; Ricoeur 60–2; Weil 60

PoieticScape, theological: interaction with power relationships of *SocialScape* 139

PoieticScapes of the North: bring death 93

PoieticScapes, EarthScapes, SocialScapes, SelfScapes tightly coupled 91–2

preferential option for the poor 97–9; and capitalism 106–7; in conflict with the logic of capitalist structures 100–1; Vatican response to 100–1

Prigogine, I. 12, 32, 43, 61, 70–1, 142

Primavesi, A. 1, 12, 22, 29, 33–4, 38, 41, 44, 57, 87, 123, 125, 128–9, 131, 133, 138, 149, 169, 174, 178

quality and inequality 84–5

quality of life: having, loving, being 84; how to achieve it 87–8

Rachels, J. 42, 43, 55, 56, 59, 118

rationality 43–4

rationality bounded 32

reality mapping 14–15

reason and emotion 130–1

redemption 35; and Nature 20–1

Rees, W. 85–6

resource use: measured by ecological footprint 86; measured by environmental space 87

respect in science and theology 33–4

revelation 21, 35, 44–5, 46, 172; Christian 89, 121–2; dependent on distinguishing sacred from profane 68; doctrine of 40–1; within hierarchical ordering 123

Richard, P. 91, 147

Ricoeur, P. 30, 60–3, 113–15

rights model of justice 74–6

Rime of the Ancient Mariner 176–7

Robb, C. S. 128

Rogers, P. 24, 26–7, 29, 49, 51, 59, 63

Rothenburg, D. 160

Ruether, R. 125

rules: consequences for when based on metaphor 113–15

Ryan, M. A. 57, 93

Rydin, Y. 62

sacred: and Gaia theory 171; and the scapegoat 169; concept of 168–72; consequences of its dissection 173; its Latin roots 173–4; relationship between God and world 168–9; the whole in which all exist 170

sacredness: and differentiation 171; of eucharistic elements 174–5; of food 174–5

salvation history 21–2

Samuelson, N. M. 31

SAP, IMF, World Bank 74–5

scapegoats 161–7; in Christianity 162, 164; in Jewish ceremony 162; *pharmakos* in classical Greece 162–3; sacred and profane 171; today 157, 163–4, 167

scarcity: in Darwinism: 55–6; in sociobiology: 56

Schrift, A. D. 159

Schwartz, R. 125, 140, 143–9, 175, 178

science: distinct from theology? 34–6; first reactions to Gaia theory 33; use of paradox in 31–2

scientific enquiry: its poetic quality 61; Prigogine and Stengers 61

Segundo, J. L. 95, 97, 100–1

self-description 1, 2

self-making and conformity 113–16

self-renewal 4

SelfScape: interaction with *SocialScape* 159–60

SelfScapes, SocialScapes, EarthScapes, PoieticScapes tightly coupled 91–2

Sen, A. 84–5, 88, 105

Shekhinah: and the Jewish Holocaust 150–3, 171; and the sacred 171

Snyder, G. 160

Sobrino, J. 97, 107

social imaginaries 91

SocialScape: and human uniqueness 33–4; effect of competition in 118–19; interaction with *SelfScape* 159–60

SocialScapes, SelfScapes, EarthScapes, PoieticScapes tightly coupled 91–2 sociobiology 55–8; Fox-Keller 57–8; Haraway 57–8; Hrdy 56; Wilson 55–6

socio-economic slavery: who most at risk from 107

Solomon, J. 82

South as poor and developing 83

Spapens, P. 87–8

species: pre-Darwinian view of 39

Stengers, I. 12, 61, 71

Stone, C. D. 42

structural change: and new emergent selves 4; and self-renewal 4

structural coupling 3–4, 24–5, 27, 82, 109–10; and poiesis 60; in reimaging the idea of nature 133–5; specific human forms of 158–9

structural sin 19, 164–5; theological remedies for 165–7; violence against the earth community 166–7

Suchocki, M. 137, 142, 166

suffering validated by God concepts 150

sun, the primary giver 178

survival of the fittest 54–5

sustainable development: as object of theological reflection 102

Suzuki, D. 59

Swartley, W. 146

symbiotic events as gift events 158–9

Tannen, D. 116

taxonomies: as sanctioning violence 22–3; the context for discrimination 22–3

Taylor, M. C. 38, 66

theological apartheid 170–1, 173

theological presuppositions: in scientific thinking 15–16

theological questions and answers: their context today 89–90

theology: and environment 13–14; and Gaia theory 13–14; and lifestyle 17, 19; and ontology 122; and science 13–14, 15–16, 17; and the preferential option for the poor 97–9; as an earth science 17, 19–23; as *PoieticScape* 20; distinct from science? 34–6; emerging from a coevolutionary perspective 45; emerging from *EarthScape* 20; from a coevolutionary perspective 12–14, 16–17, 19–23, 26; militarist 146–47; natural 34–6; of mutual care 150–3; partiality in 12–13, 19–21; use of paradox in 31

theology in the North: contrasted with that in the South 95–7, 100–2; function of God concepts in 95–6; in tension with liberation theology 100–1; inimical to multiple perspectives 96; its characterization of theology in the South 95; its preoccupations 94–5

theology in the South: contrasted with that in the North 100–2

Thomas, L. 17–19, 21, 26, 40, 55, 114, 116, 166

tight coupling 3–4, 24–5, 27, 82, 109–10; and poiesis 60; in reimaging the idea of nature 133–5; specific human forms of 158–9

trade and justice 74–5

transcendence and immanence 67

translation 14–15

Trias, E. 173

Tuana, N. 130

UN development programme report, 1996 83–4

UNCED 13; declares who most at risk 75–6

value: intrinsic/commodity 77–8

Varela, F. J. 1–3, 10, 17–18, 24, 27, 30, 33–4, 47, 51, 56, 61, 82

Vatican II: *Declaration on Religious Freedom* 59

Vincentian canon 96

violence: against Nature 48–9; and liberation 149–50; endemic in Christianity 68; from theological apartheid 170–1; in Christianity 38–9; in theological metaphors for God 173–4; sanctioned by eucharistic doctrines 172–4; sanctioned in the name of God 144–7, 149; theological remedies for 165–7; validated by hierarchical ordering 22; validated by taxonomies 22–3; validated through God concepts 19, 178

Volk, T. 1–2, 5, 7, 12, 31, 62

vulnerability: and justice 81; demonstrated by ecological footprint 87; demonstrated by environmental space 87; from permeability and interdependence 81

Wackernagel, M. 85–6

water wars 111–12
Watts, M. 82, 91–2
Weil, S. 60, 63, 72–4, 79–80, 98, 103–6, 158; her experience as unskilled labour 103–4; her experience of capitalism 103–4; on justice 72–4, 79–80
welfare and gift event 177–8
Welker, M. 70
Wertheim, M. 89
Whitmore, T. D. 57, 93

Wiesel, E. 178
Wittgenstein, L. 70
women and God: in concentration camps 150–3
women and Nature 131–3; devalued by hierarchical ordering 128–30
women's identity defined by men 131
World Bank, SAP, IMF 74–5
world views: Christian alien to modern 89–90
Wren, B. 143